Rescuing the Bible from Fundamentalism

OTHER BOOKS BY JOHN SHELBY SPONG

Honest Prayer

This Hebrew Lord

Dialogue in Search of Jewish-Christian Understanding,
     with Rabbi Jack Daniel Spiro

Christpower

Life Approaches Death: A Dialogue on Medical Ethics,
     with Dr. Daniel Gregory

The Living Commandments

The Easter Moment

Into the Whirlwind: The Future of the Church

Beyond Moralism,
     with the Venerable Denise G. Haines

*Survival and Consciousness—An Interdisciplinary Inquiry into
     the Possibility of Life Beyond Biological Death*

Living in Sin? A Bishop Rethinks Human Sexuality

RESCUING THE
BIBLE
FROM
FUNDAMENTALISM

A Bishop Rethinks the Meaning of Scripture

John Shelby Spong

HarperSanFrancisco
A Division of HarperCollins*Publishers*

RESCUING THE BIBLE FROM FUNDAMENTALISM: *A Bishop Rethinks the Meaning of Scripture.* Copyright © 1991 by John Shelby Spong. All rights reserved. Printed in the United States of America. No part of this book may be used or reproduced in any manner whatsoever without written permission except in the case of brief quotations embodied in critical articles and reviews. For information address HarperCollins Publishers, 10 East 53rd Street, New York, NY 10022.

FIRST EDITION

Library of Congress Cataloging-in-Publication Data

Spong, John Shelby.
    Rescuing the Bible from fundamentalism : a bishop rethinks the meaning of Scripture / John Shelby Spong.—1st ed.
      p. cm.
    Includes bibliographical references and index.
    ISBN 0-06-067509-8 (alk. paper)
    1. Bible—Criticism, interpretation, etc. 2. Fundamentalism—Controversial literature. I. Title.
    BS511.2.S69 1991
    220.6'01—dc20
                                  90-41697
                                      CIP

91   92   93   94   95   RRD(H)   10 9 8 7 6 5 4 3 2

TO
CHRISTINE MARY SPONG
my wife

Contents

Preface

In January of 1989 I appeared on ABC's "Good Morning America" show to be interviewed by host Charles Gibson. I had made a public speech earlier that month in which I had raised questions about how we Christians could continue to call the Bible the Word of God when many of its passages reflected facts that twentieth-century Christians simply do not acknowledge as true and attitudes that twentieth-century Christians do not share.

In ABC's desire to present a counter point of view, Jerry Falwell, a well-known television evangelist, was also invited to participate in this discussion. The interview was set for the normal segment of five and a half minutes. However, when the discussion was interrupted for a commercial, Charles Gibson immediately canceled his next scheduled guest and ordered the dialogue to go on for an additional segment of five and a half minutes. An eleven-minute segment on one of these national morning television talk shows is very rare indeed. We clearly had touched a vital nerve in the religious soul of this nation and were debating a question that interested many.

Following this interview I wrote Jerry Falwell with the idea that he join me in a series of national debates on the Bible. I suggested to him that a debate between the two of us on the Bible had the potential to excite this nation and to turn our people anew toward serious reading of Holy Scripture. Jerry Falwell was not impressed by this proposal and responded, not personally but through the media, that "he did not want to lift me out of my anonymity." I was not surprised, for Jerry is not well equipped for such a debate.

A lesser-known evangelist, John Ankerberg, did, however, accept the challenge, and we had three hours of debate that played across the nation on cable television in six thirty-minute segments in the fall of 1989. The response to these public media opportunities convinced both me and my publisher that a book on these issues would meet a very present need in the religious life of this nation and perhaps in the Western Christian world.

There are many well written and even brilliant works of biblical scholarship available to the clergy, the scholars, and the academicians. There are many tracts, pamphlets, and books from the pens of fundamentalist Christians designed to defend biblical inerrancy and to shore up sagging weaknesses in the defensive armor of the literalists. There are, however, few volumes that take seriously the current levels of biblical scholarship and make that scholarship available in an understandable form to the average lay person who sits in the pews of our churches or to that person who wants to be a Christian but who does not find in his or her church a sufficient reason to invest life in that institution.

Most Christians who are generally unaware of this scholarship seem to believe that they must either be biblical literalists or admit that the Bible contains nothing of value for them. I am convinced that there is another alternative, that intelligence does not have to be a casualty of church life, that God can be worshiped with our minds, and even that biblical ignorance is unworthy of a disciple of Jesus Christ. It is my desire to make that alternative universally available. I want to place the biblical and theological debates that are commonplace among scholars at the disposal of the typical churchgoer.

So it was that the idea of this book was born under the encouragement of both my editor, Jan Johnson, and my publisher, Clayton Carlson at HarperSanFrancisco. For the next two years, my study life was reorganized around this task. The result has been not only the completion of this volume but an ever-deepening renewal of my love for Holy Scripture and my search for that elusive truth of God that lies beneath the literal words of that sacred text. In many ways I have Jerry Falwell to thank for these gifts to me.

I also wish to thank Charles Gibson and the staff of ABC's "Good Morning America" for sensing a story in this discussion and for risking a religious controversy in order to bring that story to their audience.

As this book developed, I tested its material in various places around the country. St. Barnabas' Episcopal Church on Bainbridge Island in the state of Washington invited me to be their "scholar in residence" in the summer of 1989. For a period of time, I sat on a deck above the magnificent Puget Sound with books scattered about me, writing great chunks of this manuscript. In exchange for their hospitality, I also lectured on this material to the members of this congregation and any of the Bainbridge Island public who cared to attend. There was tremendous interest. More than one hundred people attended these lectures on weeknights in July! The response of the people of Bainbridge Island convinced me anew that such a book was not only desired but badly needed.

My special thanks go to the Episcopal bishops of that part of the State of Washington, Robert Cochrane and Vincent Warner, for their welcome of me as a teacher into their diocese. I also thank the past and present rectors of that church, the Reverend David L. Heaney and the Reverend Joseph J. Tiernan, for inviting me to that exquisitely beautiful spot on not one but two occasions, and the adult education committee, headed by Linda Fullerton, Christine Shrader, and Barry Mills, who designed the scholar-in-residence program.

I also tested this material in a Lenten series of addresses at my former parish, St. Paul's Church in Richmond, Virginia, at the invitation of the Reverend Canon Robert Heatherington, rector, and the Right Reverend Peter Lee, bishop of Virginia.

I worked further on this manuscript and preached and lectured out of its content at The Church at Point O'Woods, New York. This quiet summer community, where I have been the guest pastor for over ten years, has been an oasis of tranquillity for me in my swirling and controversial life as a bishop. For that gift of peace I am most grateful.

To the clergy and people of the Episcopal Church in the Diocese of Newark, I express both my thanks and my gratitude for the opportunity they have given me to serve them as their bishop. This community of faith has inspired me almost daily to pursue my calling as a bishop who dares to take seriously the scholarly teaching function of the episcopacy. I do not know any Christians anywhere who live out so consistently their baptismal vows to "seek Christ in all people" and to "respect the dignity of every human being." I salute them as my partners in the journey of faith, which I believe to be nothing less than a journey into the reality of God. I especially want to acknowledge the Reverend John Branson and the Reverend Elizabeth Wigg-Maxwell of St. Paul's Church in Chatham, New Jersey, and the Reverend Richard Shimpfky and the Reverend Bonnie Perry of Christ Church in Ridgewood, New Jersey, who hosted lectures that I gave as part of the New Dimensions lecture series, which made public the content of this book for the first time in our diocese.

I also acknowledge my debt to my close friend and mentor the Right Reverend John Elbridge Hines, the former presiding bishop of the Episcopal Church, who has been my "father in God" for more than twenty-five years, and whose wise counsel I have received in weekly telephone calls and semiannual visits since I was elected bishop.

Over the last three years, as a gift to me from the Diocese of Newark, I have been privileged to enjoy a sabbatical study month each February. I have spent that month first at Union Theological Seminary in New York, then at Yale Divinity School in New Haven, and finally at Harvard Divinity School in Cambridge. My thanks go to the deans at each of these institutions, to the faculties, to the librarians, and to the students, all of whom enriched my life and opened my mind during these refreshing study times.

My associates on the core staff of our diocese have also played a major part in this publication, and to them I am deeply grateful. That core group includes the former Christine Mary Barney (to whom, under another name, this book is dedicated), the Right Reverend Walter C. Righter and his wife, Jane; the Venerable James William Henry Sell and his wife, Ellen; the Venerable Leslie Carl Smith and his wife, Lois; and Mr. John George Zinn and his wife, Carol. These people live and work closely together in a vital and electric diocese, and I am proud to be identified with them. My vocation as an author has not made their lives simple or easy.

Other members of our staff to whom thanks are due include Marge Allenspach, Cecil Broner, Rupert Cole, Gail Deckenbach, Olga Hayes, Wendy Hinds, Kathryn King, Robert Lanterman, Barbara Lescota, Australia Lightfoot, Ginnie Maiella, William Quinlan, Lucy Sprague, Barry Stopfel, Philip Storm, and Elizabeth Stone.

I save one person for special mention. She is Wanda Corwin Hollenbeck, my executive secretary. In a very real way, this book is uniquely her book. Not only did she type, edit, and reedit it many times, but she was a source of enormous encouragement to me as the book developed. The words in the manuscript seemed to speak to Wanda more deeply than those of any book I've written on which she had previously worked. To find her excited by its content as each chapter rolled off her word processor, and to hear her proclaim that "this is the best thing you've ever written," were for me moments along the way that made the task most enjoyable. I often wonder how my office or the Diocese of Newark ever functioned before Wanda joined our life in 1984. She brings to her position outstanding ability, personal integrity, and an incredible sensitivity. She and her husband, Richard, are among my close friends. No words are adequate to convey to her my deep appreciation.

Finally, I salute my family—my wife, Christine; my daughters, Ellen, Katharine, and Jaquelin, and their husbands, Gus Epps, Jack Catlett, and Todd Hylton, respectively; my granddaughter, Katharine Shelby Catlett; my stepson and stepdaughter, Brian and Rachel Barney; my mother, Doolie G. Spong; and my brother Will and sister Betty, all of whom surround my life with a sustaining love. Seldom has one person lived inside a more supportive family.

I write this book in the confidence that if I can succeed in lifting up the Christ so that this unique figure can be seen by people living in our century, then this Christ will complete the process by drawing all of God's people into that holy presence where God can be experienced as real. That, to me, is not only a worthy task for a Christian but it is also a biblical imperative. Shalom!

John Shelby Spong
Newark, New Jersey
January 1991

Rescuing the Bible from Fundamentalism

1

A Preamble:
Sex Drove Me to the Bible

Sex drove me to the Bible!

This statement is literally true, but not in the sense that most would interpret it. In 1988 my book entitled *Living in Sin? A Bishop Rethinks Human Sexuality* was published by Harper and Row. In that book I was led to question traditional religious attitudes and traditional religious definitions on a wide variety of sexual issues, from homosexuality to premarital living arrangements. There was an immediate outcry from conservative religious circles in defense of something they called biblical morality.

Proof Texting and Prejudice

This appeal to the Bible to justify and to sustain an attitude that was clearly passing away had a very familiar ring to me. I grew up in America's segregated South with its rich evangelical biblical heritage. Time after time I heard the Bible quoted to justify segregation. I was told that Ham, Noah's son, had looked on Noah in his nakedness, and for this sin he had been cursed to servitude and slavery along with all his progeny (Gen. 9:25–27). It did not occur to those quoting this Scripture to raise questions about what kind of God was assumed in this verse, or whether or not they could worship such a God. Since they could not identify themselves with those who were the victims of this cruelty, the God to whom they ascribed this victimizing power did not appear to them to be seriously compromised.

It also did not seem to matter that this corporate condemnation of millions of people to servitude because of their ancestor's indiscretion might also contradict other parts of the sacred text. The prophet Ezekiel, for example, writes: "What do you mean by repeating this proverb concerning the land of Israel, 'The fathers have eaten sour grapes, and the children's teeth are set on edge'? As I live, says the Lord God, this proverb shall no more be used by you in Israel. Behold, all souls are mine; the soul of the father as well as the soul of the son is mine: the soul that sins shall die" (Ezek. 18:2–4). The only concern of the one who quoted the texts in my early life was to maintain that person's prejudice, to enable that person to avoid having to change destructive attitudes.

I lived in Lynchburg, Virginia, in the late 1960s, when independent Baptist preacher Jerry Falwell was just beginning his rise to national prominence. Intense racism was certainly in the air at that time, and Jerry Falwell played to these feelings as his popularity grew. To start a "Christian school" in that period of history was a popular response to the Supreme Court order to dismantle the segregated school system endemic to the South since the Civil War. Teachers in Falwell's school had to take an oath of conformity to biblical inerrancy, and by that same view of Scripture, Jerry Falwell could justify his emotional commitment to segregation, although, in fairness to Mr. Falwell, it needs to be said that he has moved away from these negative attitudes as the years have gone by.

It was in this period of history that the segregationist governor of Georgia, Lester Maddox, became a candidate for president of the United States and was supported by many southern fundamentalists. Maddox was a Georgia restaurateur who battled for his "constitutional right" to serve only a segregated

2

public. He gave out ax handles at his restaurant as a hint of the way he thought those who wanted to desegregate public businesses might be discouraged from doing so.

With ease, many texts out of the Hebrew Scriptures could be quoted to justify the need for God's chosen people to keep themselves separate and apart from those judged to be unchosen, heathen, or evil. That was, and is, a major theme in the books of both Ezra and Nehemiah, for example (Ezra 10:12, 15; Neh. 13:1–3). Of course those texts could be countered by other texts to produce ambivalence or relativity in biblical truth, but fundamentalists could not tolerate this. Those whose religious security is rooted in a literal Bible do not want that security disturbed. They are not happy when facts challenge their biblical understanding or when nuances in the text are introduced or when they are forced to deal with either contradictions or changing insights. The Bible, as they understand it, shares in the permanence and certainty of God, convinces them that they are right, and justifies the enormous fear and even negativity that lie so close to the surface in fundamentalistic religion. For biblical literalists, there is always an enemy to be defeated in mortal combat.

Sometimes that enemy is Satan—the devil literalized and made very real and serving the primary purpose of removing responsibility from the one who has fallen into sin. Onetime-popular American evangelist Jimmy Swaggart, when caught in a New Orleans motel with a prostitute, explained his behavior by just such an appeal to Satan. His evangelistic enterprises were so successful, he stated, that the devil was being hurled back into darkness by this white knight of a preacher. So the devil launched a counterattack and lured evangelist Swaggart into a trap and dealt a mortal blow to his soul-winning ministry. If the devil can ensnare a heroic figure like Swaggart, so the argument went, think what he (the devil is always male, witches are always female) can do to the lesser persons who are mere church members.

In evangelical circles, child discipline tends to be quite physical, both because children are thought to be "born in sin" and therefore evil and because the Book of Proverbs teaches parents that "he who spares the rod hates his son, but he who loves him is diligent to discipline him" (Prov. 13:24). One disobedient lad, facing corporal punishment in "the woodshed," is said to have argued for a suspended sentence by saying, "It wasn't my fault, father. The devil made me do it." To which the father replied, "Well son, I guess it is my duty to beat the devil out of you!" Blaming the devil is a popular but not always successful maneuver. It did not work for Mr. Swaggart.

If the devil is not the enemy, then, according to the fundamentalists, a rival church frequently is the focus of the negative energy that roots in fear. The story is told of a little town in east Tennessee, hardly big enough to support one church, where on opposite sides of the main street stood the First Baptist Church and the Second Baptist Church. When a visitor inquired as to why there were two Baptist churches in this single tiny town, the visitor was told, "This Baptist church says, 'there ain't no hell,' and this other Baptist church says, 'the hell there ain't.' "

If not a rival church, then religious liberals, secular modernists, God-denying communists, or some other incarnation of evil becomes the enemy. Irrational religious anger demands a target. Television evangelists use physical and verbal means to act out their negativity and thereby to relieve some of this energy in the lives of their congregations. It is an interesting exercise, when viewing television evangelists, to turn off the sound and watch the facial contortions and violent gestures. Seldom do they communicate the love of God.

When a fundamentalist Christian sees the Antichrist in someone who is disturbing his or her religious security, it becomes not merely justifiable but downright righteous to utter words of condemnation and prayers for the early demise of that enemy. Indeed, you can even believe that you are God's anointed one to rid the world of this demonic figure.

One irate reader of a newspaper article wrote that he was praying that the next plane I took would crash, carrying me to my grave. The next time I boarded a flight I felt I should stop

4

at the front of the plane and say, "Folks, there is something you need to know before this plane takes off." If I did so, it might result in a wider seat selection. I wonder, however, at the incongruity of that letter writer who sincerely believes himself to be a Christian and yet somehow does not calculate the fact that his prayers for the early demise of someone he abhors might also require the sacrificial deaths of a planeload of supposedly innocent people. Yet that is the nature of religious anger. Once again, the words spoken and the deeds proposed are simply not in touch with the gospel of the God who so loved the world and who, in the person of Jesus, invited all to "come unto him."

A major function of fundamentalist religion is to bolster deeply insecure and fearful people. This is done by justifying a way of life with all of its defining prejudices. It thereby provides an appropriate and legitimate outlet for one's anger. The authority of an inerrant Bible that can be readily quoted to buttress this point of view becomes an essential ingredient to such a life. When that Bible is challenged, or relativized, the resulting anger proves the point categorically.

The same mentality exists in the more sophisticated mainline churches on more rational levels and with more complex and emotional issues. These churches would be embarrassed if they had to defend the patterns of segregation among southern fundamentalists, but many of them are quite convinced that their prejudice toward women, for example, is a justified part of God's plan in creation. It is for them God-given and biblically based. It is no surprise, then, that the twentieth-century battle for the rights of women in the church and for the casting off of the male-imposed definition of women has produced heated and emotional ecclesiastical conflict.

From the Pope, John Paul II, to the former Presiding Bishop of the Episcopal Church, John Maury Allin, to the Archbishop of Canterbury, Robert Runcie, to the outspoken Anglican Bishop of London, Graham Leonard, the most remarkable words have been spoken to prove that the "unbroken tradition of two thousand years of an all-male priesthood" is not a manifestation of the prejudice and sin of a patriarchal, sexist society, but is rather a manifestation of the unchanging will of God supported by "the word of God" in the Bible. Each spoke for that point of view that was distinctly uncomfortable as the sexual stereotypes of the past began to be discarded.

In separate ways, but with a patriarchal consistency, the various Christian leaders accepted a definition of women that precluded the possibility that a woman could represent God at the altar. Without daring to say so outright, they were nevertheless suggesting that women are not created in the image of God. Only men share that honor. Paul had made that argument in the First Epistle to the Corinthians—"For a man ought not to cover his head, since he is the image and glory of God; but woman is the glory of man. (For man was not made from woman, but woman from man. Neither was man created for woman but woman for man.)" (1 Cor. 11:7–9). Paul drew in that same epistle the conclusion that, therefore, "the women should keep silence in the churches. For they are not permitted to speak, but should be subordinate, as even the law says. If there is anything they [women] desire to know, let them ask their husbands at home. For it is shameful for a woman to speak in church" (1 Cor. 14:34, 35).

If this passage is taken literally, if the Bible is regarded as the "inerrant word of God," then no woman can sing in a choir, participate in a liturgy, teach Sunday school, or be ordained as a pastor or a priest. Churches with women participating in any of these areas, and that includes every church in Christendom on some level, have thus ignored, reinterpreted, dismissed, or relativized these biblical passages. The new sexual consciousness, and most especially the feminist aspect of that consciousness, is clearly on a collision course with "sacred tradition" as both church and Scripture have defined it. At every point thus far, "sacred tradition" has been bent to accommodate the emerging insights. This will not change. It is only a matter of time before all vestiges of the ecclesiastical oppression of women will come to an end. A woman bishop of Rome, sitting on the throne of Saint Peter as pope, is inevitable. The Bible

6

quoted to oppose this rising tide of consciousness will itself be a casualty unless it is freed from the straitjacket of literal fundamentalism.

The issue of homosexuality is another reality in sexual thinking and practice that places pressure on Holy Scripture. Once again, this prejudice is so deep, so widely assumed to be self-evident, that all major churches have in the past simply quoted the Bible to justify their continued oppression and rejection of gay and lesbian persons. The Sodom and Gomorrah story is cited uncritically to be a biblical account, and therefore a justification, of God's condemnation of this behavior. Yet a closer reading of this narrative reveals it to be a strange story involving hospitality laws in a nomadic society that our world of superhighways, bright lights, and chain motels cannot even imagine. It is a story about gang rape, which cannot ever be anything but evil. It is a narrative that expresses violent malevolence toward women that few people today, even among the fundamentalists, would be eager to condone.

In the biblical world of male values, the humiliation of a male was best achieved by making the males act like women in the sex act. To act like a woman, to be the passive participant in coitus, was thought to be insulting to the dignity of the male. This, far more than homosexuality, was the underlying theme of the Sodom story. The hero of this tale was Lot, a citizen of Sodom, who offered the sanctuary of his home to the angelic messengers and who protected them from the sexual abuse of the men of Sodom. Few preachers go on to tell you that Lot protected these messengers by offering to the mob for their sexual sport his two virgin daughters. You may "do to them as you please" (Gen. 19:8), Lot asserted.

The story goes on to say that Lot, despite this violent betrayal of his daughters, was accounted righteous by God. As the tiny righteous remnant of Sodom, Lot and his family were spared by God from the destruction that befell that infamous city. The story continues to tell us of Lot's subsequent drunkenness and his seduction into incest by his scheming daughters (Gen. 19:30–36). Once again, the purpose of a claim of biblical literalism is revealed to be not to call people to the values of justice, but to justify existing prejudice by keeping oneself secure inside a way of life that cannot be challenged by any new insight. Among fundamentalists, the selective use of a text, ignoring vast areas of reality, is commonplace.

There are certainly other places in Scripture where homosexuality is condemned. Both the Torah and Saint Paul can be cited. However, the question of biblical authority arises anew when scientific data, which the fifth- and sixth-century B.C.E. authors of the Torah and Saint Paul could not have imagined, throws new light on the origin and cause of homosexuality. Such data available today suggest that homosexual orientation is not a matter of choice but a matter of ontology; that is, it is of the being of the individual, not the doing.

It also suggests that this phenomenon has been present in human life since the dawn of human history, that it is present in higher mammals that presumably fall below the level of volition, and that there has been no appreciable success despite all the efforts of modern science, including psychiatry, in changing the givenness of this reality for the vast majority of persons. Then perhaps it begins to dawn on us that life has within it wide varieties. We have male vocal ranges from countertenor to bass and female vocal ranges from lyric soprano to a contralto that could be and sometimes is a baritone. We have male physical ranges from the muscular athlete to the soft, delicate man and female physical ranges from the well-conditioned athlete who can compete on an equal basis with the vast majority of males to the frail woman who lives out the male stereotype of helplessness.

So also we have ranges in male sexual orientation from those who constitute the majority and who relate to women sexually, though, it might be added, with a wide variety of sexual appetites; to those who, because of the way their brains were sexed in utero, as many scientists would now suggest, find desire only in their response to those of their own gender. (Lest some reader make too quick and simplistic a correlation of these categories, let me quickly say that I know countertenors who are heterosexual and basses who are homosexual. I know male athletes who are gay and I know heterosexual males who in physical appearance would be called effeminate. The stereotypes of the ages do not hold when scrutinized.)

The authors of the Bible did not have the knowledge on this subject that is available to us today. The sexual attitudes in Scripture used to justify the prejudiced sexual stereotypes of the past simply are not holding in this generation. They are not in touch with emerging contemporary knowledge.

So it was that sex drove me to the Bible. The new emerging sexual consciousness and the passing of ancient stereotypes challenged the authority of Scripture, raised profound questions about the authenticity of biblical insights, and created for me and for many others a crisis of faith.

The Rescue Effort

It is not a new crisis. Tension has existed between the church and the scientific community for hundreds of years. Galileo was excommunicated for his suggestion that the earth was not the center of the created order. Isaac Newton and his clockwork universe were at odds with those who pray to an intervening deity. People like Bishop Samuel Wilberforce and his modern-day descendants, called creationists, were sent into orbit as they tried to neutralize the impact of Charles Darwin. This tension has increasingly resulted in an anti-intellectual approach to Christianity on the part of literal-minded, conservative Christians and a departure from the organized Christian church into the secular city by scores of modern men and women for whom the mythological framework of the Christian story no longer has any translatable meaning.

Above all, it has placed the Bible in jeopardy. If the only people who talk about the Bible are fundamentalists and their more sophisticated city cousins, who wince defensively when the "traditions of the church" are challenged by new insights, then fewer and fewer people are going to take seriously a book or a church that appears to them to be so antiquated.

When attention is turned to the mainline churches, where a well-educated ministry has always been required, it becomes obvious that they have, by and large, simply ignored the Bible. The average pew sitter in the average mainline church, both Catholic and Protestant, is, to say it bluntly, biblically illiterate. The offering to the world by the mainline churches of a viable option and alternative to biblical fundamentalism is, therefore, not forthcoming. The options, our people are made to feel, are either to live in continued ignorance or to abandon the church altogether for life apart from any religious convictions. The biblical scholarship of the past two hundred years has simply not been made available to the man or the woman in the pew. So mainline Christians allow the television preachers to manipulate their audiences, most times to their own financial gain, by making the most absurd biblical claims without their being called to accountability in the name of truth.

It is for these reasons that I have found it imperative to put another voice into the public arena. My purpose in this volume is first to rescue the Bible from the exclusive hands of those who demand that it be literal truth and second to open that sacred story to levels of insight and beauty that, in my experience, literalism has never produced. I hope to call people into an appreciation of the living "Word of God" that lurks so often hidden and undiscovered beneath the literal words of the text.

For biblical scholars, this volume will be very elementary. For those who have only vague recollections of biblical stories, it will be both insightful and expanding. Depending on how much the Bible has been made into an idol for my readers, my book will be regarded as either enlightening or disturbing. My hope is that it will help members of the Christian churches to allow their soon-to-be-twenty-first-century minds to become aware of and to embrace a biblical truth that, while not literal, is certainly timeless.

I write as a Christian who loves the church. I am not a hostile critic who stands outside religion desiring to make fun of it. I am not a Marxist who believes that religion is the opiate of the people. I am not a Madalyn Murray O'Hair who believes

10

that God should be expunged from public life. I am a bishop in the Anglican (Episcopal) church who was raised as a biblical fundamentalist and who, when I left that fundamentalism, did not leave my love of the Bible or my desire to serve God through the church.

There will be some who, upon reading this volume, will be disturbed and even angry. I regret that. I have no desire to make uncomfortable anyone's fragile life. In a strange way, discomfort and even anger bear witness to the dawning of new possibilities; so while it saddens me to cause distress, it also awakens in me a sense of gratitude. At the same time, I suspect that voices will be raised among the liberal Christians proclaiming that there is nothing new here and, therefore, no reason to take this book seriously. Or they will fasten on a date or a fact that they can challenge, even successfully, to discredit the whole work. There is not much new here, and some of my dates and "facts" are still debated in theological circles. Nonetheless, I will continue to argue that these insights, drawn largely from that deep and impressive literature of biblical scholarship over the past one hundred years, have not yet become operative in the church primarily because they have not yet become operative in those very clergy who will dismiss this as "old hat."

It is my deepest hope that there will be others who will discover in the pages of this book a means through which they can return to church in honesty or be enabled to worship God with a renewed integrity in the church that they have never left. I believe that their name is legion. They are members of my family and among my closest friends. I write for them because the goal of my professional life has been to combine scholarship with faith, to bring honesty and the authenticity of citizenship in the modern world to the activity of worship while continuing to walk in the faith tradition established by Jesus of Nazareth whom I call Lord and Christ. Time will tell whether or not so lofty a goal has been achieved.

11

2

Raising the Issues

When I was a lad of twelve, my mother gave me a Bible as my primary Christmas present. It was a fat volume, leather-bound, printed on tissue-thin paper and in the King James Version. That was, in fact, the only version that I knew existed. This Bible had lots of maps, an index, and various notes on things in Bible times. It also had the words of Jesus printed in red letters, even when Luke was quoting the already ascended Christ in the Book of Acts as saying, "It is more blessed to give than to receive" (Acts 20:35), and when Paul related in 1 Corinthians the words of Jesus at the Last Supper, "take eat, this is my body" (1 Cor. 11:23). It did not occur to me at the time that neither Luke nor Paul ever knew the historical Jesus, so that these quotations, if authentic at all, had to have existed for some time as part of the church's memory and oral tradition.

It is revelatory of the value system of my family that I received that Christmas gift with the greatest of joy and placed this Bible prominently on my bedside table, where it could conveniently remind me of my vow to read it daily. And read it I did; and I still do. I was drawn powerfully to that book. My father had died some four months before that Christmas, plunging my family into radical emotional and economic insecurity. Somehow that Bible ministered to my insecurity. I pored

13

over its words with all the intensity and depth a twelve-year-old boy could muster.

My mother had not finished the ninth grade in school; she was a woman of a simple faith. No critical problems ever bothered her understanding of God. He was father and judge—ever watching, protecting, and keeping records of our behavior so that reward or punishment could be meted out fairly at the Day of Judgment. It did not occur to me at the time to see how similar that divine image was to Santa Claus, who every December emerged to be perceived as one who was "making a list and checking it twice, gonna find out who's naughty and nice."

In my junior and senior years of high school, my knowledge of the content of Scripture was greatly enhanced when I was allowed to take two classes in Bible in the public schools of Charlotte, North Carolina. That was still possible in the late 1940s. My teacher for both of those classes was a lovely lady, named Janet Robinson, who declined to wear any makeup because it was "against the teaching of the Bible." She believed that God had dictated every word of Holy Scripture, that it was in a literal sense "the Word of God." But that premise did not stop her from making the stories of the Bible live with dramatic power. King David, Nathan the prophet, Elijah on Mount Carmel, the journeys of Paul, and the story of the cross—all became gripping dramas that seared their way into my memory. Under her tutelage I memorized vast portions of the Bible. Passages such as 1 Corinthians 13, Romans 12, the Sermon on the Mount, the Lucan birth narrative, as well as many salvation-oriented proof texts, became part of my reflex Christian life. There was for me no authority beyond the affirmation "the Bible says."

I mention this brief bit of autobiography to set the stage to talk about the Bible. I come to this study as one who has had a lifetime love affair with this book. I look at the authority of the Scriptures as one who has been both nurtured by and then disillusioned with the literal Bible. My devotion to the Bible was so intense that it led me into a study that finally obliterated

14

any possibility that the Bible could be related to on a literal basis. My relationship with the Bible became and remains so significant that I cannot ignore it, forget it, or walk away from it. I have to engage it, probe it, dissect it, transcend it. It is a volume that has been a source of genuine life for me.

For years in my writing career, I have examined such parts of the sacred text as the person of Jesus, the Ten Commandments, the resurrection narratives, and the biblical teaching on human sexuality. In each instance, I narrowed my focus to the subject at hand and studied it with great intensity. But increasingly I felt a need to look at the Bible itself as a whole. How can this book be used with integrity by men and women of faith? How can it be lifted out of the prejudices and cultural biases of bygone eras? How can it be a source of life to a twentieth- and soon-to-be-twenty-first-century generation? If it continues to be viewed literally, the Bible, in my opinion, is doomed to be cast aside as both dated and irrelevant.

Can modern men and women continue to pretend that timeless, eternal, and unchanging truth has been captured in the words of a book that achieved its final written form midway into the second century of this common era? Would not such a claim be dismissed as ludicrous in any other branch of human knowledge? Is it less ludicrous because we have surrounded it with a religious aura? Have we embraced the meaning of the subjective quality of a particular language, the truth lost at worst and distorted at best in the translations?

The Underlying Issues: Language and Concepts

Christians have almost no words that Jesus spoke in Aramaic, the tongue he employed. The exceptions are "Talitha Cumi" in Mark (5:41); "Ephphatha" in the story of the deaf mute (Mark 7:34); and the best known, the cry from the cross, "Eloi Eloi lama sabathani." This cry is, of course, a quotation from Psalm 22 and may or may not have been actually uttered by the dying Jesus of Nazareth. But before we can confront the Jesus of history, we have to move from English to Greek (the language in which the New Testament was written) to Aramaic. To move into Aramaic is to move into a world of oral tradition where no written records exist. Did Jesus say, for instance, "It is easier for a camel to go through the eye of a needle than for a rich man to enter the Kingdom of Heaven"? It is a strange analogy, an inappropriate mixing of metaphors. Camels do not go through eyes of needles, not even tiny camels. But when the word *camel* is translated into Aramaic, one sees that in Aramaic the word for camel and the word for rope are almost identical. Was the original word of Jesus "It is easier for a rope to go through the eye of a needle"? It would be an appropriate metaphor, still possessing the power of the impossible but not violating the imagination of the hearers. If this is a saying that was garbled in translation, are there others? How substantial are they to our understanding of the essential elements of our tradition?

When I became aware that neither the word *virgin* nor the concept of virginity appears in the Hebrew text of Isaiah that Matthew quoted to undergird his account of Jesus' virgin birth, I became newly aware of the fragile nature of biblical fundamentalism. The understanding of "virgin" is present only in the Greek word *parthenos*, used to translate the Hebrew word *'almah* in a Greek version of the Hebrew Scriptures. The Hebrew word for virgin is *betulah*. *'Almah* never means "virgin" in Hebrew. I had to face early on in my priestly career the startling possibility that the virgin tradition so deep in Christianity may well rest upon something as fragile as the weak reed of a mistranslation. I will develop this point more fully in chapter 13.

Beyond the difficulties with the ancient languages, there are concepts in the Bible that are repugnant to the modern consciousness. There is a vicious tribal code of ethics that prohibits internally behavior that is actually encouraged in dealing with outsiders. Moses was a murderer, but this was not a character flaw because his victim was an Egyptian (Exod. 2:11ff). Joseph was an arrogant and spoiled favorite son upon whom his father heaped lavish gifts and special favor (Genesis

37). It is hard to be critical of Joseph when the people of Israel believed God related to them in a similar fashion. Adultery was said to be evil, but both Abraham and Isaac tried to pass their wives off as their sisters, even though this meant having them sexually used by Abimelech, king of Gerar (Gen. 20:1–18; 26:6–11).

Tribal hatreds are extolled as virtues in parts of the Hebrew Scriptures. Captive peoples, if spared from death, were reduced to slavery. Captive women were used for sexual sport by their Hebrew conquerors. Judah treated his daughter-in-law Tamar as a prostitute and then proposed to kill her when she became pregnant (Genesis 38). Bearing false witness was prohibited by the Ten Commandments, but that is exactly what Moses did in his conversations with Pharaoh. His request was for temporary leave for the people of Israel so that they might hold a religious feast in the wilderness (Exod. 5:1). Later Moses promised that it would be for only three days (Exod. 9:27). Obviously neither Moses nor Pharaoh believed this. Whenever the Pharaoh relented in response to the plagues, the Bible would say that God hardened his heart so that more plagues could be visited upon the Egyptians (Exod. 10:1ff). Not a very fair portrait of God, one could certainly argue.

God appeared in some passages to be not only a nationalistic deity but also a sadistic one who delighted even in killing the firstborn in every Egyptian household (Exod. 11:4–6). The purpose of this exercise, said the biblical writer, was so that all would know "that the Lord makes a distinction between the Egyptians and Israel" (Exod. 11:7). The Torah said "do not steal," but at Moses' command, the Exodus from Egypt was accomplished after the Israelites had robbed the Egyptians of their jewelry, silver, gold, and clothing (Exod. 12:35–36). When the Hebrew people decided to make a golden calf in the wilderness, they made it with their Egyptian loot (Exodus 32). Where else does a former slave people come upon such wealth in the wilderness? The picture of God that began to emerge from the Bible for me was neither a pleasant one nor one to which I was drawn in worship. It did not get better.

The Bible confronted me with the picture of God rejoicing over the drowning of the Egyptians at the Red Sea (Exodus 15). Was this God not also the God of the Egyptians? I wondered. Later this God suggested that the children of the Edomites should have their heads dashed against the rocks for what the Edomites had done to the Jews (Ps. 137:7–9). In another instance, God was called "a man of war" (Exod. 15:3), a concept far removed from the one I had come to call the "Prince of Peace."

Then, as the Law of God unfolded in the remaining books of the Torah, I found myself more and more repelled. Slavery was assumed, and the master could beat the slave mercilessly, for the Law said, "The slave is his money" (Exod. 21:21). The child who struck or cursed a parent shall be executed (Exod. 21:15, 17). Anyone who sacrificed to a God other than Israel's God "shall be utterly destroyed" (Exod. 22:20). Menstruation was unclean, and whatever the menstruating woman touched was unclean (Lev. 15:19ff). A man who had a wet dream "shall be unclean until the evening" (Lev. 15:16). You could not be a priest if you were blind or lame or had a mutilated face or were a hunchback or a dwarf or had a defect in sight or an itching disease or scabs or crushed testicles (Lev. 22:16–22). If you blaspheme God you shall be executed (Lev. 24:16). "When a man causes a disfigurement in his neighbor, as he has done, it shall be done to him, fracture for fracture, eye for eye, tooth for tooth; as he has disfigured a man, he shall be disfigured" (Lev. 24:19–20). If a "spirit of jealousy" came upon a man, he could order his wife to undergo an ordeal of drinking a poisoned potion. If the woman died, her guilt was assumed. If she survived, she was presumed to be innocent (Num. 5:11ff). One shudders to think of the mentally unbalanced males who put their wives to death wrongfully under this male-inspired law that was said to be "the word of God."

Religious purity was also assured by the execution of anyone who deviated from true worship by serving a false God (Num. 25:1–6). If we had such a law today, who would define the true God? There are many religious people who are quite sure that their God is the only God and that their way of worship is the only proper way to worship. The claims of infallibility and inerrancy are familiar religious claims. This is the very stuff of religious imperialism. All of this seemed to me more like religious bigotry than divinely inspired Scripture. But there it was in the Bible.

Womanhood was insulted in verse after verse of the Torah. The woman was thought to be incompetent to make a vow, so her father was given veto power (Num. 30:1–5). Later in her life her husband had to approve of her utterances if they were to have any force (Num. 30:8).

Non-Israelite groups, such as the Midianites, were ordered to be destroyed by the God of the Bible (Num. 31:1, 2). Israel obeyed: "They warred against Midian as the Lord commanded Moses and slew every male" (Num. 31:7). They spared the women and children and took as booty all their cattle, flocks, and goods (Num. 31:9). So much for "You shall not steal"! Then they burned the Midianite cities (Num. 31:10). Moses was angry that they had let the women live (Num. 31:15). He then ordered all the male children to be killed. So much for "You shall do no murder"! Then all the females who were not virgins were ordered to be killed, but Moses allowed the Israelite men to keep all the virgins "for yourself." So much for "You shall not commit adultery"!

I was repelled by the arrogance of the biblical claims made on the land of others in the name of the God of Israel. The Hebrews in the thirteenth century before this common era were, from the Canaanite perspective, a marauding band of looters, killers, and destroyers, but they saw themselves as a people of destiny, as those whose national vested interest was, in fact, the will of God. Because the Hebrews won that ancient struggle, their point of view rather than the Canaanite point of view prevailed in the biblical record. There is always a danger in believing that you and your people are somehow God's specially chosen. The obvious corollary is that your enemies are

God's specifically "unchosen," and very soon they are thought of as God's rejected. If God had rejected these others who are not Hebrew, then Israel's rejection and even murderous behavior could be justified. Every nation, including the United States when it operates under a theory of divine election or manifest destiny, can be especially distorted. This chauvinistic nationalism reached the force of law in the Torah by the suggestion that Hebrews not take the health risks that aliens must endure, and that these risks can be used for profit by Hebrews in dealing with foreigners. For the Torah says, "You shall not eat anything that dies of itself. You may give it to the alien who is within your towns that he may eat it or you may sell it to a foreigner" (Deut. 14:21). This verse comes from the same book that asks, "What does the Lord your God require of you, but to fear the Lord your God, to walk in all his ways . . . and to keep the commandments and statutes of the Lord" (Deut. 10:12–13). Time after time the things this God was thought to have commanded became repulsive to me. If all of these things were part of a Bible that had to be believed as the literal word of God, I found that increasingly I could not give myself in worship to such a deity.

This list of objectionable passages could be expanded almost endlessly. I could quote passages condemning witches and mediums that were used until the eighteenth century to justify the murders of countless women. I could point to passages that condemned homosexuality that were used to justify the burning at the stake of many a person either thought to be living or actually living a responsible gay or lesbian life. I could quote passages glorifying war used to justify the nationalistic ambitions of many a political leader who, under the guise of patriotism, used war to build fortunes.

It was still on a superficial level that I confronted these surface anomalies, but I could not believe that anyone who had read this book would be so foolish as to proclaim that the Bible in every literal word was the divinely inspired, inerrant word of God. Yet the claim continued to be made and continues to this day. Have these people simply not read the text? Are they hopelessly uninformed? Is there a different Bible? Are they blinded by a combination of ego needs and naivete?

When one turns from the ancient Hebrew texts to the New Testament, the problems do not disappear. There are passages in the Gospels that portray Jesus of Nazareth as narrow-minded, vindictive, and even hypocritical. Jesus exhorted people to love their enemies and to pray for their persecutors (Matt. 5:44) and never to call others by demeaning or hurtful names (Matt. 5:22), yet he called his enemies a "brood of snakes" (Matt. 12:34), "sons of vipers" (Matt. 23:33), "blind fools" (Matt. 23:17). He called gentiles "dogs" (Matt. 15:26). He said he had come to set a man against his father and a daughter against her mother (Matt. 10:35). He disowned his own family (Matt. 12:46–50), hardly obeying the commandment to "honor your parents." These do not appear to be the words of one dedicated to preserving and strengthening the family, as the fundamentalist preachers have constantly asserted.

Are we drawn to a Lord who would destroy a herd of pigs and presumably a person's livelihood in order to exorcise a demon (Mark 5:13)? Are we impressed when the one we call Lord curses a fig tree because it did not bear fruit out of season (Matt. 21:18, 19)? How divine is the message that says for your finite failings you will be cast into the outer darkness, where there will be weeping and gnashing of teeth (Matt. 25:30)? If the Bible is read literally, it must be said that Jesus seems to have accepted without question the language of hell employed by his religious contemporaries. Is eternal punishment the plan of the all-merciful God? Was Jesus mistaken? Was the interpretation of Jesus given in these passages, which come primarily from Matthew, untrustworthy?

No matter how this question is resolved, the literal authority of the Gospels is compromised. Was belief in hell so common that Jesus simply reflected the values of his time unquestionably? Hardly, since the Sadducees did not believe in any life after death, either as a reward or punishment. We know only that someone was convinced that Jesus did believe and teach that eternal punishment in a fiery hell was an appropriate

21

sentence to pronounce on sinners. Is it? I for one do not believe it. Am I false to Jesus? False to Jesus' interpreters? False to God? I pray not!

Jesus is also depicted, especially in the Book of John, as being guilty of what we today would surely call antisemitism. Indeed, the hatred of the Jews that has been the dark underside of Christianity for two thousand years is fed by the pejorative attitudes found in the Christian Scriptures and even in the supposed words of Jesus. It has led to pogroms, ghettos, segregated housing and clubs, defaced synagogues, Krystallnacht, and Dachau. In the name of Jesus, damnation has been pronounced on those who do not accept Jesus' messiahship—a charge leveled historically by Christians at the Jews. "His blood be upon us and upon our children," Matthew had the Jewish crowd say when Pilate sought to set Jesus free. From this phrase of Holy Writ the epithet "Christ killer" (Matt. 27:25) has been leveled at Jewish people ever since. When John used the phrase "The Jews" (John 5:10; 10:19, 24, 31, 33; 19:7, 12, 14, 15) instead of "the Jewish leaders," he fed that corporate guilt that bloomed as bigotry and prejudice. John said that the Jewish people loved darkness more than light, for their deeds were evil (John 3:18–20), and he said the Jews were children of the devil, who was the father of lies (John 8:39–44). These words are hardly designed to build mutual respect. They are, to me, repugnant. Yet they are part of the Bible that many Christians even today ask me to take literally.

Paul added to this fuel by suggesting that Jews were possessed with "a spirit of stupor" that produced "eyes that should not see and ears that should not hear down to this very day" (Rom. 11:8). Finally, the history of the church from Tertullian and John Chrysostom to Jerome to Augustine to Aquinas to Luther to this generation has reflected a killing antisemitism that was rooted in the New Testament. Can a book responsible for these things be in any literal sense the Word of God to me?

If Jesus was wrong in fact or in attitude, either Jesus himself or Jesus as viewed through Scripture has been compromised. Yet Jesus is presented in the Bible as believing that epilepsy is caused by demon possession (Mark 9:14–29). That is hardly a viewpoint that any of us would share today. He is portrayed as accepting the assumption that deaf muteness results from the tying of the tongue by Satan (Matt. 9:32, 33; 12:22, Luke 11:14). A spirit of infirmity was said by Jesus to result from Satan's binding (Luke 13:11, 16). He seems to have accepted the Davidic authorship of the Psalms (Mark 12:36; Luke 20:42), an attitude and concept quickly dismissed in the circles of biblical scholarship today. Jesus also seems to have accepted the theory of Mosaic authorship of the Torah (Mark 7:10; 10:3; Luke 5:14).

Yet in the Torah there are two creation stories that vary in detail and contradict each other in order (Gen. 1:1–2:4 and Gen. 2:5ff). These stories cannot be harmonized. Poor Moses contradicted himself radically in the first two chapters of the Torah. He also seemed not to know the nationality of the people to whom Joseph's brothers sold Joseph, who took him down to Egypt. In one version it was the Ishmaelites (Gen. 37:25), and in another version it was the Midianites (Gen. 37:28). They are not the same. Moses, as a single author, seems to have been quite confused.

If this were not enough, there are three separate and distinct versions of the Ten Commandments in the Torah that cannot be reconciled (Exodus 20, Exodus 34, and Deuteronomy 5). God was portrayed, if one seeks to maintain a literalism about Holy Scripture, as terribly inept. He (and it *was* he) could not even get the essence of the divine law clear. In the story of Sodom and Gomorrah, God was portrayed as not knowing what was going on in those two cities, so he had to send divine messengers to bring him a report. This is hardly a portrait of divine omniscience.

If one doesn't read the Bible constantly, these issues can be ignored—lost in ignorance. But if one does read the Bible regularly and seriously, these issues are disturbing and unavoidable. They call into question so many of the attitudes upon which our faith is built. When these attitudes, based on a literal view of Scripture, begin to shake, our faith also shakes, and we either refuse to look again at the Bible and continue our religious game of "let's pretend" or we walk away from this resource for the faith of our fathers and mothers and conclude that religion as we know it has lost its power and is dead. If we fall into the former camp, the voices of the television evangelists who traffic in certainty, who claim biblical authority in the hope that no one will challenge them, might compel our attention and our response. But it will not last. Religious hysteria always burns itself out in emptiness. If we are in the latter camp, we live in a world of dreadful transcendent emptiness. We enter the pathos of a modern poet who suggested that God is dead and modern folks gather nightly at the divine grave to weep.

A literal Bible presents me with far more problems than assets. It offers me a God I cannot respect, much less worship; a deity whose needs and prejudices are at least as large as my own. I meet in the literal understanding of Scripture a God who is simply not viable, and what the mind cannot believe the heart can finally never adore.

Is there a truth beyond biblical literalism to which my life can be dedicated? Can I find this truth by probing the words of the Bible? Or, as many secular critics of religion maintain, has time run out on the Judeo-Christian tradition as it did on the gods of Olympus? Are those who refer to this age as the "post-Christian" era more correct than Christians have cared to believe?

The answers to these questions are not yet clear, but the issues are drawn—powerfully and provocatively drawn. There is no way out except to walk into these questions deeper and deeper until either there is nothing left or a wondrous new meaning begins to dawn. For those who are willing to make this journey, the stakes are high. But not to make this journey means, in my opinion, certain death to all that we have believed. So the task moves on.

3

The Pre-Scientific Assumptions of the Bible

The Bible is not a scientific textbook.

Jesus could not have imagined such an idea as Albert Einstein's theory of relativity. The medical understanding among biblical writers was the common wisdom of their time and place, not remotely close to our understanding of medical science. Studies of plant life, animal life, and human life available in centuries past were primitive, to say the least. Concepts commonplace today in the world of physics, subatomic physics, astrophysics, and cosmology would have drawn from Matthew, Mark, Luke, and John, to say nothing of the author of the Book of Genesis, nothing except blank stares of incredulity.

The fact is that every human experience is interpreted by the experiencing person or it is not passed on. It is always interpreted within the framework by which that person comprehends what is real. When knowledge expands, it renders the interpretive framework of ancient people inadequate, and it reveals the ignorance of the past. For people living in one age to try to cling to the objective truthfulness of the concepts of another age is to participate in a doubtful enterprise.

Yet a popular television evangelist has written, "The Bible is the inerrant . . . word of the living God. It is absolutely infallible, without error in all matters pertaining to faith and practice, as well as in areas such as geography, science, history, etc."[1] One can only conclude that this is the statement of one who is simply unaware of vast areas of reality that are common knowledge to people of this century.

The Genesis Stories and Science

The earth is not flat. We now have the empirical proof of this fact taken from a spaceship hurtling away from this planet, revealing the earth to be an incredibly beautiful sphere of blues and whites continuing its lonely path of orbit around the sun. That fact alone renders the cosmological assumptions of the Bible to be woefully inadequate in understanding this world.

The earth is also not the center of the universe. That realization has been alive since the days of Copernicus and Galileo, but only since World War II has the study of the universe expanded so dramatically until it has leaped beyond our ability to grasp with our finite minds. Everything written by biblical writers about the heavens or the earth assumed that the earth was the center of the universe. To the degree that the Bible makes these assumptions, the Bible cannot be literal for us.

Of course these things have been known for years, but the task of rethinking the Bible's story in terms of these new realities has not been done by many, indeed by most, people. We still perpetuate our myths in the daily weather reports on television, where reporters tell us, with straight faces, what time the sun will rise and set each day. The sun does not rise. The sun does not set. The earth turns on its axis. Our language, however, perpetuates our illusions. Perhaps there is an unconscious conspiracy abroad fueled by the deep sense of human anxiety that refuses to allow us to embrace the vastness of space and the insignificance and loneliness of this planet, our island home. The mythology of the Bible serves that conspiracy.

In the creation story, in the creeds of Christianity, and in countless stories in the biblical drama, a nonoperative, prescientific, and clearly false view of the world is perpetuated.

Those who seek to preserve these biblical understandings have to become anti-intellectual or must close off vast portions of their thinking processes or twist their brains into a kind of first-century pretzel in order to maintain their faith system. It is no wonder that they are afraid of knowledge. Their faith security system is built on sand. It cannot and will not survive, and they have no sense that there is any alternative save despair, death, and meaninglessness. This is enough to cause fear to erupt in anger.

Most of us are not aware that there are a number of creation accounts in Holy Scripture. The two with which we are most familiar open the Book of Genesis. The first account, actually thought by biblical scholars to be the newest narrative, has a vision of the cosmos that no educated person could today assume. For the author of this account, the earth is flat, surrounded by water on all sides. Water, indeed, is also underneath the dry land, making it possible for human beings to dig wells and cisterns in order to release the waters of the deep. The sky is a dome over the earth into which a sun has been placed to illumine the day as it journeys through the heavens. A moon is also hung in that ceiling by God to illumine the night, regulate the tides, and help people count the passage of time.

The image we need to embrace, if we wish to understand the biblical narrative, is that of a domed stadium, expanded to embrace the scope of the earth but self-contained. There was water above the sky that fell as rain. There were also stars—tiny lights, perhaps candles or maybe even peepholes through which the light of heaven could be glimpsed. One of the images of heaven was that of eternal day. In our neon and artificially lighted society, we moderns have a difficult time embracing the meaning of darkness as it was experienced by our ancient forebears. Danger lurked in the night from predators and human enemies, and in their minds, from ghosts, witches, and goblins.

This fear continues to be present in our language where *darkness* and *night* are words still used by dramatists to connote fear and the need for vigilance. The childhood prayer "If I should die before I wake, I pray the Lord my soul to take" also participates in this ancient meaning of night. Heaven, the realm of God, knew no night, and the stars were peepholes into the heavenly realm. When moralism and judgment became a major part of religious thinking, the stars were looked upon as the openings through which an all-seeing deity watched human behavior. It was even suggested that if one wanted to misbehave, that person might choose a cloudy night, for under those conditions, God could not see as well! From time to time in the ancient world, a meteor would plunge to the earth. Our forebears called them "falling stars," and the sense that the sky was very near was enhanced by these phenomena, for that which could fall to the earth could not be an infinite distance away.

God was thought to live just beyond the sky in the biblical understanding, and God was understood after the analogy of earthly kings. God was a male, sat on a throne, and lived in a heavenly palace. God caused to happen everything that occurred, so that storms, floods, thunder and lightning were thought of quite simply as the expressions of God's anger and the means whereby God punished the real or imagined human failings. Sun, seasonal rains, warmth, and even seasonal cold were thought to be gestures of God's beneficence.

These assumptions are present in the creation story. The sky (the heavens) and the earth were created first. They were separated by a firmament that was created to keep the waters below from the waters above. Then the sun was made to give light to the earth by day and the moon to give light by night. Then the waters were gathered together so that dry land could emerge. Then came the fish, the birds, the animals, and the "creeping things," and finally, when all things were ready, God created the man and the woman in the divine image. Then God rested on the seventh day to validate the Jewish custom that the seventh day was to be a day when all activity ceased so that life would have a rhythm and all days would not be a monotonous procession.

In the second creation story, thought to be written some four hundred to five hundred years earlier, the drama is told anew; somewhat differently but with the same cosmological assumptions. The language was much more anthropomorphic. God molded the man Adam out of the dust of the earth, much as a child would make a mud pie. In the first narrative, God created by divine fiat—"Let there be," and there was. Here God must actually breathe into Adam the *nephesh*, the soul, the life-giving spirit. One gets the impression in this earlier narrative of God giving to Adam artificial respiration so that the breath of life, the divine life, now rested in the human creature.

This second story was also cast in a heavy patriarchal mold. The man was created first, in the image of God. Then the animals were created, one by one, in a vain divine attempt to make a fit partner for the man. None satisfied, but the man named them each in turn—cow, horse, cat, sheep—until all the species that Noah later was to save were in existence. Then in one final divine gesture, God created out of the man, and specifically not in God's image, the woman to be the man's helpmate. Neither the scientific nor cultural suppositions of these creation narratives are accepted, believed, or acted upon by people in this century.

This same view of the created order also underlay the story of the great flood and Noah. Most people remember that narrative only in terms of rain for forty days and forty nights, but a careful reading of the biblical text will reveal that it was the fountains underneath the dry land, accompanied by the rain, that brought about the flood. The separation of the waters in the heavens from the waters of the earth, which had been the primary act of creation, was allowed to be undone. "On that day all the fountains of the great deep burst forth and the windows of the heavens were opened" (Gen. 7:11).

The literal account in the Bible says that the waters covered the whole earth. "And the waters prevailed so mightily upon the earth that all the high mountains under the whole heaven were covered; the waters prevailed above the mountains, covering them fifteen cubits deep" (Gen. 7:19, 20). A cubit is an ancient unit of length varying from eighteen inches to sometimes twenty-one inches, or more. The Himalayan mountains soar to 28,028 feet in Mount Everest. For the flood story to be literally true, water more than five miles deep would have had to cover the earth. Since the earth is round, not flat, the water could not simply fall off the edges so that dry land could appear. If the polar ice cap melted, it might place coastal cities under water, but a five-mile depth of water covering the entire earth is more water than any of us could imagine. It is also a quantity that could not ever be absorbed by the earth. A universal flood that covered the whole earth to the depth of fifteen cubits is not a fact of human history. It exists only in our mythology.

In the Book of Joshua, this view of the cosmos once again was operative when Joshua ordered the sun to stand still in the sky so that the slaughter of the Amorites by the Israelites might continue to occur without the interruption of nightfall (Josh. 10:12, 13). Ignoring the rather dubious reason for such a miracle and the tribal hostility that made Israel assume that the killing of the Amorites was God's holy cause as well as theirs, this account is still not something our modern minds can accept. The sun cannot be ordered to stop, for it is not journeying through our sky. Rather, the earth is turning on its axis. If, out of an inadequate cosmological knowledge, Joshua really caused the earth to cease turning, the gravitational effects would have destroyed this planet forever. From every side, this story is based upon pre-scientific conclusions that are today believed by no one.

It gets a bit stickier and far more emotional when these observations are applied to events in the life of Jesus. However, the fact remains that a literal, physical understanding of Jesus' ascension is also open to serious questions, for the same reasons. The ascension story, as Luke tells it in the Book of Acts, assumes a flat earth covered by a domed ceiling beyond which heaven exists and God dwells. Jesus rises in order to enter the keyhole in the sky to be enthroned at the right hand of God. But in a space age, rising from this earth into the sky does not result in achieving heaven. It might only result in achieving orbit. The image of Jesus in eternal orbit with white tunic flying in the breeze does nothing for my spiritual understanding and trivializes the deeper meaning of the biblical story.

Luke did not comprehend the vastness of space. No one in his day did. He could not have imagined space travel. Under the popularizing influence of astrophysicist Carl Sagan, we can now put the ascension into a new physiological context that reveals the inadequacy of biblical literalism. If Jesus ascended physically into the sky, and if he rose as rapidly as the speed of light (186,000 miles per second), he would not yet have reached the edges of our own galaxy. There are more stars in our single galaxy than there are human beings who have ever lived on the face of this earth in all of its history. There are more galaxies in our universe than there are stars in our single galaxy. Our galaxy is only one of billions and billions of galaxies in the universe. Space is incomprehensibly vast. The cosmology of the Bible is incredibly limited in terms of the knowledge available to us today.

The Imperative to Reinterpret

We could cite other biblical passages that reflect a pre-scientific attitude toward the world or the universe. There is the account of the wandering star in Matthew's birth narrative, or the view of Sheol in the center of the earth as found in numerous places (Gen. 37:35; Num. 16:30; Isa. 7:11; Amos 9:2). But the point is made; only the implications have not yet been fully drawn. As those implications begin to invade our consciousness, we realize that we have all assumed a biblical literalism in the construction of our theological understandings of God, Jesus, and salvation. Unless theological truth can be separated from pre-scientific understandings and rethought in ways consistent with our understanding of reality, the Christian faith will be reduced to one more ancient mythology that will take its place alongside the religions of Mount Olympus. Those who insist on biblical literalism thus become unwitting

31

accomplices in bringing about the death of the Christianity they so deeply love. Ironic though it may seem, the success of fundamentalism in many ways guarantees the death of the very things these Christian folk affirm.

At the very least, those who want to be Christians in the twenty-first century must embrace this data. Geologists estimate today that the age of the earth is between four and five billion years. This means that the earth existed for more than 99 percent of its physical history to date before human life appeared. If human life was the purpose for the earth's creation, it certainly took a while for it to appear. This earth may well exist for billions of years beyond the age of the mammals, including human life. It is thus hard to argue that human life is the sole, or even primary, purpose for which creation occurred.

Far from being the center of the universe, we now are aware that our tiny planet is insignificant in size and in the scope of the universe. Suddenly the ancient myth of creation, together with all those biblical stories that assume its worldview, have no geological or astrophysical meaning. God, thought once to be so intimately near that God could actually walk with Adam and Eve in the Garden of Eden in the cool of the day (Genesis 3), is now increasingly perceived in distant, impersonal terms. The traumas of nature, even hurricanes and tornadoes, droughts and floods, are explained apart from any divine reference. The God living just above the sky who would intervene in the life of this world to effect a cure, save a nation, or deliver one from peril is no longer a certain deity to those who embrace the knowledge available in this century. If there is no other way to think about God, many will be forced to acknowledge that the God who was once a major actor in so much of our recorded history has simply been lost in the new insights of this century. No appeal to an inerrant Bible will bring back such a limited deity.

The issue in the creation story and in the Bible as a whole is not evolution versus creationism, as many conservative Christians like to maintain. This irrelevant issue only scratches the surface of the problem. The real issue is that the suppositions that underlie the Bible are today held by no one, not even those who define themselves as "Bible believing Christians." Their value is only historic. The Bible relates to us the way our ancient forebears understood and interpreted their world, made sense out of life, and thought about God. Our task is the same as theirs. We must interpret our world in the light of our knowledge and suppositions.

We must, as they sought to do, make sense out of life in terms of our understanding of meaning and values. We must think about God in the light of our perceptions of divinity. The Bible becomes not a literal road map to reality but a historic narrative of the journey our religious forebears made in the eternal human quest to understand life, the world, themselves, and God. We walk in their company as fellow pilgrims. We affirm some of the values they affirmed.

We call life good. We look for and find meaning and divinity, not always so much in an external God as in the very depths of our humanity, but it is divinity nonetheless. We discover transcending spirit within ourselves. We explore the enormous range of our consciousness looking for ways to leap our barriers in every direction. We seek to penetrate the life experience of animals. We delve into the limitations of our own brains. We look for hints that might free us from our limits— mind-altering drugs, hypnotic explorations into some previous incarnations, the possibility of finding and communicating with other forms of intelligent life in the universe. We have in our space probes learned to escape the effects of gravity and to experience weightlessness. The possibility of colonizing another planet is discussed today as a reality, albeit farfetched but definitely not science fiction. We have come to the dawning realization that God might not be separate from us but rather deep within us. The sense of God as the sum of all that is, plus something more, grows in acceptability. When theologians are pressed, however, to define that *something more*, the inadequacy of language becomes gallingly apparent.

We modern Christians grapple with these ideas as we journey through our life in our time. On that journey, we read the

Scriptures but not for their historic accuracy so much as to be able to receive and enter into the experience of those who journeyed before us. Like them, we explore the human capacity to discover meaning, community, and deity. As with the fine knife of a skilled surgeon or perhaps even a laser beam of cutting light, we can separate in the myths of the past, the truth, from the containers of that truth, and to that truth we can still pledge allegiance. It is not easy.

We say that God created human life to be good. But the assumption in our religious tradition is that this human life was created in a perfected, recognizably Homo sapien form. Our myth does not accommodate itself to a period of time of some one and a half million years in which the barrier between human and nonhuman or subhuman was indistinct. If only human beings have souls, as the church has taught, one must be able to say when humanity became human and was infused with its divine and eternal soul. Without an instantaneous creation, that becomes quite problematic. Is Homo erectus human? Or is that human definition to be reserved only for Homo sapiens? If so, at what stage in the development of Homo sapiens? Language appears to be no more than thirty-five thousand to fifty thousand years old. If biologists cannot pinpoint the moment at which Homo erectus became Homo sapiens, except to say that it occurred over a period of one and a half million years, can theologians dare to be more specific?

On what real basis do we suggest that the creation began good and then fell into sin? Where is the evidence? Did the animal nature in us that drives us to survive, reproduce, satisfy the basic needs for food, water, and procreation, which formed our values, suddenly become evil? Was it not always there and would we have survived without it? Did these ancient and basic urges come into existence only in "the fall"? Or is it not more accurate to say that they were part of creation itself and in time had to submit to the civilizing influences first of life in the clan, then in the tribe, then in the nation, and finally today in our vastly interdependent world? Are not the human qualities we now call selfishness or self-centeredness the result of

34

the drive to survive far more than of the fall into sin? Do not those very qualities that once served our need to survive now threaten to annihilate us as we struggle to be the keeper of our brothers and sisters in a shrinking, overpopulated world that can no longer absorb the garbage we selfish Homo sapiens create in our quest for individual pleasure?

If the "fall of man," as the traditional Christians like to describe the story of sin entering human life in the Garden of Eden, no longer makes sense, the traditional way of understanding the Christ story also sinks into a sea of inadequacy. For the Christ has been portrayed as the divine rescuer—sent to save the fallen human creature from sin and to restore that creature to the goodness of his or her pre-fall creation. Again and again we discover painfully that our central Christian affirmations make assumptions based upon a literalized view of the biblical narrative that are no longer believable. Hence when we cast light on those assumptions, they fall apart. They are not based on a reality we can grasp or believe. The Christian church, if unwilling to rethink and reformulate the very basic understandings of its faith, will increasingly not have much to say to a world that will understand neither our language nor our symbols. The Christian church is living now on the basis of capital from the past; traditional patterns of thought that have not yet been challenged sufficiently in the minds of the masses. That will not long endure.

The only churches that grow today are those that do not, in fact, understand the issues and can therefore traffic in certainty. They represent both the fundamentalistic Protestant groups and the rigidly controlled conservative Catholic traditions. The churches that do attempt to interact with the emerging world are for the most part the liberal Protestant mainline churches that shrink every day in membership and the silent liberal Catholic minority that attracts very few adherents. Both are, almost by definition, fuzzy, imprecise, and relatively unappealing. They might claim to be honest, but for the most part they have no real message. They tinker with words, redefine concepts, and retreat slowly behind the rear guard protection of a few pseudoradical thinkers. I have sought to live in this arena. It shrinks daily. In contradistinction to this liberal wing are the conservatives, who seem to be expending all of their meager energy on the hopeless task of doing a facelift on the corpse of the traditional Christian religion, employing images that have lost their meaning. They, too, will ultimately fail.

No one seems yet ready to invest the energy that will be required to engage the task of reformulating the Christ story for our day if, indeed, it can be reformulated. Yet that alone, in my opinion, is the pathway to a living Christianity and a living Christ. Until the choices before us are clear, the path ahead will not be apparent.

Dismissing the pre-scientific assumptions in which the biblical narrative is captive is a necessary first step. I invite my readers to take that step and to let everything built upon those assumptions fall with them. It will not be easy for believers, but even this level of religious vulnerability is not the only problem we face, as the next chapters will reveal.

4

The Formation of the Sacred Story

The biblical writers had no sense at all of the sweep of historic times, nor did they have any concept even of the size of the earth. They did not know that there was a China or that the "new world" populated by tribes of people, all of whom would mistakenly become known as Indians, existed.

There was for the writers of Scripture no communication system beyond word of mouth. There were no newspapers, television sets, or radios. Events were recorded not on film for future viewing, but only in the memory of the observer. When the observer passed the news on, it was filtered through subject after subject until it was either forgotten or took its place in the tribal folklore to be repeated generation after generation.

We need to be reminded that even in this modern world with its technological genius, there is still no such thing as "objective" history. Our view of history is shaped by our own national interests, by those who have the power to make their view of life the standard view, and by those who have won the wars. If this is so for us, how much less would objectivity be served in the ancient world with its narrow focus, its limited embrace of reality, its pre-scientific mind-set of miracle and magic, and by its nationalistic tribal understandings of deity itself.

Despite these realities, many of the Christian people of the world are still taught that the Bible is inerrant or in a literal sense "the word of God." This conclusion continues to have power and is, in my opinion, one of the primary reasons why educated young adults find themselves abandoning organized religion in droves. Adding piety to ignorance does not temper the ignorance, no matter how real and beautiful the piety.

In this chapter I want to place the biblical narrative into a frame of reference that will enable my readers to embrace the reality of time and see what that reality does to ancient religious claims, as well as the possibilities it creates for new biblical insight.

History According to Science and According to the Bible

For years the church taught that creation itself could be dated in the year 4004 B.C.E. (before the common era). An Irish prelate named Bishop James Ussher painstakingly went through the Bible in the seventeenth century, counting the ages attributed to various persons in order to arrive at this date. Even before Bishop Ussher had been quite so specific, the general consensus located the beginning of time somewhere after 6000 B.C.E. Our ancient forebears did not know about the Ice Age, Neanderthal man (and woman), or the cave dwellers of antiquity. Every child in every school today learns about prehistoric people that run our dates back at least twenty-five thousand to fifty thousand years.

Geological evidence today indicates that this planet earth is between four and five billion years old. Life itself seems to have come into existence about three and a half billion years ago in the sea, where it continued to develop until it was ready to leave the watery depths of its first womb. Somewhere around 450 million years ago that life climbed out of the sea in primitive amphibian forms. One hundred million years ago the reptiles ruled the earth, with dinosaurs being the dominant reptile.

38

When the dinosaurs were destroyed, the way was opened for mammals to inherit the earth, where they have now been dominant for about sixty million years. Somewhere between five hundred thousand and two million years ago, Homo sapiens came into being, probably in the grasslands of east Africa or in the area of southeast Asia, including what are now the islands of Indonesia but in that ancient time were still connected by land with what we now call Vietnam, Cambodia, Thailand, and the Malaysian peninsula.[1]

If the beginning of the Judeo-Christian faith can be documented in history, the story of the call of Abraham would stand for that moment. Abraham and his wife, Sarah, according to the Hebrew folktale, responded to the call of God to leave Ur of the Chaldees to journey out into the unknown to a strange land in a foreign place and there to build a great nation. Abraham was to be the new nation's father. (In a patriarchal age, nations did not seem to have mothers.) His descendants were to be more numerous than the sands of the sea or the stars in the sky, figures of speech designed to represent an infinite number, which, of course, Israel never achieved.

If Abraham was a real person in history, or even if a kernel of historic truth lies at the core of the Abraham saga, he is dated by most historians somewhere in the nineteenth century B.C.E. The biblical portrait of Abraham depicts him as a nomad who lived in a tent, kept great flocks, had many servants, wives, and children, and as one who roamed the wilderness so that his flocks could find adequate pasture.

There are two things to note about Abraham. First, if we accept the latest date put forward by anthropologists concerning the emergence of Homo sapiens of 500,000 years ago, Abraham is placed into that time frame about 496,000 years after the first human being arrived on this planet. This means that if Abraham is the starting point for our faith story, human beings were on this earth 496,000 years before our faith story was born. Can one realize this and still claim that ultimate saving truth resides only in our understanding of God? Would it not be a strange God who would leave human beings with no saving revelation of the Divine One for all but .8 percent of human history? The presumption of those who make such a claim for the infallibility of their version of truth is awesome.

The second noteworthy fact to consider is that biblical scholarship today seems to indicate that the earliest continuous written material contained in what we call the Old Testament is no earlier than the tenth century b.c.e. This does not preclude the presence in these continuous narratives of material that in isolated forms is much earlier. If this date is right, Abraham existed in solely word-of-mouth narration for some eight hundred to nine hundred years before stories about him achieved written form. For eight hundred to nine hundred years, the only things anyone knew about Abraham were passed on around camp fires from generation to generation. Who, knowing this, is willing to support the claim of inerrancy for a nine-hundred-year-old oral tradition?

In the Abrahamic saga, we are told that Sarah conceived despite the fact that she was ninety years of age (Gen. 17:17); that Abraham actually drew a knife to slay his own son (Genesis 22); that God rained fire and brimstone upon Sodom and Gomorrah (Gen. 19:24–25); and that Lot's wife, because she looked back at Sodom, was turned into a pillar of salt (Gen. 19:26). Can these narratives be literal truth?

If we could assume for a moment the truth of the Mosaic authorship of the Torah, we would still have to face a time gap between Moses and Abraham of 400 to 550 years. The earliest date I have ever seen for Moses is 1400 b.c.e. Most scholars, however, date Moses around 1250 b.c.e. Even assuming a higher quality of oral transmission among ancient people than is the case in our technological society, how much confidence does one want to place in the inerrant quality of a story passed on only in spoken form from person to person for even 400 years?

The consensus of Bible scholars locate the earliest written Old Testament material in or around Jerusalem and dates it shortly after the death of King David (ca. 960 b.c.e.). If this is true, then even the escapades of Moses and the words of the Torah, the Jewish law, did not achieve written form until at least three hundred years after the death of Moses. The Torah as presented in the first five books of the Bible could thus hardly be material that Moses received directly from God at Mount Sinai. Yet this Hebrew tradition still feeds a lively Christian fundamentalism.

This means that even the historic Moses himself is lost in the darker recesses of historic memory and that the biblical image we have of Moses has been significantly tempered by the history of a much later time. Was Moses an Egyptian? His name certainly was. *Mose* was the Egyptian word for child. Most of his religious ideas can be linked with the dawning universalism of a most unusual pharaoh named Amenhotep IV, who ruled Egypt from 1375 to 1358 B.C.E. and who later changed his name to Ikhnaton. Yet some of the ideas attributed to Moses are anything but universal, caught as they are in tribal patterns.[2] Were there really two persons who have been subsumed under the name Moses in the memory of Israel? Was the God of the original Moses a broad God whose ideas gave rise to approaching universality while the God of the second Moses was a tribal deity who embodied the prejudices of his people? Could this explanation account for the tension between the lofty idea that "God is creator of all and all are in God's image" and the barbaric orders to "kill every man, woman and child of the Amalekites," both of which are said to emanate from the God of Moses?[3]

Is the story about Moses needing someone to speak for him, which resulted in bringing one identified as Aaron the brother of Moses into the drama, a vestigial remnant of the memory that Moses was a foreigner, perhaps an Egyptian, who did not speak Hebrew? Was the original Moses killed in the wilderness in one of the many rebellions against this leader that the biblical narrative speaks of? And was he then replaced with a Hebrew whose warlike tribal experience reflected a God who was conceived of as a warlike tribal deity? In time were these

41

two figures merged into a single person with a continuous, although not always compatible, narrative in the folklore around the camp fires?

Is not the story of the crossing of the Jordan River, which is so repetitive of the story of the crossing of the Red Sea, but one illustration of how two separate traditions around two separate people got merged in the corporate memory? Who were the Levites? How did a priestly tribe emerge? Were they also connected to the original Moses as a priestly group whose roots were likewise Egyptian? Are they the ones who kept the original Egyptian Moses and his ideas alive in Israel so that they could challenge year after year and generation after generation the narrow, angry tribal deity that dominates the pages of Hebrew Scriptures? Did the prophetic movement rise out of the Levitical heritage?

These are just a few of the issues that scholars raise about this hazy period of Israel's prewritten history. Obviously these are difficult possibilities to entertain if the Bible must be regarded as literally true.

There is also a strong possibility that Abraham, Isaac, and Jacob, far from being the founding ancestors of Israel, were in fact Canaanite holy men, connected with the religious shrines at Hebron, Beersheba, and Bethel. Did the marauding Hebrews simply take over these shrines and their stories, adapt them to Israel's history, link these patriarchal figures together as father, son, and grandson and then use them to legitimize their invasion and conquest of Canaan? From the Canaanite point of view, the claim that God had promised Canaanite lands to the forefathers of the Israelite people some five hundred years earlier must have had a strange sound. It was in Israel's political vested interest, then, to claim ancestors associated with three Canaanite holy places and to show how the Hebrew people left this area for Egypt to avoid famine only to fall into the oppression of slavery from which they now escaped to reclaim their ancestral lands.

Every nation justifies the violence of its aggressive foreign policy with self-serving rationales. Israel was no different, but can such a tale be called the "inerrant word of God"? Can these words be treated as literal truth?

The Making of the Hebrew Scriptures

[handwritten: THIS WAS TAUGHT AS FAR BACK AS I CAN Remember]

The prevailing point of view among biblical scholars regarding the way the Hebrew Scriptures came to be written still revolves around the four-document theory originally proposed by the Graf-Welhansen school of biblical scholars in the nineteenth century. That theory brought into biblical scholarship the familiar symbols of J (Y), E, D, and P. These symbols stand for the separate strands of biblical narration (Yahwist, Elohist, Deuteronomic, and Priestly), each with its own agenda that later came to be merged into the one continuous biblical narrative. Although this theory is constantly being modified as knowledge expands in biblical research, it nonetheless continues to be affirmed almost incontrovertibly in its broad sweep. The tragedy is that the typical woman or man in the pew has not been introduced to these insights, whether in a refined form or not. If the Bible is so important to us, it seems essential that we understand how it came to be written. It did not drop from heaven in a complete and final form, written in Elizabethan English. I will offer here a brief explanation of these four sources of the Hebrew Scriptures and illustrate their influence.

The Yahwist

The source theory concludes that at some point, probably during the early years of the reign of Solomon in Jerusalem (960–920 B.C.E.), an unknown person took pen in hand to write an epic story about how this Jewish nation came into being. The result was the first narrative history of Israel—a sort of Hebrew *Iliad.* It was a story that reflected what is surely a fact of history, that some portion of this now-mighty nation enjoying the opulence and wealth of the Solomonic years had its origin in slavery in the land of Egypt. The Jews had once been weak and powerless, but by the hand of their God they had been built into being a powerful nation.

This writer called God by the name of Yahweh in this narrative, and for this reason, the narrative itself is referred to as the Yahwist document. No personal detail of the life of this anonymous author is known to us today. The assumption is that he was a male because women were not educated in that era to read or write. His work had been lost for centuries despite the fact that for all of those years it had been read as part of the Hebrew Scriptures. When the Yahwist document was finally identified and isolated by German scholars, it was lifted out of its hiding place where it had been preserved—buried inside the biblical text itself.

The Yahwist writer recorded the genius of Israel and made that genius normative for the future of the Hebrews. The Yahwist document opens with what is now the second creation story (Gen. 2:46–4:26) and moves through the sagas of Noah, Abraham, Isaac, Jacob, and Joseph until it culminates in the account of Moses, who is this writer's great hero. Each of these stories has been impacted from other sources but under the scrutiny of the biblical scholars the Y material begins to stand in clear relief. It is fresh, colorful, and full of power; clearly the work of a single great mind. He does not whitewash his heroes. He calls Abraham a liar (Gen. 20:1ff), tells the story of Noah's drunkenness (Gen. 9:20), and relates the account of Lot's incest (Gen. 19:30–36).

The Yahwist's purpose in telling his story is easy to discern. He chronicles a history of his people from slavery to the establishment of a great nation and then argues powerfully that the slave heritage of Israel was an accident of their history. Behind their slavery the Hebrews were free, noble, and rich. They are a people of promise in whose life Yahweh is constantly intervening to make good the divine word.

The Yahwist writer asserted that Yahweh was the only divine power at work in the universe. The seeds of a crude monotheism are clearly present. This God created the heavens, the earth, the plants, the herbs, the male, the animals, and the woman (Gen. 2:4–25). Since Adam and Eve were thought to be the primeval parents of all humanity, this single God was the only God and must ultimately be the God of all nations.

Yet this universal God was very humanlike. Not only did God mold the man out of the dust of the earth (Gen. 2:7) and breathe into that creature the divine *nephesh*, or spirit, but God also planted a garden (Gen. 2:8) and took walks in that garden in the cool of the evening (Gen. 3:8). God called to Adam when Adam could not be found, as if the Divine One were limited and as if the human creature could successfully hide from this limited deity (Gen. 3:9). God made the woman by a process of trial and error in the attempt to create an adequate partner for the male (Gen. 2:18–23). Even after the sin of disobedience, Yahweh clothed the first family (Gen. 3:21).

For the Yahwist writer, the human and the entire created order were inexorably bound up together. All things were touched and brought into ruin by human weakness. He was also a writer whose narrative gave answers to the questions of ancient people: Why has the human being been given dominion over the animals? Why do human beings use language, have religion, and wear clothing? Why do briars and thorns grow in cultivated areas? Why do seasons return and different tribes speak different languages? Why are there rainbows?

As the human family grew, the Yahwist writer, recognizing a distant kinship, told of how the other nations of the earth came into being. The Ammonites and the Moabites came through Lot's incestuous relationship with his daughters (Gen. 19:30–38). The Arabs were descended from Ishmael, Abraham's first son born to Hagar, the Egyptian slave woman (Gen. 21:8–21), and the Edomites were the children of Esau, Isaac's first-born son who sold his birthright to his twin brother, Jacob (Gen. 25:29–34; Genesis 27; Gen. 36:1). Even when the Yahwist writer narrowed his story to Israel, he still portrayed God as interested in all humanity. All nations are to be blessed through Abraham (Gen. 12:3). It was a remarkable view to hold in the tenth century before the common era and represents part of the genius of Israel.

45

The Yahwist writer viewed his nation from the vantage point of the province of Judah. The monarchy and the temple at Jerusalem were the twin authorities for him. He saw the king and the priest as God's anointed and suggested that they ruled by divine right. Rebellion against the royal family or the temple worship was rebellion against God and was, therefore, not allowable. So the Yahwist writer extolled the monarchy and the temple and established the lines of authority to be from God to the hierarchical leaders and only then to the people. The people related to God by supporting God's chosen ones. Even Moses was portrayed by this writer as chosen by God and sent to the people as God's emissary (Exod. 3:1ff).

Thus the first strand of Israel's written history was royalist, hierarchical, and strongly supportive of the institutions of monarchy and priesthood as they were being lived out in Jerusalem in the tenth century B.C.E. It needs to be noted that in the Yahwist version of the Ten Commandments (Exodus 34), there is no reference to God having rested on the seventh-day as the justification for the observance of Sabbath. The reason for this omission is obvious to biblical scholars because the seven-day creation story of Genesis 1:1–2:4 had not yet been written. It was a much later work of art.

Around the year 920 B.C.E., following the death of Solomon, there was a rebellion and a civil war in the Hebrew nation, and the land was split into a northern kingdom, called Israel, and a southern kingdom, called Judah. In the south, the Jerusalem temple and the royal house of David continued to be the dominant institutions. But in the north, rebellion against both institutions had to be justified, and a new form of "church and state" relationship had to be designed. These realities found expression in a new version of Jewish history that was to be the product of the northern kingdom.

The Elohist

Somewhere near the year 850 B.C.E. another court historian—this one not in Jerusalem but in Samaria—began to put together another story of Israel's life, another interpretation of its history. This story reflected the value system alive in the northern kingdom—a value system that was antidynastic and antiking. It suggested that God made the original covenant not with the leaders or Moses or the royal family but with the people, who then chose their leaders and empowered them. For this reason no priest, leader, or king could claim permanent status over God's people. The power the people gave their leaders could be withdrawn by the givers if the leaders failed to be sensitive to the people's needs. This was the budding of democracy and helped the people of the north to justify the rebellion against Solomon's son Rehoboam and the resulting creation of a new state that had neither a temple nor a sustaining royal family.

This document called God by the name Elohim and for this reason is known as the "Elohist" document. It forms the second major written narrative in what is now known as the Old Testament. The author of this document is likewise unknown, but he was obviously a citizen of the northern kingdom and was possibly a priest associated with the sacred shrine of Bethel. His work is also an epic and qualifies to be called the Hebrew Odyssey. It is a tale full of romance and emotion.

This author gives the northern kingdom's version of many of the stories in the Yahwist document. He is somewhat more provincial, less sweeping, and more nationalistic. He began this tale not with creation but with Abraham, whom he identified with eastern Bedouins rather than with Ur of the Chaldees. But Abraham was not his hero. He did dwell on the story of the near sacrifice of Isaac, an Elohist masterpiece, but he passed Isaac quickly to get to Jacob, who was the focus of his tale.

Under the skillful pen of this author, Jacob emerged as a flesh-and-blood figure whose life was chronicled in intimate detail. He was the chosen one, elected over his older brother to receive Isaac's blessing (Gen. 27:1ff). He dreamed of ladders to heaven (Gen. 28:10–17) and wrestled with an angel (Gen. 32:22–32). He went to his uncle Laban, fell in love with Laban's daughter Rachel, worked seven years to gain her hand in

47

marriage only to be tricked into marrying Rachel's older sister, Leah (Gen. 29:15ff). Leah, the mother of Judah, the dominant tribe in the southern kingdom, was described in very derogatory terms ("Leah's eyes were weak" Gen. 29:17), while Rachel, the grandmother of Ephraim, the dominant tribe in the northern kingdom, was flattered constantly, "Rachel was beautiful and lovely" (Gen. 29:17).

Joseph, Rachel's son and Ephraim's father, was the favorite son of his father Jacob (Gen. 37:3) and the recipient of a long robe with sleeves that was thought of as possessing many colors (Gen. 37:3). He was also the bearer of his brothers' abuse (Gen. 37:20ff), the source of their salvation in Egypt (Gen. 42), and the reason the Hebrews went to Egypt to live (Gen. 47). They went as noble people, and at the invitation of the Pharaoh they took up residence in Egypt in the land of Goshen. In time, however, they fell into slavery when a pharaoh arose who "did not know Joseph" (Exod. 1:8).

Was this accurate history? No. Like all history, it was intermingled with the values of those who created it. It was an attempt to explain the history of the present moment by shaping the folklore of a past that could have been at least one thousand years earlier. It contained kernels of history, but little more. Certainly it could not be literalized. It suggested that perhaps the division among the Hebrew people that broke into civil war in 920 B.C.E. was a division that had always existed. Perhaps the original Moses led only the Joseph tribes out of slavery, and at a place called Kadesh they entered into an alliance with the Leah tribes, the dominant one of which was called the tribe of Judah. The Leah tribes were semitic people, but they had never known slavery. These two groups then formed an alliance based on their common ethnic kinship and sought to build a single nation. In time the history and folklore of both groups blended into a unified story and folklore. The story of Jacob having two wives accounted for both their sense of kinship and their separateness. Together the two groups conquered Canaan under Joshua, who was also a hero to the Elohist writer.

48

The people then divided up the land—Ephraim dominating the north, Judah dominating the south, until the alliance fell apart years later. Some of the Hebrew people intermarried with the Canaanites, and this was recognized and explained in the folklore by giving Jacob not only Leah and Rachel as his wives, but also a maidservant of Leah's named Zilpah (Gen. 30:9) and a maidservant of Rachel's named Bilhah (Gen. 30:7) by whom Jacob could produce the half-breed children who made up part of the nation.

Over and over the Elohist writer identified the patriarchal heroes Abraham, Isaac, and Jacob with the shrines of Hebron, Beersheba, and Bethel, respectively. At this moment in history, the northern kingdom had to resist the allure of Jerusalem, and they did so by heightening the power of the northern kingdom's religious shrines so that its people would not yearn for the holy places of Jerusalem.

The Elohist writer may have been familiar with some aspects of the Yahwist document but, time after time, he blunted its Judean emphasis to allow the glory of the northern kingdom to be seen. He used dreams to convey God's power in his drama. Jacob, Joseph, Pharaoh, and Samuel all dream in the Elohist material. Most of the miracle and magic of the plague stories in Egypt are Elohist material. This writer had God establish the covenant with the people first. The people then made Moses their mediator. In the Elohist material, the people participated in the covenant, whereas in the Yahwist material, bounds were set around the holy mountain to prevent the profaning of the holy place by the people. From the Elohist writer we receive the version of the Ten Commandments with which we are most familiar. In the Elohist version, the covenant was sealed when Moses sprinkled blood on all the people (Exod. 24:8), which differs substantially from the Yahwist account, which had the covenant sealed only by Moses, Aaron, two priests, and seventy elders, who climbed the mountain, had a heavenly vision, and ate the sacramental meal (Exod. 24:9–11). The Elohist writer built up Moses but said rather pointedly that there had not since arisen a prophet in Israel like Moses. There

49

was to be no dynasty. God would raise up prophets as God needed them. Hosea and Amos, for example, were to rise from the northern kingdom.

When Samaria, the capital of the northern kingdom, fell to the Assyrians in 721 B.C.E., the people were carried into exile and eventually were amalgamated into the general population of that foreign land. But some citizens of the northern kingdom did manage to escape captivity and to rescue the Elohist document by taking it to Jerusalem, where, in time, it was blended into the Yahwist narrative, so that this second step in the formation of the Hebrew Scriptures was accomplished near the turn of the eighth century B.C.E. So many of the textual contradictions present in the Old Testament result from the fact that these two versions were originally separate and distinct and the attempt to harmonize them was never complete.

The Deuteronomists

In 621 B.C.E. another major revision of this sacred story occurred in Jerusalem during the reign of King Josiah. According to the tradition, during a period in which repairs were being made on the temple, a scroll of law purporting to have been written by Moses was discovered in the temple (2 Kings 22:18). This sacred text was, not surprisingly, completely responsive to the prophetic tradition of Hosea, Amos, Isaiah, Micah, and especially Jeremiah, who was alive and at work when this new book was "discovered." This book called for the kind of religious reform the prophets had been calling for, and it rekindled a kind of national pride that helped to keep this soon-to-be-conquered nation intact through the period of exile. The book was called the second (*deutero*) giving of the Law (*nomas*) and came to be known as Deuteronomy.

When discovered, the book was taken immediately to King Josiah, who had the reputation for doing what the prophets desired. The young king read the book then tore his clothes in an act of ceremonial repentance, gathered the people, publicly read to them the words of this text, and called the people into a renewed covenant and a religious reform movement that was the most rigorous in biblical history. Over the next twenty-five years, the Book of Deuteronomy was added to the Yahwist-Elohist combination, and the newly merged text was edited anew in the light of the deuteronomic insights. The author of Deuteronomy was eager to purify worship, to purge from Judah all foreign rites, to centralize worship in all the land under the supervision of the Jerusalem priesthood, and to bring the people into a realization of the love Yahweh had for them. He was also a writer of considerable ability and beautiful prose. Before the deuteronomic revision of the Hebrew sacred story was complete, it was clear that more than a single person was involved, but all worked from a single perspective.

The deuteronomic writers reflected a high spiritual monotheism: To Yahweh belonged the heavens, the earth, and all within them. God was both sublime and awesome. It was the deuteronomists who insisted that no image of God could be used in worship. At Horeb "you heard the sound of words, but saw no form; there was only a voice" (Deut. 4:12). Yet Yahweh was still a nationalistic deity in Deuteronomy, and here are found the seeds of divine pettiness in the service of a national deity that became so destructive later. Finally, the authors of this strand of biblical material closed down all religious shrines save for the Jerusalem temple and decreed that the Passover itself could be celebrated only in Jerusalem, a practice that plays such a large part in the later life of Jesus of Nazareth.

By the time the deuteronomists had finished their work, they had colored the books of Joshua, Judges, 1 and 2 Samuel, and 1 and 2 Kings. They had supplied their nation with a philosophy of history, and they had touched up the books of the prophets. They had taught the Jewish people to see the past through their eyes.

Twenty-five years after the discovery of this book in the temple the nation of Judah was defeated and destroyed by the Babylonians. Into captivity the people went, but they carried with them their growing sacred story—the Yahwist-Elohist-deuteronomic blended version together with other religious

51

traditions kept alive particularly by the priests. These traditions may also have been ancient in origin, but they had not yet been fully incorporated into Israel's growing sacred story. During the exile, however, this sacred story would undergo its final and most dramatic editing and revision under the impact of this priestly material. Thus it would emerge in the postexile world more or less in the form that we have it in our Bibles today.

The Priests

In 596 B.C.E. the city of Jerusalem fell to Nebuchadnezzar and his Babylonian army. The city was sacked, and, in keeping with Babylonian policy, a program of deportation into exile began. In the ancient world this policy normally meant the end of a nation's life. In captivity the conquered people tended, after a period of time, to intermarry with their captors and to lose their national identity. This is exactly what had happened when the people of the northern kingdom of Israel were resettled after their defeat by Assyria some 130 years before. For Judah this moment was the supreme challenge. Everything she stood for—her worship, her God, her Law, and even the values that resided at that moment only in the genes of her people—was put in jeopardy. In 596 B.C.E. most of the elite of Judah were marched into captivity. In 586 B.C.E., following an abortive attempt at revolution, another deportation occurred that all but obliterated the nation. Other peoples were brought in to resettle Judah. These people intermarried with the few natives left and became known as the half-breed Samaritans.

Many of the Psalms were written during this period of exile, including the plaintive cry of Psalm 137: "By the waters of Babylon, there we sat down and wept, when we remembered Zion. On the willows there we hung up our lyres. For there our captors required of us songs and our tormentors, mirth, saying, 'Sing us one of the songs of Zion!' How shall we sing the Lord's song in a foreign land?"

The Jews of the exile, however, were a hardy breed. Led by their priestly class, headed at the beginning of this period by the prophet-priest Ezekiel and culminating in such priests as Nehemiah and Ezra many years later, they rose to meet this national crisis in a way no captive people had ever done. They did it primarily by asserting the power of the religious tradition of the Jews over the total life of the people. In the process they also edited and rewrote massive parts of their sacred story.

For people to maintain their national identity in captivity, they had to be perceived as different. The priestly leaders accomplished this in two primary ways. Out of their Jewish past they lifted two traditions that actually had fallen into general disuse—circumcision and Sabbath day observance—and they invested these with such meaning that they became the distinguishing marks of a Jew. Every Jewish male had on his body the physical sign of his Jewishness. All Jewish people were those strange folk whose religion required that they do no work on the seventh day. Under pressure from these priestly writers, the familiar seven-day creation story that opens our Bibles was written to root Sabbath day observance in the moment of creation. The God who rested from creation on the Sabbath hallowed this day and mandated its observance by all those who would be the people of this God.

This account of creation was in fact one of the last parts of the Hebrew Scriptures to be written. It is a poem of praise to the God of creation, culminating in the Sabbath day command to take cognizance in rest of the goodness of God's world.

Synagogues were built under the leadership of the priestly group in the exile to indoctrinate the coming generation, who would not remember Jerusalem, including in time those who had never known Jerusalem. The details of worship, the rules of worship, the observance of worship became all important and resulted in the creation of much of the Book of Exodus, almost all the Book of Leviticus, and major portions of the Book of Numbers. The Yahwist-Elohist-deuteronomic version of the Hebrew sacred story was thoroughly edited by the priestly writers to include the ancient priestly traditions and to affirm the sanctity throughout all of Jewish history of the traditions now being required of faithful Jews.

The Noah story was altered so that Noah took seven pairs of clean animals and only one pair of unclean animals (Gen. 7:1–10). This would enable Noah to have animals available for the ritual sacrifices and still preserve the species.

The story of manna in the wilderness was altered so that the people gathered two days' supply on the sixth day of the week and would not therefore have to work by gathering manna on the Sabbath (Exod. 16:4ff).

The Ten Commandments of Exodus 20 were edited to place the rationale from the newly written creation story into the words of Moses requiring the Jews to keep holy the Sabbath day. All the chronologies in the Old Testament are from the hand of the priestly writers. They wanted to make sure that links with the past were kept intact. A history of every ritual observed in Jewish worship entered the sacred story. The story of Abraham was altered to place the origin of the practice of circumcision into the life of the founding father of Israel. Strict dietary laws were written into the Torah as part of the separatist movement. Kosher food is a gift to Jewry of the priestly writer in exile in the late sixth and early fifth century B.C.E.

The historic saga of Israel that begins in slavery in Egypt and wanders through the wilderness to the conquest of Canaan, to the establishment of a united kingdom that endured division and civil war, defeat and exile, only to return to their holy land, is a narrative written by a variety of persons over more than half a millennium. It is filled with geographical misinformation and the biological, geological, and astrophysical information only of this ancient time. It reflects cultural traditions long since abandoned as unworthy of civilized people—polygamy, child sacrifice, and slavery, for example.

To suggest that this text is in any sense the "literal Word of God" is to place extreme limits on both its truth and its power. Out of our sincere religious need to possess in some written form an infallible source of truth, we run the risk of reducing our treasured book to irrelevance. If the religiously alienated, which in many cases includes our own children, can ridicule our sacred tradition by an appeal to our own sacred Scriptures for which we have claimed too much, then we will have little to offer the world. If those elements of organized religion are allowed to claim for the Bible such words as "inerrant," "infallible," "the literal Word of God," so that it is their limited understanding that becomes the only perception of Christianity in the public arena, then the Christian church, so heavily burdened, will not be able to speak with power to our own generation.

Beyond the historic portions of Scripture that we have just analyzed so quickly, there are some additional works that fill out the sacred text substantially. These writings consist of the works of the prophets that constitute close to one third of the Hebrew Scriptures, the liturgical literature, including Hebrew hymnody, the wisdom writings, and some works of protest. In order to complete our brief survey of biblical literature, we must now turn to look at these additions before we explore the deeper meaning of these ancient parts of the Bible itself.

5

Prophets, Psalms, Proverbs, and Protest

We have traced ever so briefly, and some would doubtless say shallowly, the sacred history of the Jewish people as found in their Holy Scriptures. That history embraced a sweep of time from the call of the shadowy figure of Abraham, who is dated in the nineteenth century before the common era, to the postexilic period that includes Ezra, Nehemiah, and others, who lived between the late sixth and early fourth centuries B.C.E. From that time until the birth of Jesus, the story of the Jewish people was recorded for us in texts that are in large measure now included in the Apocrypha. The primary exception to this was the Book of Daniel, which, though purporting to be an episode that took place during the exile, was in fact a book written in the Maccabean period of the second century B.C.E.

The Prophets

The second-biggest section after the books of history in the Hebrew Scriptures was the work of the various prophets. They stood as giants speaking their messages at critical points in Jewish history. Contrary to the way the prophets were understood in early Christian history, they were not predictors of the future. Jerry Falwell has written:

> I believe the Bible is God's word also because of fulfilled prophecy. Dozens of predictions are made in the Old Testament that were fulfilled in the New Testament in every detail. There are so many cases of fulfilled prophesies in the Bible that only the atheist or agnostic would believe them to be merely coincidental. Over two dozen prophesies have been fulfilled relating to the death, burial and resurrection of Christ alone. At least twelve of those are found in the 53rd chapter of Isaiah, which was written several hundred years before Christ was born! Fulfilled prophecy is an indisputable evidence that the Bible was written under the inspiration of the Holy Spirit.[1]

That quotation will hardly stand in the world of biblical scholarship. What this pastor calls fulfilled prophecy represents one of two things, both of them far removed from what he claims. Either the Christian author was writing the story to conform with prophetic hints (Did Psalm 22 predict the events of the cross, or did the Gospel writers pattern their story of the cross after this very familiar psalm?) or the author was employing a dreadful and disturbing method of wrenching Holy Scripture out of its context in order to make it serve Christian missionary aims. For example, the Matthean words "He shall be called a Nazarene" (Matt. 2:23), a quotation not easily identified with any verse in the Hebrew text, was made by the author of this Gospel to refer to citizenship in the town of Nazareth. This suggestion, which will be developed fully in chapter 10, is about as farfetched an idea as one might imagine.

The prophetic movement was a Jewish gift to the world. It was in touch with the Elohist mentality that placed all things, including temple and royal family, under the judgment of the living God. It offered a divine challenge to the established Jewish priesthood. It was validated by no external authority. It stood or fell on the basis of its participation in truth alone. It embodied many elements that later came to be seen as part of the emphasis of Protestantism.

For me, the father of the Jewish prophetic movement was Nathan, the prophet who confronted the powerful King David with his sinfulness in the name of the righteous God and on behalf of the cuckolded and murdered Uriah the Hittite (2 Sam. 11:1ff). In most ancient societies, what David did in claiming Bathsheba as his paramour fell within the divine right of kings. In Israel, however, even the kings were called to judgment and accountability before the God of Israel. This was the concept that made the prophetic movement both possible and uniquely Jewish. Elijah and Elisha kept the movement alive predominantly in the northern kingdom during the ninth century B.C.E., and then the great writing prophets began to appear in the eighth century.

There was Amos, the herdsman and keeper of sycamore trees in the southern kingdom of Judah, who journeyed to Bethel in the northern kingdom of Israel to pronounce his message on behalf of those who "sell the righteous for silver and the needy for a pair of shoes—they that trample the head of the poor into the dust of the earth and turn aside the way of the afflicted" (Amos 2:6, 7). There was Hosea, who followed Amos; but Hosea was a citizen of the northern kingdom, not a strident alien visitor like Amos. Hosea stood in the midst of his own people and pronounced a message of judgment that fell upon him as surely as it fell on anyone else. He saw God as the infinite and patient lover who craved his beloved Israel no matter how often she was unfaithful to the God who had chosen her. His own life, his own domestic woes, led him to see God in this way.

Then, when the northern kingdom of Israel was being besieged and finally destroyed by the Assyrians, the prophetic movement came south to Judah in the persons of the first Isaiah (Isaiah 1–39) and Micah. Isaiah was of royal blood and served as a kind of court adviser to the king. He was the one who promised King Ahaz a sign that God would deliver his nation from the threat of Rezin, king of Syria, and Pekah, king of Israel. That sign was that a young woman in the royal family would bear a son as a symbol of the continuity of the nation.

59

The name of the son was to be Immanuel (Isa. 7:14). That promise would hardly represent much hope to Ahaz if this event was to occur some 730 years later in Bethlehem. His city of Jerusalem was at that moment at the mercy of these two warring kings.

Micah was a country lawyer. He was the kind of man who envisioned practicing before the high court of his land in Jerusalem. That, however, did not occur, so he put his nation on trial figuratively before the mountains and the hills. When Judah stood condemned and asked how restitution could be made for her sins, Micah replied: "He has showed you, O man, what is good; and what does the Lord require of you but to do justice, and to love kindness and to walk humbly with your God?" (Mic. 6:8). Micah was also the prophet who suggested that Bethlehem, the city of David, might one day produce again a ruler of Israel (Mic. 5:2, 3). This passage helped to create the Bethlehem birth tradition of Jesus, who was almost certainly born in the town of Nazareth.[2] Moving into the seventh and even into the sixth centuries B.C.E., we confront the work of Jeremiah, Nahum, Zephaniah, Habakkuk, and Ezekiel.

Jeremiah and Ezekiel were the central prophetic voices when Jerusalem fell to the Babylonians. Jeremiah fled to Egypt and disappeared there from the scene of history. Ezekiel went into exile in Babylon and probably played a key part in keeping the nation of Judah intact to return from exile 50 to 140 years later. Ezekiel had wonderful dreams and visions that enliven both his work and our black spirituals. Ezekiel, in one vision, did see "the wheel way up in the middle of the sky" (Ezek. 10). Ezekiel also saw his nation under the symbol of a valley filled with dead, dry bones that were infused with life when the wind of God (the *ruach*) blew over that valley, causing the toe bone to become "connected to the foot bone, the foot bone connected to the ankle bone, the ankle bone connected to the leg bone" and so on until those bones and Judah were alive again (Ezek. 37).

The prophets of the late exile and the postexilic period were Obadiah, Haggai, Malachi, and that prophet who has become known as Second Isaiah (Isaiah 40–55). This Isaiah represented one way of dealing with the trauma of exile; the others represented another way. The small minds like Haggai, Zechariah, and Obadiah saw the exile as a punishment for the Jewish lapse in their observance of the Law, and so they returned as almost religious fanatics, zealous to purge Judah of all alien influences and to make the Law of God the law of the land in every jot and tittle.

Second Isaiah saw Judah as a people called by the experience of suffering into a vicarious life of sacrifice, healing, and doing for others. It produced a new dimension in the evolving portrait of what the Jewish messiah was destined to be.[3]

Later still would come the Book of Daniel, called "a major prophet," thus linking it with Isaiah, Jeremiah, and Ezekiel; but it was major only because of its length not its message. Daniel is dated around 160 B.C.E. and is chiefly noted for the story of Daniel in the lion's den (chap. 6), for the account of Shadrach, Meshach, and Abednego being delivered from the fiery furnace (chap. 3), for the time when King Belshazzar saw "the handwriting on the wall" (chap. 5), and for the apocalyptic chapters that are quoted by all those who wish to predict the exact moment of the end of the world (chaps. 7 and 12).

The prophets were intensely human people and spoke to remedy intensely human problems of injustice and the loss of meaning. They are thus worthy of our study and attention. The social gospel that later bloomed in our century was rooted in large measure in the works of the prophets. From the fourth century B.C.E. to just a century ago, organized religion in the Western world moved its primary attention away from the task of building a just society and into an increasingly individualistic focus on life after death. In many ways it was justice postponed. Heaven and hell became the ultimate means whereby the injustices of this world were redressed. Only when confidence in life after death began to disintegrate in the explosion of scientific knowledge did society once again move to a major concern for justice here and now. By this time the issues of human justice had lost most of their religious roots and had assumed a primarily secular form, so social justice concerns, in various political arenas, were called the New Deal, the Fair Deal, the Great Society, socialism, Christian socialism, Marxism, and communism. All represented a secular form of the social gospel that was begun in the movement of the eighth-century prophets in Israel. Perhaps one of our apologetic tasks today is to give these secular programs their original roots and thus to reclaim the Word of God found in the ancient but now time-warped words of the prophets.

Poetry and Wisdom

Beyond works of history and the writings of the prophets, the other books in the Hebrew Scriptures are primarily post-exilic, at least in their final form. Major among these works are the Psalms, the strange Book of Esther, and the wisdom literature, which would include Proverbs, Ecclesiastes, and the Song of Songs.

The Psalms, because of their liturgical use in the churches of Christendom, are probably among the more familiar parts of the Hebrew Scriptures. The 150 psalms contained in the Psalter have roots that may go back to Egyptian sources as early as the third millennium B.C.E., as well as to Canaanite and Sumerian origins. Psalms 2, 16, 18, 29, 68, 82, 108, and 110 may actually date from the time of David. The vast majority, however, were composed in that period of pre-exile, exile, and postexile when temple worship was dominant in fact, in memory, or in the hoped-for restoration. Those psalms that were not composed in these defining years of history were still shaped by their usage during that period.

The Psalms became the hymnbook of people of Judah as indeed they have continued be for Christians. Many of the psalms made liturgy out of the recitation of Israel's history. Others were dedicated to the cycles of planting and harvest. Still others were sung in praise of the king. The writers of the psalms, probably never a single person, seemed aware that the deity they adored was beyond their human encompassing—

"The earth is the Lord's" (Ps. 24:1); "In his hand are the depths of the earth; the heights of the mountains are his also. The sea is his, for He made it; for his hands formed the dry land" (Ps. 95:4, 5). "Let all the earth fear the Lord, let all the inhabitants of the world stand in awe of him!" (Ps. 33:8).

The Book of Proverbs, the words of Qoheleth—the preacher that we know as Ecclesiastes—the Book of Esther, and the Song of Songs offer the reader of the Bible a rich variety of literary forms. Solomon had achieved in Hebraic folklore what seems to me to be the totally undeserved reputation of a wise man. The facts of the biblical story seem to indicate anything but wisdom in his management of the nation and in his relationships with his thousand wives and concubines. He did not succeed even in passing on his kingdom intact to his son Rehoboam, and he left a legacy of intrigue and the oppression of many of his people into enforced labor or slavery. Despite this, the Book of Kings attributed vast wisdom to Solomon: "Solomon's wisdom surpassed the wisdom of all the people of the east, and all the wisdom of Egypt" (1 Kings 4:30). Furthermore, this book also stated that Solomon "uttered three thousand proverbs" (1 Kings 4:32). Solomon, who became the patron for the wisdom tradition in Israel, was thought therefore to be the author of the wisdom literature, including Proverbs.

Though the wisdom movement may have its roots in the court of Solomon, it did not flourish as a major part of the Jewish tradition until the postexilic period of Judah's history from the days of Ezra to the time when the Book of Sirach, also called Ecclesiasticus,[4] was published in the second century B.C.E.

Ecclesiastes also dates in its final form from the third century. It reflected a growing philosophical inquiry into the meaning of life that could not have been found earlier in Judah. Indeed, the questioning, godless quality of the Book of Ecclesiastes led to much dispute among Jewish scholars as to whether it should have been included in the sacred writings.

The Book of Esther seems to have had its origin in a festival called Purim, which the exiled Jews brought home with them from Babylon. It is the story of a beautiful Jewish queen who uses her position to save her people from a cruel persecution. The name of God never occurs in the Book of Esther, which prompted later scribes to write additions to this book that would make the book properly religious. These additions are now in the Apocrypha.

The Song of Songs was originally a series of sensuous love songs that had nothing to do with God and God's beloved, Israel, or with Jesus and his beloved, the church. They were earthy bits of writing that probably could not have survived the antiflesh crusades of the Western church without being allegorized. They serve to remind us that the Puritan tradition has been imposed on Scripture; it is not original to Scripture. There is no Jewish Queen Victoria. The Adam who upon beholding Eve for the first time could shout with lustful joy (Gen. 2:23) reflected the attitude toward bodies and sex that is biblical and that the Song of Songs captures. Seldom is this book used for readings in the liturgy of the churches. Even more seldom, regrettably, is it preached on from the various religious pulpits—Jewish or Christian.

The Protesters

The final literary category in the Hebrew Scriptures is what I call protest literature, and it includes the books of Job, Ruth, and Jonah. These were stories that provided a counterpoint to a prevailing attitude. They were never intended to be literalized. It is fairly clear that Job, Ruth, and Jonah were literary creations, not persons of history. To treat them literally is to miss their meaning, power, and point. For this reason, I focus on them, for they illustrate better than anything else in Holy Scripture what is lost when literalism prevails.

Job

The Book of Job, in its finished form, was probably written fairly late in Hebrew history, but it has ancient roots. Indeed, suggested dates run from 1100 B.C.E. to 500 B.C.E. Its dramatic poetry builds on a tale, probably from a much earlier time, about the sufferings of a righteous man. It is a protest against the point of view expressed in the Book of Proverbs, a point of view that did not yet embrace fully the problems inherent in individualism. As we have it today, it is certainly postexilic, sixth century B.C.E. or later.

Individuality is a relatively recent idea, historically speaking. It seems not to have appeared anywhere on earth in any substantial way, except as an aspect of royalty, much before 4000 B.C.E. Among the Hebrews it seems to have become a powerful idea much later, making its way into Scripture in a clear form, as I have previously suggested, in the writings of Ezekiel. Prior to the rise of individualism, the tribe was thought of as the basic unit of life. A tribe was a corporate singularity. It was not a collection of individuals. One stood before God as a people, not as individuals. The people of the tribe were interrelated, interdependent, and mutually responsible. It was their destiny to thrive or to perish together. When evil was in their midst, the whole of the people suffered. When faithfulness marked their common life, the whole of the people were blessed.

Sin itself was conceived of corporately. The sins of the fathers "shall be visited upon the children to the third and fourth generations" proclaimed the commandments (Exod. 20:4–6). When Achan sinned at Ai, his whole family was destroyed and no one thought that to be unjust (Joshua 7). Even the first Jewish messianic thought was corporate rather than individual. Through the descendants of Abraham all the nations of the earth would be blessed. Only later, in the postexilic period, did the messianic vocation of Israel come to be thought of as a vocation of the supreme Israelite. The servant passages from Second Isaiah could be interpreted either corporately or individually, but when Ezekiel wrote "the soul that sins shall die" (Ezek. 18:46), individualism had dawned as a dominant idea among the Hebrew people. It was destined to grow in importance, and it received the fullest biblical expression in the

65

wisdom literature of the Hebrew people, especially in such biblical works as Proverbs, Ecclesiastes, the Song of Songs, and in the apocryphal books of Ecclesiasticus and the Wisdom of Solomon. In these works a radical individualism was assumed.

"Wisdom" in the Jewish tradition was defined as the ability to discern the pattern of God in the world and the ability to conform the individual self to that pattern. Wisdom for a person began with the acknowledgment of God as the primary reality of the cosmos. "The fear of the Lord is the beginning of wisdom" (Prov. 9:10). The wise men of Israel taught that those who seek wisdom conform to that wisdom and will be rewarded by God without qualification. There were no extenuating circumstances out of the past, no connecting antecedents, no web of relationships. Each person was a solitary individual who by seeking wisdom would be led to happiness. He or she would by wisdom discover God's plan and then, by an act of the will, would conform to it. To the degree that a person was successful, God's blessing would be upon that person. To the degree that one failed, God's curse would be pronounced.

The happy life of wisdom was spelled out in the Book of Proverbs. It involved hard work, high morals, moderation, kindness to the less fortunate, loving one's family and home, sincerity, modesty, self-control, chastity, a willingness to live and learn, an attitude of forgiveness, and even being kind to animals. The author of Proverbs never discussed the nature of right and wrong. This was supposedly self-evident. Nor did this author see conflicting duties. Every choice was clear, direct, and individual. The central idea was simple: Wisdom brings happiness, the lack of wisdom brings misery. Every life got what that life deserved. The name for this credo was "moral retribution."

The one who held this point of view believed that God's world was so organized that the exact reward for each person's conduct was meted out before that person died. The transfer of this justice to a life beyond this life was not yet a major factor in their thinking. The individualism first mentioned in Ezekiel had by the time of the Proverbs been given the weight of un-

66

questioned dogma. As Proverbs asserted: "The fruit of the righteous is a tree of life, but lawlessness takes away lives. If the righteous is requited on earth, how much more the wicked and the sinner!" (Prov. 11:30–31). If this were not so, then God is not just. Since wisdom is open to all who will learn it, those who did not possess it were assumed to have refused even to seek it, and therefore they could be blamed. If they were poor and afflicted, they deserved it. Likewise, if they were rich and healthy, they deserved it. Life was its own rewarder and punisher. Nothing was said about the handicaps of environment, security, education, or temperament, which differ so widely from person to person. The assumption was that everyone began life even—at an objectively equal starting line.

This was a fascinating view of life. It still has power, especially in ultraconservative circles where it is important that both wealth and power be thought of as deserved by either the life of virtue or, in its absence, the life of laziness. But even life in this ancient time defied so simple an explanation. There was still apparent injustice visible to all who would look. Good people did suffer. Evil people did prosper. Finally, one articulate, skillful Jewish poet rose to challenge this prevailing point of view. He did so by creating a political work based on an ancient narrative. It was a literary device that would dramatize the issues.

A wise Jew, faithful to God, obedient to the Law, a practitioner of wisdom would suffer calamity after calamity. He would be visited by representatives of the prevailing wisdom who would seek to force his life and his tragedies into their frame of reference. Through this means, this author would seek another answer that still preserved the power of God but also made sense out of the experience of life. This ancient writer wanted to bear witness to the insight that Archibald MacLeish, in his play *J.B.,* placed into the mouth of his modern-day Job: "If God is God [i.e., all powerful] he is not good. If God is good [just, fair, loving] he is not God."

So the character of Job entered the biblical story. In the biblical book that bears his name, Job was a creation of his author. He was certainly not a literal, historic figure. He was the epitome of the wise man. He feared God and turned away from evil. He even quoted the proverbs. He always did right in both his concern for others and in his personal morality. He shunned falsehood and deceit. His neighbor's wife he let alone. He gave his servant justice in every dispute. Toward his enemies he kept goodwill. His ethical standing was higher than any other person in the Jewish sacred story. He performed every possible religious duty. He refrained from the worship of heavenly bodies and never allowed his wealth to come between himself and his God.

With the lines of his chief character clearly drawn, the author asked, How did the promises of retribution work in his case? As his story unfolded, he stated that for years the promises seemed to come true. Job was blessed with wealth, health, long life, a large family, and high public esteem. He was the greatest man in the east. Then a terrible change came. In one day he lost all that he had—children, wife, slaves, cattle, and health. With these losses he also found that honor and prestige had been withdrawn from him, for disaster was itself a sign of deserved evil. Even the outcast spat in Job's face.

Job's friends came to him to call him back to the wisdom that he had so obviously forsaken. The dialogue between Job and his comforters turned on the meaning of life itself. It is still a powerful drama. If life was to be understood individualistically, and if there was both a sense of God's goodness and a sense of God's justice, then the problem of evil was unsolvable. The idea of moral retribution did not work. Life was not fair. It never had been and it never would be. Should the problem of evil be extended into the next life? Is the primary function of heaven and hell to make fair an unfair world, to make sense out of the problem of evil?

Our popular view of both heaven and hell still assumes the fundamental error of the Book of Proverbs—namely, that individual judgment of individual behavior is the basis upon which divine reward and punishment are to be meted out. The presence of evil still confronts us with a threat to the reality of God. It suggests that either the all-powerful God desires evil or that the presence of evil reveals the impotence of God. Perhaps it argues that there is no God at all, and that all of us are at the mercy of a power called fate. Perhaps it suggests a dualism, a theological schizophrenia between God and Satan, good and evil, the spiritual and the physical, or wisdom and chaos. Perhaps the presence of evil pushes us to see the shadows present in both God and life that Carl Jung talked about and to seek that interrelatedness that makes even suffering a pathway to God.[5] Those are the options posed for us by Job. In some sense these options are both posed and lived for us by Jesus of Nazareth.

But to talk of these things is to open Scripture to depths so far beyond literalism that many simple yet sincere Christians would not even comprehend the words being used. I, for example, do not believe in a God who willed Jesus to suffer for my sins. I do not believe in a God whose inner need for justice is satisfied when his son is nailed to a cross. I regard the substitutionary version of the atonement as a barbaric attack on both the truth of God and the meaning of human life. Even Scripture, in my opinion, condemns this individualistic idea that has so distorted the Christ. But it does not do so unless one is willing to go beneath the literal words of the biblical text where one can meet the living Word in the questions raised by the Jewish poet who years ago created for us the character Job. There Scripture opens us to new possibilities.

Ruth and Jonah

When we turn to the protest works of Ruth and Jonah we discover the art forms of Scripture to be exquisite, but the issue here is not so much justice as it is the narrow-minded religious bigotry of the times. These protests also grew out of the same mentality that created Job. A central idea in the Jewish Scriptures was the sense of being chosen. The Jews believed themselves to be God's elect. This was a dominant concept throughout most of Israel's history. It was rooted, I believe, in the experience of Moses choosing to identify himself and his God with the slave people in Egypt. The great danger present, however, in believing yourself to be especially chosen is that it becomes easy to view those who are not of your people as God's especially unchosen. The step between being God's unchosen and being God's rejected constitutes a very small distance in human emotions. If you can convince yourself that those you regard as strangers, aliens, or even enemies are also rejected by God, then prejudice runs free and unchallenged.

Being God's elect had other problems. Suppose God's elect were defeated, exiled, all but destroyed? This would be a strange way for God to treat the especially chosen people. It would call for major explanations without which the power of this God would be in serious question. The nation of Judah, so deeply convinced of her chosen status, had been defeated by the Babylonians. Jerusalem had been destroyed. The people had been marched into captivity. They had died there. Their children had died there. Some of their grandchildren had died there before finally they were allowed to return to their homeland. When they returned, they found their holy places destroyed and reduced to rubble. Their nation would never be powerful again. They were viewed by their neighbors as pitiful, and the sense that this broken, defeated, enslaved people was the glory of their God, Yahweh, was laughably anachronistic.

For the minority of the Jewish people, this produced a new and profound concept that saw meaning in suffering and called the Jews to accept this vocation as the means by which the world could be served and thus called into the worship of Yahweh. This point of view lived almost hidden in the Jewish tradition. It was the minority underside of their corporate life, at least until it fueled one Jesus of Nazareth to live out historically the meaning of this possibility. We need to be reminded that it was the religious establishment of first-century Judaism that executed this Jesus for being a blasphemer and a destroyer of sacred tradition.

The majority tradition of Judaism, out of which the chief priests and members of the Sanhedrin operated, attempted to interpret being chosen quite differently from this minority understanding. The pain of defeat and exile came, they argued, only because the Jews of the past had been unfaithful to the terms of the covenant. They were thus determined to prevent that from happening again. The newly restored nation of Judah would be one that kept the law—every jot and tittle of the law. They were rigorously religious. This restored nation would worship properly and obey every rubric. Their nation would be a religiously zealous theocracy from which no deviation would be allowed. In this way they could guarantee that defeat and exile would never again be the experience of God's elect, for religious faithfulness would be rewarded with wealth, power, and renewed prestige. This was the vision they sought to live out.

As they meditated on their past failures that had brought such pain to their nation, they became increasingly uncomfortable with their own critical judgment pronounced so vigorously on their grandparents and on other forebears who had failed their God so miserably that the nation had had to undergo the divine punishment of defeat and exile. Searching for a means to alleviate this judgment, they pounced on the idea of ethnic purity.

Some of our forebears had married non-Jewish spouses, they declared. These alien influences had polluted and corrupted God's elect. These strangers and foreigners had brought into Judah their alien gods and their alien worship practices, which had weakened the Jewish resolve to serve Yahweh faithfully. This explanation became exceedingly popular. It justified the punishment they believed that God had rendered upon them, but it also exonerated their own forebears. Foreigners were the culprits. The scapegoat had been identified.

So it was that ethnic purity became a dominant theme in postexilic Judaism. The bloodlines of the new nation were to be pure. Those who were not contributors to this purity were to be banished. Under Ezra and Nehemiah, laws were passed

71

making it a crime to live in Judah unless you were a full-blooded Jew to the tenth generation. Married couples were split by these laws, for less than full-blooded Jews had to be banished. Families were torn asunder by these laws, for half-breed children also had to be banished. Political purges were justified under these laws, and the ability to prove one's Jewish heritage became all important in case there was a knock on the door in the middle of the night. It was a terrible period in the history of the Jews. Eras that are dedicated to racial or ethnic purity are always terrible.

So dominant were these ideas that no one could counter them politically. To do so would open up the critic to the telling charge that she or he was eager to have the nation conquered and exiled yet again. Still, this consensus was not universal, and it demanded some response in the midst of the systematic purges that were zealously being carried out, ripping apart the fiber of Jewish life.

At this moment in history two anonymous Jewish story-tellers took pen in hand to write biting pieces of protest literature. Their works hooked readers into making judgments, causing them to realize by the time the story was unfolded that they were making those judgments against themselves. It was in this way that two mythical heroes entered the stream of Jewish consciousness. One written story was named Jonah, and the other was named Ruth. Both stories were clearly fictional. Both were never meant to be literalized. Both countered the common wisdom of the day in profound and provocative ways.

Jonah was a prophet who reflected the prevailing prejudice. He did not believe that God could care for the people of Ninevah. They were gentiles, warlike and outside the boundaries that the Jews had placed around the love of God. Through a series of adventures, including three days in the belly of a great fish (called a whale only in folklore—never in Scripture), Jonah was finally led to see that something was seriously wrong with a religious system that enabled him to be more compassionate toward a tree than he could be toward those

Ninevites whom he could not believe were meant to be the recipients of God's concern.

Ruth was a citizen of Moab who married a Jewish man named Chilion while he sojourned in her country with his mother, Naomi, and his father, Elimelech. Chilion had a brother named Mahlon who also married a Moabite woman, named Orpah. In time all three Jewish men died, leaving Naomi, Ruth, and Orpah widows and childless women and therefore outside the economic and political protection present in that patriarchal society. Naomi tried to send her daughters-in-law back to their father's home in Moab, where the law of tradition insisted that they be received into care and safety. After much negotiation Orpah agreed to go, but Ruth clung tenaciously to Naomi. Ruth said to Naomi: "Entreat me not to leave you or to return from following you; for where you go I will go, and where you lodge I will lodge; your people shall be my people, and your God my God; where you die I will die, and there will I be buried" (Ruth 1:16, 17). These words have been set to music and are not infrequently sung at weddings. Bride and bridegroom alike are blissfully unaware that this apparently romantic ballad in fact relates Ruth's words to her mother-in-law, not to her husband or even to her intended.

Ruth, despite her vulnerability as an unprotected woman, acted out the highest standards of the Jewish Torah by caring for her widowed mother-in-law, Naomi. She went into the fields after the harvest to glean enough food to survive, winning the admiration of the owner of the land and all the men who tilled the soil for him. Then, through a series of maneuvers, each in accordance with the law of the Jews, Ruth was married to the owner of that field, a man named Boaz. At this point in the story it seems like just a good tale, romantic and entertaining and with a happy ending, for Boaz is capable of caring adequately for both the faithful Ruth and the unfortunate Naomi. The reader's sympathy is deeply drawn to the character of Ruth, who so persistently tends to the needs of her mother-in-law and so completely fulfills the Jewish law in her dedicated love for Naomi. She is in fact a sterling character. The reader is not prepared for the closing lines of the narrative, which are indeed the whole purpose for which this tale was created.

Ruth and Boaz had a son named Obed. Obed grew up, married, and had a son named Jesse, who was in fact the father of the greatest king in the history of Israel—a man named David. The message slowly penetrated the consciousness. King David was not a full-blooded Jew. His great-grandmother was a Moabite woman named Ruth. David himself would have been purged by the laws under which the Jewish state was now operating. It was an exquisite, timely literary attempt to puncture the pomposity of the moment. The fact that it got included in the canon of Scripture for the Jewish people is evidence that it succeeded. The same could be said for the books of Jonah and Job. Literalism would be a serious block to meeting, confronting, and understanding the Word of God in these wonderful books of protest.

We have now skipped lightly through the Hebrew Scriptures. It has not been my intention to be exhaustive. Libraries contain great volumes that explore these narratives in depth. I wanted only to taste the power in the text, to place its timeless truth into a proper historic context, to challenge the narrow focus of those whose need is to be literal and to point to new possibilities once our limiting biblical prejudices can be set aside. The Hebrew Scriptures are not accurate in geographical, historical, geological, or astrophysical details. They are punctuated with contradictory facts and with narratives, like those of Jonah and Ruth, that become nonsensical if they are literalized. The Scriptures are acculturated stories of a specific people.

There is so much more biblical truth and biblical beauty once we escape the strictures of a literalistic approach to the Bible. If we could be assured of this possibility, we might be able to surrender our concept of biblical inerrancy. But to surrender biblical inerrancy is not to surrender the Word of God! For if we mean by "the Word of God" that we can discern the

74

hand of a transcendent deity underneath these literal words, we have taken a major step forward. Then we can lift that transcendent presence out of its ancient context and place it with integrity inside our own spiritual journeys as a resource. Surely then we can proclaim with great joy that in this sacred book we can meet and know the Word of God and that this living Word can be for us a source of life even two thousand years removed.

We hear that Word in creation, where this God proclaimed that everything divinely created was good and that male and female had both been created in God's image. That "Word of God" fueled every human movement for justice from the fight to end slavery and segregation to the feminist movement to the peace movement to the gay and lesbian rights movement. That Word of God challenges the prejudice that grows out of our limited knowledge, our tribal identities, our economic systems, and our sexual fears.

The Bible is the Word of God in that it touches universal, timeless themes. The sense of being created for union with God, the sense of being alienated from that union, and the yearning to be restored to that union are in the depths of every human psyche. Yet here they are external and objectified in the narratives of Scripture. The Bible is the Word of God when it captures in its remembered history archetypal and eternal truths that we can experience, enter, and live, even today.

All of us know what it means to live in bondage to some power that is beyond our ability to manage and from which we cannot escape. All of us know the meaning of exodus and deliverance. All of us have, in some way, come out of our limiting bondage. We know what it means to wander in the wilderness and finally to arrive at the promised land. We know what it means to be fed on our journey with manna, that heavenly food, or to be sustained with water that flows from a rock. We know what it means to receive the law, to yearn for the perfect life, to enter the darkness of death, and to believe that one can walk through even death without fear, for our faith story tells us that one has entered and conquered even death with the

75

power of the love of God. We know what it means to live in a community where there are no boundaries, no barriers, and where everyone can communicate with everyone else without misunderstanding. We know what it means to yearn for a perfect world and to be empowered to work for that perfection until the Kingdom of God shall come.

These are all biblical themes that enrich, interpret, and challenge our lives. They are themes, however, that cannot be heard, heeded, or entertained until we are free to approach the sacred Scriptures with eyes, ears, and hearts that are not bound in the straitjacket of trying to impose a literal authority that has never been the essential truth of Scripture. The Bible is not literally true in a thousand details. But the Bible does touch the deep wells of truth, and to those deep wells it calls us again and again.

We turn now to examine those books that form what Christians call the New Covenant.

6

Forming the Second Covenant

There are many members of the Christian church who might be dismayed by attitudes or distortions that occur in the Hebrew Scriptures, but their faith is not finally disturbed because, they say, "Christ has put an end to the first dispensation." They are aware that Christians do not refrain from work on Saturday, the Sabbath day, which is of course the last day of the week; that ham and bacon adorn the breakfast tables of many Christians in direct violation of the kosher laws of the Book of Leviticus; and that slavery was abolished from this land by the Thirteenth Amendment to the Constitution, making its affirmation in the ancient Hebrew Scriptures irrelevant. They also acknowledge that the polygamy practiced by the heroes of Hebrew history from Abraham to Solomon is not legal in this country, except of course in its serial form. So clearly, all of the words of the Bible are not the unchanging "Word of God." Practices that once were normative for the Bible have become for us either illegal or, in some cases, immoral.

However, when these believing Christians come to the specifically Christian Scriptures, their backs stiffen in defense of the literal authenticity of this dispensation. In the New Testament there are no kosher laws, no examples of polygamy, and the Sabbath has been replaced in the practice of the Christians by the first day of the week.[1] So questions about inaccuracies, prejudices, or outmoded attitudes are resisted more fiercely. Such possibilities strike too close to the authority of their faith system. Thus their fears rise and their defensiveness intensifies. These *are* the words of Jesus, the writings of Paul and the other disciples, they assert. These words must be trustworthy, inerrant, and infallible. One television evangelist with whom I was in a public dialogue defended the Mosaic authorship of the Torah because Jesus said Moses wrote it. "I would rather trust Jesus than you," he said, to the applause of his sympathetic audience.

But this attitude toward the specifically Christian parts of the Bible ignores important, inevitable questions. For instance, of the four Gospels, Luke and Mark do not ever claim the authority of being apostles. Neither is listed by any gospel writer as being among the chosen Twelve. So their material cannot be of the eyewitness variety. The question must also be raised as to whether we have the actual words of Jesus in any Gospel. Certainly the words of Jesus we have in the New Testament are not in the language that Jesus spoke. How much did the needs of the Christian community at the moment the Gospels were written prove stronger than the historicity of the words themselves?

Frequently one quotation of Jesus in one Gospel will not harmonize with another word of Jesus, either in the same Gospel or in a different one. And how does one reconcile Mark's emphasis, for example, on the secretiveness of the messianic movement until the ultimate revelation on Good Friday and Easter with John's Jesus publicly saying, "I am the bread of life" and "I am the resurrection"? What allowances can a literalist make for the growth in the tradition that occurred between the time of Paul and John—a period of perhaps a half century?

Clearly these difficulties have been sensed in the past, and the theory of divine inspiration has been developed to counter this threat to inerrancy claims. The divine inspiration theory suggests that the human scribes wrote as they were directed to write by the Holy Spirit. Whatever disharmony might be discovered to exist in the total text is then blamed on the humanity of the scribe, thus leaving intact the inerrancy of the ultimate source of the word of God. It is not a helpful argument, and is not normally employed until the fundamentalist's back is against the wall. It is not dissimilar from the defence of those who claim papal infallibility when that tradition begins to suggest that what the doctrine really means is that God will not ultimately let the Holy Church fall into error. Errors can then be ascribed to some of the weaker vessels in that body's history that may not have been completely in tune with this ultimate source of divine truth. Such ideas may be ingenious, but they do not finally hold water.

To our knowledge Jesus never wrote a single word save for the time he is reported to have written in the dirt, in the episode involving the woman taken in adultery (John 8:6). Jesus was a teacher, an oral communicator. With no written words or tape recorders, with a significant gap in time before the spoken words were written down, and with translation from the spoken Aramaic to the written Greek, just how authoritative or secure can one be in claiming for the New Testament a literal truth? Can the claim for the inerrant word of God reside with integrity even in this part of our Holy Scriptures? The answer is clearly "No!" Inerrancy is not a viable option for the serious Christian, even when the claim is focused narrowly on the New Testament.

In a very preliminary way it is necessary to bring certain facts of both history and literary composition into focus. The formation of what we call the New Testament also went through a process of transition that possesses fascinating levels of interdependency. Like all literature, the Christian writings reflect the issues alive when the writing took place as well as the memory of the events of the past that they intend to transmit. Frequently present history will temper or modify past memory.

First, a grasp of the time frame behind the New Testament is essential to our understanding. Most scholars who work at fixing the date of Jesus' birth focus on the years 8 to 4 B.C.E. This is determined primarily by the tradition that says Jesus was born during the reign of Herod. Secular records indicate that Herod died in the year 4 B.C.E., so the birth of Jesus is fixed prior to that death. There seems no reason to drift back more than four years from the date of Herod's death, so the 8 to 4 B.C.E. range emerges.

The date of Jesus' death is more difficult. A reference in John has a person in the crowd say, "You are not yet fifty years old, and have you seen Abraham?" (John 8:57). The general consensus in the early Christian tradition is that Jesus was in his early thirties when he was crucified. He was at the beginning of his ministry—thirty years of age, according to Saint Luke (Luke 3:23). The exact length of that ministry is uncertain, but one to three years is the range within which the debate is carried out. So, a date of around 30 C.E., with a range from 27 to 34 C.E., is generally accepted as the fixed point to mark the end of his life in human history. To simplify things I will accept 30 C.E. as the point of reference.

Paul's first letter to the Thessalonians or his letter to the Galatians is thought by various scholars to be the first book written by a Christian that was later incorporated into the Bible. If it was written about 48 or 49 C.E., as scholars believe, this means that eighteen to nineteen years passed between the life of the historic Jesus and the writing of the first book of what we now call the New Testament.

The last of Paul's writings, perhaps Colossians, is dated about 62 C.E.[2] Paul is believed to have been put to death by the Emperor Nero in 64. When Paul died, not a single Gospel had yet been written, and at the time of Paul's death none of the Pauline letters were regarded as anything more than what they were—treasured letters from a revered Christian leader. These letters certainly had not received in Paul's lifetime the status of

Scripture. Paul was too controversial a person for that. One has only to read Galatians to see that Paul was in great tension with both Peter and the leaders of the Jerusalem church and to know, therefore, that his words could not have been thought of as "Bible," much less inerrant. The Book of Acts, written some twenty to twenty-five years after Paul's death, still bristles with accounts of this tension.

Between Paul and the Book of Acts, which purports to describe Paul's activity, there is an irreconcilable gap—not just in time, but in context. Paul defended his apostolic status by claiming to be an eyewitness to the resurrection. The Easter appearance to Paul, he argued, differed in no way from the Easter appearances to other disciples save in that his was last—to one born out of due season. The Book of Acts, however, portrays Paul's conversion not as a resurrection experience but as a vision on the road to Damascus. In Acts this is a vivid narrative. It seems peculiar, though, that Paul never mentions it. Paul never refers to the road to Damascus. He never speaks of Ananias, whom Acts claims to have been instrumental in Paul's baptism. One wonders if Paul would have recognized the Damascus road experience or whether this met some of Luke's own journalistic and apologetic needs. At the very least, the reader of the Bible has to face this conflict, assign the weight of probability to one or the other, and, above all, recognize that it would be the second century before either Paul or Acts would begin to be thought of as Bible.

Placing Paul's writings accurately in Christian history as antecedent to any other part of the New Testament leads us to wonder just how much we have distorted Paul's meanings by unconsciously allowing the Gospels to color Paul's words. Have we noticed that Paul seems to know nothing of Jesus' supernatural birth? Jesus was, says Paul, "descended from David according to the flesh and designated Son of God in power according to the Spirit of holiness by his resurrection from the dead" (Rom. 1:3, 4). It is also interesting to note that Paul overwhelmingly uses a passive verb, "was raised," to describe the resurrection. His image of resurrection appears to be much more exaltation into heaven than a resuscitation back to this life. Paul even goes so far as to say that flesh and blood cannot inherit the Kingdom of Heaven, which surely must give pause to those who assert that the resurrection must be a physical event in history.

Paul's date of conversion is placed by the vast majority of Christian scholars no earlier than one year after the crucifixion and no later than six years. The fact remains that Paul, whom no one believes to have been an eyewitness to the life of Jesus and who wrote in Greek (which Paul spoke and wrote fluently), was the first Christian to place into writing what later came to be regarded as Scripture. This fact, in and of itself, should make humble the excessive claims for the Bible of many well-intentioned Christians. Furthermore, since Paul could not possibly write about that which he had neither seen nor heard, he had to write about what he had been told, and what he had experienced in those days after the events of the first Easter. Yet very little of what we know about Jesus is recorded in Paul. That comes to us through the Gospels, and that fact stretches our time span between Jesus and written records significantly.

Biblical scholars are today fairly unanimous in according to Mark the status of being the oldest Gospel. Mark is usually dated no earlier than 65 c.e. and no later than 75. This means that before the first Gospel was written, thirty-five to forty-five years had passed since the life of this historic Jesus came to an end. Mark, however, included only a portion of the events in the life of Jesus and the words of Jesus that form the biblical heritage of Christian people.

When we move from Mark to the other Gospel writers, we move farther and farther away from the Jesus of history. Matthew, usually dated near the midpoint of the 80s, appears to have been written in Antioch. The Gospel of Luke, along with its second volume, the Book of Acts, is thought to be the work of an evangelist who lived in Caesarea and who produced his monumental work sometime between the years 83 and 90. John's date is more debated than any other book in the New Testament, but a general consensus is that the final form of the

Fourth Gospel appeared around the turn of the century. This means that we have to reckon with thirty-five to seventy years between the life and spoken words of Jesus and the written versions of that life that recorded firmly those words. A thirty-five- to seventy-year gap, when added to the fact of translation from Aramaic to Greek, presents a literal view of the Bible with insurmountable problems.

The Evangelists: Their Styles and Audiences

A second problem for this literal view arises in the realization that the Gospels also reflect different perspectives and abilities on the part of the authors and reveal quite distinct audiences to which each is addressed. The gospel message of each is shaped dramatically by these two considerations. Mark, for example, used the Greek language very poorly. His syntax was often confusing, and occasionally he ended sentences with dangling participles.

Luke, on the other hand, was a master of the Greek language. Jerome, who translated the Bible into the Latin Vulgate in the fourth century, called the author of the Third Gospel "the most polished" of all the evangelists in the use of Greek. It is not surprising, therefore, to discover in comparing Mark with Luke that Luke frequently cleaned up Mark's bad grammar. When speaking of the widow's mite, Mark wrote rather cumbersomely "everything she had her whole living" (Mark 12:44). Luke, perhaps appalled at that sentence structure, edited it in his Gospel to read "all the living that she had" (Luke 21:4). Mark began one episode by saying "and a great multitude from Galilee followed; also from Judea and Jerusalem and Idumea and from beyond the Jordan and from about Tyre and Sidon" (Mark 3:7, 8). Luke could not stand that, so he altered Mark in his Gospel to read "and a great multitude of people from all Judea and Jerusalem and the seacoast of Tyre and Sidon who came to hear him" (Luke 6:17). It was as if Luke was a professor grading a first-year student's thesis. Sometimes it was more than he could bear.

Matthew, sensitive to the pious tradition of his primarily Jewish audience that the holy name of God was not to be spoken, regularly changed Mark's phrase "the Kingdom of God" to the more acceptable "the Kingdom of Heaven."

Luke, writing as a gentile to an audience that was primarily gentile, systematically deleted from Mark words and names that would not be familiar to non-Jewish readers. In Luke you will not find such semitic words as *Boanerges*, the Aramaic word meaning "sons of thunder" applied to the sons of Zebedee, or *Iscariot*, thought by some scholars to be a reference to the Judean village of Kerioth that came in time to be thought of as part of the betrayer's name. Semitic words like *Abba* (father) and *Hosannah* (we pray) do not appear in Luke. *Rabbi*, for Luke, became master, and *Satan* became the devil. Once more it becomes obvious that neither Matthew nor Luke regarded Mark as inerrant.

It is fascinating, furthermore, to see how both Luke and Matthew used the Markan material. Matthew recorded 600 of the 661 verses of Mark in his Gospel. He accepted Mark's basic style and framework and then added to, editorialized on, and expanded Mark. Luke, on the other hand, used only about half of Mark. When he had in a different source a similar version of an episode in the life of Jesus recorded by Mark, Luke seemed always to prefer his alternative material. When he used Mark, he used large sections, which he inserted into his narrative with only editorial, not substantial, revision. Furthermore, both Luke and Matthew brought into written form a vast amount of material that perhaps had not achieved written form before. At the very least, it had not achieved a written form that would survive.

Disagreement Among the Gospels

A third problem for the literal view comes when there is disagreement among the evangelists about events in the life of

Jesus. Was the cleansing of the temple an event at the beginning of Jesus' ministry as John asserts (John 2:13–17), or was this an event of the last week of his life as Matthew (Matt. 21:12, 13), Mark (Mark 11:15–19), and Luke (Luke 19:45–48) maintain? Did the miraculous catch of fish occur in the Galilean phase of Jesus' ministry as Luke records (Luke 5:4–7), or was it an account of a postresurrection event as John maintains (John 21:4–8)? Did the public ministry of Jesus last one year as the synoptics suggest, or was it three years as John asserts? Was the last supper the Passover meal as Matthew (Matt. 26:17ff), Mark (Mark 14:12ff), and Luke (Luke 22:17ff) prefer, or a preparation for the Passover as the Fourth Gospel believes (John 13:1–9, 12–16)?

These are but a few of the contradictory references in the biblical text itself that resist reconciliation and that make difficult to impossible a literal, inerrant approach to Scripture.

The Source Discoveries of Modern Scholarship

Once we are willing to lay aside literalism, new possibilities do begin to open before us. The thirty-five- to seventy-year gap between Jesus and the written Gospels can be probed with exciting results. Scholars in the last 150 years have in fact discovered some bright new insights in that dark and quiet period of what was assumed to be a period of oral history. Foremost among these insights has been the recovery of an ancient document, or documents, that underlie both Matthew and Luke.

This lost work, which for convenience I shall treat as a single work, is called Quelle—the German word for "source" —and it was discovered when the form-critical period of biblical scholarship was born. (By "form-critical" I mean that aspect of biblical scholarship that seeks to isolate the building blocks used by the Evangelist to create his final product.) Scholars first recognized significant portions of Mark in both Matthew and Luke. When Mark was deleted from the text of the other two Gospels, an amazing phenomenon became visible for the first time: even without Mark, there were still some two hundred verses of Matthew and Luke that bore a striking similarity. These verses mostly involved the teachings of Jesus. Sometimes the resemblance was slight, such as in the account of the giving of the Lord's Prayer, where the "Our Father who art in heaven" for Matthew is simply "Father" in Luke. The Beatitudes in Matthew appear to be spiritualized when compared with the Beatitudes in Luke. Matthew has Jesus say, "Blessed are the poor in spirit" (Matt. 5:3) and "blessed are those who hunger and thirst for righteousness" (Matt. 5:6), while Luke quotes Jesus as saying, "Blessed are you poor" (Luke 6:20) and "Blessed are you that hunger now" (Luke 6:21). Furthermore, Matthew has Jesus deliver these words on the mountaintop, while Luke says they were spoken only when Jesus "came down with them and stood on a level place" (Luke 6:17).

At other times, however, material is all but identical, including the account of the temptation of Jesus (Matt. 4:1–11; Luke 4:1–13), the discourse on the Pharisees (Matt. 23:13–36; Luke 14:42–45), and the teaching on loving one's enemies (Matt. 4:43–48; Luke 6:27, 28, 32–35).

Since there is no reason to believe that either Matthew or Luke knew of the existence of the other, the conclusion emerges that they must have had a common written source. Once this source was identified, it was subjected to enormous scrutiny. The Dutch Roman Catholic scholar Edward Schillebeeckx now suggests that "Q" had three editorial phases —an Aramaic phase, a Jewish-Christian phase, and a gentile phase. It appears to represent a primitive written source that could carry us back into the early part of the sixth decade of the Christian era (50–55 C.E.) for some of the words of Jesus or to within twenty to twenty-five years of the historic Jesus.[3]

Once Q was removed from both Matthew and Luke, there still remained a substantial amount of material in each Gospel. This material peculiar to the Gospel of Matthew was called M and the material peculiar to Luke was called L. There is no suggestion that either M or L is from a single source, or even always a written source. In all probability it represents in each

Gospel a series of sources perhaps both written and oral. This material gives each Gospel a unique and special flavor.

Once this material was isolated, some other fascinating insights appeared. There seems to be a more than coincidental affinity between that material peculiar to Luke (L) and the Fourth Gospel. For example, both L and John agree that there were two apostles named Judas (Luke 6:16; John 14:22). Both suggest that the act of betrayal occurred because Satan entered Judas, making Judas less responsible (Luke 22:3; John 13:2). Both record the episode in which the slave of the high priest has his ear cut off at the arrest of Jesus (Luke 22:50; John 18:10). Both record Pilate denying Jesus' guilt on three occasions (Luke 23:4, 14, 20; John 19:4, 6, 12). Both are aware of a close relationship among Mary and Martha and Jesus, but there are no common illustrations of this friendship included in either Gospel. There is not sufficient identity to suggest that John was leaning on Luke, but only that a major portion of the special Lucan material was part of a tradition with which John was also familiar.

With Q we may probe that shadowy period between the life of Jesus and the writings of the Gospels and perhaps shrink it from thirty-five to seventy years down to twenty-five to seventy years. Next, the study of the Gospels reveals that each of them has only one continuous narrative: the passion story that carries us from the Palm Sunday procession to Easter. It is reasonable to argue that this passion narrative, so much at the heart of each of the Gospel narratives, could have achieved an earlier written form for use in worship in each of the major metropolitan centers. Each Gospel is identified with a different center: Mark with Rome, Matthew with Antioch, Luke with Caesarea, and John with Ephesus. The differences that appear in each of the passion stories may reflect the differences that were present in the local urban churches. If this is so, there is at least the possibility that parts of the passion narratives could have been placed into a semipermanent written form even as early as the 40s. This is speculative, however, and we can get no closer than this.

This analysis of the written sources behind the Gospels is far too sketchy and brushes ever so lightly over issues to which scholars have devoted lifetimes. It represents, nevertheless, significantly more information than most lay people have ever been given, as strange as this possibility may seem. Obviously, it also still leaves us with important questions about the trustworthiness of this primary source of the Christian tradition in regard to the literalness of the details. If we deal with this material honestly, we will have to journey far more deeply into the meaning of biblical truth than most people in this generation of Christians, either fundamentalists or liberals, seem willing to do.

From Oral Vignettes to Written Canon

There is, however, one more step that we can take. It is a step from written sources into oral history. The material in the New Testament is written and therefore frozen into a more-or-less permanent form, with some fragments of it (the passion stories) perhaps being written ten or so years after Jesus' life; perhaps a few more fragments (the Q material) twenty years or so after Jesus' life; significantly more (the Markan narrative) thirty-five to forty-five years afterward; and the Johannine material as much as seventy years afterward.

But since the Gospel writers did not create the material they incorporated, we must look at that period of history in which this material existed only in oral form being passed verbally from person to person or from an itinerant preacher to various congregations. It was not cohesive material. It existed rather in various segments, called "pericopae." These were not generally related to a time or a place in Jesus' life but stood as solitary vignettes that circulated in their isolated splendor. These various pericopae have been identified as pronouncement stories, designed to preserve a saying of the Lord; miracle stories, which included both healing and nature miracles; parables; stories about Jesus; and isolated sayings. The only biographical framework that Matthew, Mark, and Luke seemed to be aware of was that Jesus began his public life in Galilee, that he ended it in Jerusalem, and that to get from Galilee to Jerusalem one must undergo a journey. So these Gospels are divided into a Galilean phase, a journey phase, and a Jerusalem, or final events, phase. The various isolated episodes from Jesus' life are hung upon this framework the way one might hang ornaments on a Christmas tree. The placement matters little. When you decorate the tree another year, you might hang each of the ornaments in a totally different place. The tree would still be beautiful, however, for each episode was complete in and of itself. It would also communicate a similar total message.

In this manner, the content that later was to be written floated freely in the early Christian communities. At some point it underwent translation from Aramaic into Greek. What was lost here nobody will ever know. In time many parts of this oral tradition were not repeated and were therefore forgotten. What jewels fell by the wayside here will never be recovered. Inevitably in time the content of the oral tradition was bent and shaped by the need to speak to and to accommodate the pressures and experiences being undergone in the living community of Christianity itself. When authors did begin to write, they certainly shaped their accounts in terms of the needs and sensitivities of their audiences.

Finally the pattern of written Gospels took shape. There were in time far more than the four Gospels that now adorn Bibles. There was the Gospel of Peter, the Gospel of James, the Gospel of Thomas, the Gospel of the Hebrews, and many others. But in the middle of the second century, a group of Christian leaders, under pressure from a man named Marcion, sat down and decided what books would be included in the volume that would be known as sacred Scripture. They chose Matthew, Mark, Luke, and John from among the available Gospels, Acts from among the various books depicting the early history of the Christian church, and the body of epistles by Paul (Romans, 1 and 2 Corinthians, Galatians, Philippians, Philemon, and Colossians) and others, like Ephesians, Hebrews, Timothy, and Titus (written probably between 70 to 90 C.E.) that they thought were Pauline but that in fact have turned out, in all probability, not to be. Then a series of letters claiming to be by Peter, James, John, and Jude were added (probably none of them were authentic). Finally they chose the Book of Revelation with its vision of the heavenly Jerusalem, written in the persecution of the tenth decade of the Christian era, to close their sacred story. The New Testament had come into being.

A literal transcript of the words of Jesus it was not. Authoritative in the life of the early church it certainly became. Indeed, it froze some things into existence that would in time embarrass the Christian church. But there it was, a written account of the beginnings of Christianity.

It remains for us to determine how this ancient book with its antiquated assumptions can feed and sustain us today. Because I believe that the Bible is so important, I feel compelled first to search for the truth of this book and then to free that truth, so that it is available to this generation. Such a study of the Bible has always given me both joy and insight and has made this book possess for me a magnetic attraction. There is yet far more to embrace, so the story moves on.

7

The Man from Tarsus

The Message of the Man from Tarsus

I wish those who unsettle you would mutilate themselves! (Gal. 5:12)

Look out for the dogs, look out for the evil-workers, look out for those who mutilate the flesh. (Phil. 3:2)

Slaves, obey in everything those who are your earthly masters, not with eye service, as men pleasers, but in singleness of heart. (Col. 3:22)

If any one will not work, let him not eat. (2 Thess. 3:10)

Wives, be subject to your husbands, as is fitting in the Lord. (Col. 3:18)

. . . Let her wear a veil. For a man ought not to cover his head, since he is the image and glory of God; but woman is the glory of man. (Neither was man created for woman, but woman for man.) (1 Cor. 11:6–9)

If any one is preaching to you a gospel contrary to that which you received, let him be accursed. (Gal. 1:9)

God gave them [the Jews] a spirit of stupor, eyes that should not see and ears that should not hear, down to this very day. (Rom. 11:8)

It is shameful for a woman to speak in church. (1 Cor. 14:35)

I magnify my ministry in order to make my fellow Jews jealous, and thus save some of them. (Rom. 11:13, 14).

Is this the Word of the Lord? As such, these verses would certainly present us in this age with problems. But these words make no claim to be the words of God. They are rather the words of Paul, a first-century Jewish convert to Christianity, lifted verbatim out of his voluminous correspondence. There is no doubt but that this man Paul was a powerful shaping influence on Christianity. There is also no doubt but that he was passionate, specific, complex, emotional, frail, controversial, self-centered, and human. He was a pioneering missionary figure who felt an intense vocation to be the apostle of Christ to the gentiles. As such, he lived upon that edge of prejudice and hostility that always accompanies the crossing of a boundary.

The Jews had survived the traumas of their national history by developing a powerfully protective shell that secured them against an alien and hostile world. In the service of that shell, they had constructed interpretive layers that justified the stance of isolation. Jews did not eat, intermarry, fraternize, or worship with gentiles. Such practices as circumcision, dietary regulations, and Sabbath observances set off the Jewish people from the world as distinct, unique, and even odd. Thus separatism also served the Jews' survival needs and kept them alive as a recognizable ethnic group. The binding force on Jewish identity was the Torah.

So it was that when, in the first century, a Jewish teacher named Paul of Tarsus moved outside this defining religious system and began to question it in the light of a different experience, he loosed the fear, anxiety, insecurity, national pride, and immense hostility that ultimately cost him his life. Before he died, however, he had built a new structure that possessed Jewish roots but that also opened his followers to the startling possibility of a universal community. In time that community would enshrine the letters of this man within the corpus of its own sacred story and call them Holy Scripture. Then the line that divided the words of this Paul from what was thought to be the Word of God would begin to fade.

Among the things lost by this confusion of Paul with God would be the intense humanity of this great first-century figure and the shape of the significant issues that he engaged. Outside the heat of his conflict, his words had already lost some of their meaning, for they were but one side of the debate. And when his words became frozen as sacred Scripture, the cultural accretions and scientific presuppositions became fixed in their first-century context. As time moved on and values changed and knowledge of the universe increased, the words of Paul would begin to sink into historical irrelevance, where, unless freed from this literal bondage, they might finally lose their power completely and thus disappear.

Because I believe those words to be in touch with something eternal, transcendent, and holy, I want to rescue them from the hands of those who by claiming too much will finally accomplish too little. If the words of Paul cannot be broken loose from the cultural accretions and presuppositions of a first-century mind-set, they will never speak to this generation.

Some Christians who treasure the Bible will feel that my efforts in this enterprise will be only destructive. They will not recognize that although I work from a different perspective, I love this book no less than they. I am concerned, however, as a Christian facing the twenty-first century that my holy book presents me with the portrait of a man who believes that in religious conflict those who disagree with him should be cursed. He also appears to many to belittle women, affirm slavery, and express some measure of antisemitic hostility. Such an author is not likely to be looked upon as significant in today's world. Yet I believe the message of Paul, freed from its literal distortion, can still speak with power to the human experience. I write to realize that potentiality.

What Did Paul Himself Write?

The list of Paul's letters that are regarded as authentic does not include all of the letters attributed to Paul. He certainly did not write the Epistle to the Hebrews, despite its title "The Epistle of Paul to the Hebrews" in the King James Bible. The vocabulary, thought forms, and conclusions of that book are simply not Pauline. He did not write those words we call the pastoral Epistles, 1 and 2 Timothy, and Titus. They appear to have been written well after Paul's death, for they reflect a structure in the Christian church that did not exist in Paul's time. The issues with which these letters deal are also not the issues that were abroad during Paul's lifetime. Most scholars do not believe Paul wrote Ephesians. That letter seems to have been written by Pauline disciples in the generation after Paul's death, perhaps as an introductory piece to a collection of Paul's authentic letters that began to circulate around the Mediterranean world. There is even some doubt that Colossians is Pauline though this is a minority viewpoint.

The letters that Paul did write are Galatians, 1 and 2 Thessalonians, 1 and 2 Corinthians, Romans, Philemon, and Philippians and probably Colossians. Even within this corpus there is more refining to do. The sixteenth chapter of Romans is not always regarded as part of the original letter to the Christians of that pivotal city in Italy, and an internal analysis of the two letters to the church in Corinth reveals that there were probably as many as four letters to the Corinthians with pieces of the first and third now incorporated into what we call 2 Corinthians.[1]

A further complication is presented by the Book of Acts, written by the author of the Third Gospel some twenty to thirty years after Paul's death. Paul was the hero of much of this first history of the Christian church, and most people have had their image of Paul created for them primarily by Acts. Yet the Book of Acts seems to have had no knowledge whatsoever of the Pauline Epistles. Furthermore, in Acts there are the dramatic stories of Paul's various journeys, his appearance before Festus, Felix, and Agrippa, and his actual journey to Rome; these are nowhere referred to by Paul. An adventure story told in narrative form is more colorful and more memorable than letters, which are always monologues that present only half of the intended conversation.

Yet the aforementioned omissions combined with major discrepancies between Acts and the Pauline corpus raise significant questions of accuracy. For example, the apostolic council described in Acts 15 cannot be reconciled with Paul's description of the resolution of the same issues in Galatians 2. Paul's writings reveal that he spent two to three years in Ephesus, but the Acts narrative reveals only striking isolated episodes. A comparison of the Damascus road conversion story, which Acts records no less than three times, with what is probably Paul's account of his conversion in 2 Cor. 12:1–5 is particularly striking. Paul here tells the story of the man caught up into "the third heaven" to hear "things that cannot be told, which man may not utter."

An analysis of the Book of Acts will reveal that its author wrote long after the major controversies in Paul's life had faded. Jerusalem had fallen to the Roman armed forces in 70 C.E., and the temple had been razed. From that day until 1948, the Jewish people of the world would not have a homeland. The power of the Jewish Christians in the burgeoning Christian church diminished sharply when its center in Jerusalem was destroyed, and increasingly the Christian movement became a gentile movement, which of course meant that Paul's struggle to enable gentiles to find a place inside Christianity became an issue of antiquity. It lost its emotion, its vehemence, and its passion. For these reasons, when Acts and the Pauline corpus are in conflict, the weight of evidence seems to lie with Paul. Consequently, in this attempt to re-create Paul of Tarsus, I will rely primarily on the writings of Paul himself.

Paul is a (perhaps *the*) primary witness in the shaping of the Christian revelation. He penned his words at a time when there were no written Gospels to feed his memory or to create his images. His epistles came during the oral period of Christian history, when there was no one authoritative source of written kerygma (the apostolic proclamation). As I have mentioned in chapter 6, the source known as Q and various portions of the passion narrative may have been committed to writing before Paul wrote. But we cannot be certain of this, nor do we have any way of knowing that Paul had access to them even if these portions of the tradition were written. These facts create an interpretive problem for modern expositors of Paul. Our minds have been so shaped and informed by the Gospel content that we do not recognize how frequently we read Paul through the eyes of the Gospels. We need to embrace the fact that none of Paul's first readers read him this way, for in their lives there were as yet no Gospels. To interpret Paul accurately we need to put ourselves into that first-century pre-gospel frame of reference and to hear Paul in fresh and authentic ways. When one does this the insights into the primitive Christian experience are startling and challenging, as I hope to point out. First, however, we need to pull together the biographical material available to us in Paul's writings and seek to bring this unique person into clear historic focus.

Who Was This Man Paul?

Paul was a Jew born in the province of Cilicia in Asia Minor. In the ancient world Tarsus had been the seat of Hittite power and later a center of a Persian satrapy. During the Hellenistic period it had remained an important city that some ancient writers said actually rivaled Athens and Alexandria as a place of learning.[2] Like most cities in the Mediterranean world, Tarsus had a Jewish colony. How and when Paul's family arrived there we do not know. This colony supported the Jewish temple in Jerusalem with two drachmas for every Jewish male in their exiled community paid to the temple annually. They possessed a synagogue, where they worshiped regularly, which means, of course, that more than ten Jewish males had to be present.

Young Saul, which was Paul's Jewish name, was undoubtedly taken to the synagogue regularly. The synagogue services began with the Shema: "Hear, O Israel, the Lord our God is one Lord." It continued with prayers and readings of portions of the Law and the prophets, usually from the Septuagint (the Greek version of the Jewish Scriptures). There would also be a sermon, typically assigned to any competent male in the congregation. The synagogue had administrative officers but no official priesthood. The ancient Jewish hope that God would raise up a king in the Davidic line to restore Israel to its destiny as God's elect was inevitably part of the milieu of that community. These were shaping influences in the life of the young Paul.

Paul's family had some status in Tarsus and perhaps even some wealth. His father, who was of the ancient tribe of Benjamin, had acquired Roman citizenship, whether as a reward for some service rendered or by purchasing it we do not know. But, as C. H. Dodd notes, a person who writes of himself as "laboring with my own hands" (1 Cor. 4:12) is hardly one who was born to manual labor.[3] Yet it was the custom for every person to have a trade, and Paul was trained as a tent maker. When Paul talked about his upbringing, it is clear that he was introduced to the Law early and rigorously. "Circumcised on the eighth day; . . . as to the law, a Pharisee, . . . as to righteousness under the law, blameless" (Phil 3:4–6). It would have been typical for a prominent Jewish family from Tarsus to send their son to Jerusalem to complete his education. Perhaps then it is true, as the Book of Acts suggests, that Paul studied under Gamaliel, the learned and respected member of the Sanhedrin (Acts 22:3). But whether accurate or not, Paul's letters reveal a passion for the Law, a knowledge of the Hebrew Scriptures, and a rabbinical style both in the use of texts and in bursts of rhetorical questions and even some oratorical diatribes.

Paul spoke and wrote Greek fluently, but with the inclusion of many second-hand semitisms. His writing style, however, was the style of a speaker. He hardly ever used a period; only dashes. Sometimes his sentences would be so long, with so many parenthetical thoughts thrown in, that a reader would forget what the subject of the sentence was before reaching the verb. His writing had the rhythm of the spoken word, but he did reach heights of almost poetic elegance in such passages as 1 Corinthians 13 and Rom. 8:31–39.

Whatever else can be said about Paul, one certainly must acknowledge that on his scale of values the Law, the Torah, and his religious traditions were supreme. By this Law he lived, defined himself, shaped his life, and sought his ultimate meaning. Of himself he says, "I advanced in Judaism beyond many of my own age among my people, so extremely zealous was I for the tradition of my fathers" (Gal. 1:14). It is easy to understand how such a person would respond with fear and anger if a movement arose that threatened the supremacy or authenticity of this controlling value system.

When one discovers religious intensity this pronounced, one certainly must look at what personal needs are being satisfied, thus fueling the zeal of the religious devotee. Since Paul's religion gave him a sense of identity and meaning, one wonders what the source of the anxiety was that this imposed identity kept in check, or where the lack of self-worth came from that made the imposed meaning so powerful. Paul covered his insecurity with an exaggerated need to excel. There was in Jewish folklore a tradition that if one Jewish male could keep the entire Jewish Law for one twenty-four-hour period, the Kingdom of God would come. Paul was so constituted that it would occur to him to think that he might be the one. We will examine this aspect of Paul in detail later, but suffice it for now to recognize that there is great frustration at work in an insecure perfectionist.

Paul's writings reveal the combination of intense levels of self-negativity covered by intensely cultivated images of superiority. At first these forces fed Paul's devotion to Judaism at the same time that they created his defensiveness. Subsequently these forces became operative in his later devotion to and understanding of the gospel. But whatever was the source of Paul's anxiety, the rise of the Christian movement within Judaism threatened Paul's security and identity so severely that he responded by becoming a persecutor of this movement. Persecution is always revealing. One does not persecute something that does not scare, and it cannot scare unless it has appeal. Conversion in such a person is always dramatic. Earlier convictions, passionately held, cannot be passionately abandoned without a volcanic internal crisis. Paul recounted his career as a persecutor (1 Cor. 15:9; Gal. 1:12ff, 1:22). And when his energies were directed to Christian ends, the intensity, passion, and single-mindedness of his personality were not diminished. He became an apostle in a manner no less consuming of his life. In one of his works he elaborated the various traumas he had undergone for the sake of the gospel. They included imprisonment, beatings, and near death.

> Five times I have received at the hands of the Jews the forty lashes less one. Three times I have been shipwrecked; a night and a day I have been adrift at sea; on frequent journeys, in danger from rivers, danger from robbers, danger from my own people, danger from gentiles, danger in the city, danger in the wilderness, danger at sea, danger from false brethren; in toil and hardship, through many a sleepless night, in hunger and thirst, often without food, in cold and exposure. And, apart from other things, there is the daily pressure upon me of my anxiety for all the churches. (2 Cor. 11:24–28)

This was a man of passion, power, commitment, and energy.

What did Paul look like? From Paul himself we have only one descriptive verse, where he was actually relating words his critics had used. "His bodily presence is weak, and his speech of no account" (2 Cor. 10:10). Later in that same epistle, he defended himself by saying, "Even if I am unskilled in speaking, I am not in knowledge" (2 Cor. 11:6). The Book of Acts suggested that the people at Lystra mistook Barnabas and Paul for gods. Barnabas was identified with Zeus, which would seem to point to a physical impressiveness, since Zeus was the king of the gods. Paul was identified with Hermes (Mercury), the messenger god who was depicted usually as small, wiry, and verbal (Acts 14:8ff). A late second-century document entitled *The Acts of Paul and Thecla* referred to Paul as small in stature, bald headed, bow legged, vigorous, with meeting eyebrows and a slightly hooked nose, but we cannot trust this source for accuracy.[4]

By Paul's reckoning in the Epistle to the Galatians, his conversion occurred seventeen years prior to the writing of that epistle. During that time he went away to Arabia, returned to Damascus, then went up to Jerusalem for fifteen days to visit

Cephas, during which time he saw none of the other apostles except James, the Lord's brother. Then he journeyed to Syria and Cilicia and resided for fourteen years before going back to Jerusalem again with Barnabas and Titus (Gal. 15–21). When these figures are put together, the time of Paul's conversion is located somewhere in the early to mid-30s, depending of course on the date finally recognized as the date of Jesus' final days. Adolph Harnack, the great church historian of the nineteenth century, is still regarded as authoritative when he dates that conversion between one and six years following the life of Jesus.

Paul's career as a missionary does not seem to have begun earlier than the late 40s. No evidence points to any direct knowledge of the earthly Jesus on the part of this man. What he knew of Jesus he seems to have gotten through the oral tradition at the feet of itinerant preachers, from the various apostles, or from disciples of the apostles. John son of Zebedee, Mark, and Luke all appear in the letters of Paul as names of those with whom he had more than just a casual relationship (Gal. 2:9; Col. 4:14; Philem. v. 23; Col. 4:10).

Paul's Opinion and Assumptions

Paul was not a universal man. He was indeed a man of his times. He reflected the common assumptions of his day, assumptions that time has eroded badly. For Paul, women were clearly inferior. Yet he could say in Galatians that in Christ "there is neither male nor female" (Gal. 3:28), and these words occur in his powerful argument to demonstrate the inclusiveness of all people, especially the gentiles, in the Christian movement. He also, in this same passage, said that "in Christ there is neither slave nor free." The fact remains that Paul accepted uncritically the patriarchal attitude of his day toward women and the cultural reality of the institution of slavery.

Paul was not married. He viewed women with something less than enthusiasm. He justified his unmarried status on the basis of the imminent apocalypse (1 Cor. 7:25). He stated, "It is well for a man not to touch a woman" (1 Cor. 7:1). A woman's hair fascinated him. Paul argued from nature, he said, that long hair was degrading for a man but pride for a woman. "We recognize no other practice," he asserted, "nor do the churches of God" (1 Cor. 11:14–16). He exhorted women to keep silent in the churches "as in all the churches of the saints." Women were "not permitted to speak, but should be subordinate, as even the law says. If there is anything they [the women] desire to know, let them ask their husbands at home. For it is shameful for a woman to speak in church" (1 Cor. 14:34–35).

In these verses Paul revealed himself as uncritically part of the patriarchal system that so informed the Hebrew Scriptures. He has been quoted to support those opposed to the ordination of women to either the priesthood or the episcopacy. The argument used by these groups asserts that a woman cannot adequately represent God at the altar, which is a not-so-subtle assertion that only the male has been created in God's image. The female thus becomes from this perspective a subhuman creature, above the animals in status but lower than the lordly male. Obviously, with such a working definition, the prejudices affiliated with second-class citizenship can be justified.

By modern standards such attitudes are not only inadequate but wrong, and they are rapidly being abandoned. Margaret Thatcher, Corazon Aquino, Sandra Day O'Connor, and Geraldine Ferraro, just to name a few, are illustrations of women achieving equality in power with men in nations that have been shaped by the value systems revealed in Holy Scripture but now significantly challenged as inadequate in the practice of our daily lives. It is well-nigh impossible for this generation to believe that these Pauline ideas about women represent the Word of God, at least the words of a God they would be drawn to in worship.

Similarly Paul accepted the institution of slavery as one of the facts of life. He made no effort to call slaves into freedom. He expressed a kind of pastoral compassion for the slaves but

101

contented himself with fine-tuning the institution of slavery itself, so that it might be kinder and gentler. Paul urged the runaway slave Onesimus to return to his master, Philemon, and therefore to bondage, with the hope that Philemon would treat him kindly because of his service to Paul (Philem. 1:10ff). He enjoined the slaves in Colossae to "obey in everything those who are your earthly masters" (Col. 3:22). He balanced that admonition by urging masters to "treat your slaves justly and fairly, knowing that you also have a master in heaven" (Col. 4:1).

Apparently for Paul justice and fairness could be achieved inside the system of slavery by urging kindness. Here again is an attitude that is difficult for this generation the world over, and on the lips of any politician today it would receive overwhelming rejection, even in a nation as violently race divided as South Africa. Yet for almost nineteen hundred years, slavery lived in the Christian West justified by an appeal to Paul and other biblical texts. There was not in the Christian West a sufficient moral sensitivity to challenge this inhumane institution. The dichotomy is best seen for me in that the most overtly religious section of the United States, the evangelical Bible belt of the South, was the place where slavery flourished and segregation, the stepchild of slavery, was clung to with tenacity even into the latter years of the twentieth century.

The well-known and much-loved gospel hymn "Amazing Grace" was in fact penned on the deck of a slave ship with its writhing human cargo below struggling to survive their kidnapping from Africa, later to endure the cruelty of the master's lash, the breakup of families, sexual violations, and all the other dehumanizing marks of this evil system. Yet slavery stands approved and accepted in the writings of the Apostle Paul, whose words are regarded by many Christians as the inerrant Word of God. A God who tolerates slavery can hardly be God for this generation.

Paul also revealed a strange attitude toward legally constituted authority. He asserted in Romans that every person was to be subject to the governing authorities. For there is no authority except from God, and those that exist have been instituted by God. Therefore he who resists the authorities resists what God has appointed, and those who resist will incur judgment. For rulers are not a terror to good conduct, but to bad. Would you have no fear of him who is in authority? Then do what is good, and you will receive his approval, for he is God's servant for your good. But if you do wrong, be afraid, for he does not bear the sword in vain; he is the servant of God to execute his wrath on the wrong-doer. (Rom 13:1–4)

That may have been good advice to be given to the tiny Christian community living before the church emerged as a threat to the emperor at Rome, but from our perspective it is politically naive.

These words have been used throughout history to justify the divine right of kings and political oppression of various types and to mute the criticism of various injustices. How would these words have sounded to the framers of the Magna Charta in 1215 C.E.? Did not the English royalists quote these words during the rebellion of Oliver Cromwell, and when the monarchy was reestablished in England under Charles II? Had George Washington taken these words literally would there have been an American revolution in 1776? Would not Benedict Arnold, remembered in the United States as a traitor because he supported the established government that ruled the colonies from London, have been accorded the honor of being one who properly acted on the "Word of God"? How do these words, if interpreted literally, sound to those who lobbied for and finally went to war for the abolition of slavery? What would be their message to the leaders of the labor movement as they struggled, sometimes amid violence, for fair wages and an end to the exploitation of men, women, and children in the sweatshops of the Industrial Revolution? If these words are to be taken literally as the very words of God, what would they have done to the activities of American or South African civil rights leaders such as Martin Luther King, Jr., James Farmer, James Meredith, Desmond Tutu, or Allan Boesak? Could these

103

words be the Word of God to the leaders of the Vietnam War protest movement, the feminist movement, or the crusade for gay and lesbian rights?

Paul was a limited man captured by the worldview and circumstances of a vastly different time. It is the height of foolishness to try to claim eternal truth for his culturally conditioned and time-limited words. Paul's words are not the *Words* of God. They are the words of Paul—a vast difference. Those who try to elevate Paul's words into being what they cannot be will finally discard Paul's words in the dustbins of antiquity.

Paul was not a universal scholar. He was not even a good biblical scholar. He studied the content of his Holy Scriptures, but he was not as conversant with the background, history, and formation of the Old Testament as any graduate from an accredited seminary in England or the United States would be today. The common wisdom of Paul's day attributed the authorship of the Torah to Moses. Paul accepted that common wisdom (see Rom. 9:15; 10:5; 10:19; 1 Cor. 9:9; 2 Cor. 3:15). Paul treated Adam as if he were as literal and historic a figure as Jesus of Nazareth had been (Rom. 5:14, 18). No biblical scholar will march today under that banner. Paul viewed Abraham in a similar historic fashion, dating him, rather interestingly, some 430 years before Sinai (Gal. 3:17), which was a closer guess than he knew. He did use Abraham in a fascinating way to build his case for inclusiveness. The one whom the Jews acknowledged as the father of Judaism was in fact called to be the one in whom all nations are to be blessed, Paul's argument went (Gal. 3:8). This was a theme that Matthew was to pick up and use later, as we shall see.

Given Paul's level of biblical knowledge, the modern interpreter of Paul must face many questions. To treat the words of Paul as if they are the inerrant Word of God, however, presents us with far more problems than it solves. Such a claim suggests that to be a Christian requires the abdication of the mind to cultural patterns long since abandoned.

One could point further to such debates as to whether or

not Christians should eat meat that had been offered to idols, which exercised Paul's mind so frequently. One could also look at Paul's view of angels and demons that shaped passages in his writing such as, "If with Christ you died to the elemental spirits of the universe, why do you live as if you still belonged to the world?" (Col. 2:20); or "For I am convinced that neither death, nor life, nor angels, nor principalities, . . . nor powers, nor height, nor depth, . . . will be able to separate us from the love of God in Christ Jesus our Lord" (Rom. 8:38–39). He spoke of Satan "preventing him" (1 Thess. 2:18) from coming to visit the Thessalonians. This was for Paul not a literary device but a fully developed belief system that enabled him to take spiritual forces quite literally. These supernatural spirits were, for Paul, responsible even for the crucifixion (1 Cor. 2:8).

The attitudes that shaped Paul's writing have long ago been abandoned. If Paul's writing is to be literalized, the assumptions and presuppositions he made are impossible to separate from his words. His assumptions and presuppositions are clearly dated and, as such, are increasingly difficult for us to accept. How can Christians living in today's world abandon Paul's underlying assumptions and still relate to Paul's words as if somehow they have captured a timeless truth? This is our task.

Paul cannot be taken literally. He did not write the Word of God. He wrote the words of Paul, a particular, limited, frail human being. But he had contact with a powerful experience that changed his life, and his changed life was instrumental in changing millions of other lives throughout the years of Christian history. Can we use his words to get into the power of his experience? Can we participate in that experience and know something of that life-giving power? Can we then translate that power into words that do communicate in our day with assumptions and presuppositions that are in touch with reality as we know it?

What was Christ for Paul? Can the Christ who is the reality pointed to by all of Paul's words still be Christ for us? What did resurrection mean to Paul? Can we meet and know that power of resurrection? What was the meaning of grace for Paul? Can we enter the grace experience that changed Paul's life? These are the questions to which our attention must now be drawn if we are to sing the Lord's song in this century.

8

Christ, Resurrection, Grace: The Gospel of Paul

Describing Paul of Tarsus externally is not a difficult task. Outlining the ideas that shaped his thinking and the cultural attitudes that rooted him in history and made him less than universal and the victim, as we all are, of assumptions that time has rendered inadequate, is an ordinary assignment. It may well trouble those who have made an icon of the literal words of Paul, but icons must and will fall every day.

If a religious system requires that a literal Bible be embraced, I must walk away from that system. I walk away without fear, for any religious system based upon such an inadequate foundation will never survive, no matter how many times it undergoes a face-lift. Doing a face-lift on a corpse does not restore life, it only restores for a moment the illusion of life. Organized religion as we have known it in the Western world is considered by many a friend and foe alike to be sick unto death. The periodic revivals of fundamentalism are momentary blips on the EKG charts of religious history.

If there is a way into a living religious tradition for our time it will not come from tinkering with the cumbersome structures we have received from the past. It will come rather by setting those structures aside, finding a new starting point, a new

107

place of entry into whatever religious truth is, and being willing
to explore that new terrain openly, honestly, and courageously.
It means asking questions that have not yet been asked and
raising possibilities that have not yet been raised. Finally, it
means understanding the human experience that lies behind
the explanations, the rationality, and the theological formulations as a valid arena in which to search for meaning, for the
transcendent dimension to this earthbound existence and, ultimately, for God.

Understanding the Real Paul

At this point in our discussion it means trying to find the
real man Paul beneath the words of his epistles and the explanations of him given by institutional Christianity, from the
Book of Acts and the pastoral Epistles to this day. It means
trying to climb into his life, feel his humanity, recognize his
pain, and, from that perspective, seeking to understand who
Christ was for him and at what point Christ met him. Then
perhaps we can understand why Paul thought of Christ as he
did, what resurrection meant and why it was so crucial to him,
and, finally, what conversion itself meant to this apostolic
figure.

If this man Paul of Tarsus can become for us one at whose
depths the recesses and universal pools of the human spirit can
be fathomed, then Paul can be for us a point of entry into the
meaning of God as the life of Jesus was for Paul a point of entry
into the meaning of God. If this can occur, we will have shrunk
the span of years and the superstructure of interpretation and
theology that separates so many of us today from the timeless
moment of incarnation. If we can comprehend and touch the
experience through which the God who was in Christ met Paul,
perhaps we can also see how and where the God who is in
Christ can still meet us. Only in this way can authenticity be
restored to the tradition in which we Christians walk. So enter
with me into the realm of speculation as we probe the life of
Paul, using his words not as literal objects but as doorways into

his psyche, where alone truth that changes life can be processed.

Paul's Profound Sense of Guilt

Who was Christ for Paul? Christ was for Paul the presence and power of God that called him into authentic personhood. Who was Paul? Was it autobiographical when he wrote that he was an imposter who yearned to be true, a person unknown who yearned to be known—as one who though dying yearned to be alive? Was it of himself that Paul wrote that Christ had enabled him, who thought of himself as one who was being punished, to know that he would not be destroyed as he had once thought was his due? Was it Paul who had known himself to be sorrowful yet who now in Christ had discovered the ability to rejoice? Was Paul the one who had once thought of himself inwardly as living in intense poverty but who now found, incredible as it seemed, that he had made others rich? Was it Paul who had previously seen himself as having nothing of worth but now, because somehow Christ had given him back the very self Paul had found so rejectable, believed that he possessed all things (2 Cor. 6:8–10)? Could the Christ who forgave his tormentors, prayed for those who drove the nails into his hands and feet, restored those who denied and forsook him also love the unlovable Paul? Could the love of God in Jesus of Nazareth that loved even those who murdered the love of God also embrace Paul of Tarsus? That might be too good to be true. Yet is that not the reality that broke through the consciousness of the one who had sought all his life to be blameless before the law? With all his might he sought perfection and he failed. Over and over and over again he failed. His mind and heart were not in control. He was convinced that what he willed to do with his mind became the very thing that with his life he did not do (Rom. 7:14, 15). Paul tried to explain this spiritual schizophrenia. If I will to do what I cannot do, he reasoned, then it is no longer I who do it but sin that dwells within me (Rom. 7:18). Sin was for Paul a powerful force—a demonic power so strong it could make Paul do what he did not want to do. "Let not sin," he wrote, "dwell in your mortal bodies to *make* you obey their passions" (Rom. 6:12). "It was sin, working death in me through what is good, in order that sin might be shown to be sin, and through the commandment might become sinful beyond measure" (Rom. 7:13).

Paul also saw himself in some sense as a victim. It is not too harsh to say he loathed himself. His words reflected this self-loathing over and over again. "What return did you get," he asked (of himself, I think), "for the things of which you are now ashamed? The end of those things is death" (Rom. 6:21). Ashamed, deserving death—these are the self-revelatory admissions of Paul. Was it not of his own life that he wrote so passionately, "just as you once yielded your members to impurity and to greater and greater iniquity, so now yield your members to righteousness for sanctification" (Rom. 6:19). Impurity, greater and greater iniquity—these are harsh and revealing words.

What is a "member" of the body that Paul says has been yielded to iniquity? The Greek word translated "member" is μελος (melos). It means "a member, limb, part of the body."[1] In the Epistle to the Corinthians Paul called the ear, nose, eye, hand, head, and feet members of the body (1 Cor. 12:14ff). Then he referred to "our unpresentable parts," which, he suggested, are to be treated with a modesty "that our more presentable parts do not require" (1 Cor. 12:24). But can one loathe the head, the hand, the foot, the ears? Are these "members" operating independently of the mind? Could Paul say of them "sin reigns in my members. With my mind I will one thing, with my body I do another"? Cannot the mind direct the feet, the eyes, the ears? The only organs that cannot finally be controlled by the will are the genitalia. Sexual arousal comes sometimes despite our best efforts. Sexual impotency comes sometimes despite our mental desire to respond.

Is there any compelling evidence to believe Paul is talking here about anything other than sexual desire that seems to plague him? Listen to his words: "I am carnal, sold under sin.

I do not understand my own actions" (Rom. 7:14, 15). "Nothing good dwells in me, that is, in my flesh. I can will what is right but I cannot do it" (Rom. 7:18). "I see in my members another law at war with the law of my mind and making me captive to the law of sin that dwells in my members" (Rom. 7:23). Can these passages really mean anything other than a confession of a sexual passion or need beyond Paul's control, part of his being about which he feels a guilt so profound that it becomes an aspect of self-loathing?

Have we been prevented for all these years from seeing this because we placed a barrier between holy Paul whose words are recorded in Holy Scripture and the sexual yearnings that we could not believe were part of the life of a saint and holy man? Have we Christians not been conditioned for two thousand years by the extolling of virginity and celibacy that were said to be the very marks of a holy life? Could the holy Apostle Paul have been marked by desire so intense that he wrote about it over and over and over again? Listen to more of Paul: "With my flesh I serve the law of sin" (Rom. 7:25); "The body is not meant for immorality but for the Lord" (1 Cor. 6:13); "The immoral man sins against his own body" (1 Cor. 6:18); "I pummel my body and subdue it lest after preaching to others I myself should be disqualified" (1 Cor. 9:27).

A body that needs to be pummeled must be evil indeed. What plagues Paul that his body is deserving of such abuse? Listen once more to the ever-revealing Paul. "For ever since we came into Macedonia, our bodies had no rest but we were afflicted at every turn—fighting without and fear within" (2 Cor. 7:5). Certainly Paul's life was difficult and persecution was real, but does that adequately account for more than half of that enigmatic tag line "fighting without and fear within"? What is the fear within? What is the power so intense that Paul believes it is held over him by demonic beings? Listen once more: "Formerly, when you did not know God, you were in bondage to beings that by nature are no gods; but now that you are known by God, how can you turn your back again to the weak elemental spirits, whose slaves you want to be once more?" (Gal.

111

4:8, 9). Not to know God, says Paul, is to suffer a confusion of identity, especially sexual identity. God gives up those dominated by such passions, says Paul, "in the lusts of their hearts to impurity, to the dishonoring of their bodies among themselves, because they exchanged the truth about God for a lie and worshiped and served the creature rather than the creator" (Rom. 1:24, 25). Again and again Paul drove home his painful revelatory cry. He was under the control of that which he could not master. It had invaded his body, his flesh. He warned, "Do not use your freedom as an opportunity for the flesh" (Gal. 5:13); "Do not gratify the desires of the flesh. For the desires of the flesh are against the Spirit, and the desires of the Spirit are against the flesh" (Gal. 5:16).

What does the flesh produce? For Paul these were clearly references to sexual passion out of control. The flesh produced "fornication, impurity, licentiousness" (Gal. 5:19). But the fruit of the Spirit was "self-control" (Gal. 5:23). Yes, there was a longer list of works of the flesh and fruits of the Spirit in Galatians, but Paul was never far from the discussion of sexual passion and the need for self-control. He concluded this passage again with a startling revelatory statement: "Those who belong to Christ Jesus have *crucified the flesh* with its passions and desires" (Gal. 5:24). The flesh was for Paul the dwelling place of the evil that possessed him, over which he had no control and which produced in him a self-rejection that descended to the intensity of self-loathing.

One aches for the pain of Paul, who, out of this pain, exhorts the people of Colossae to "put to death therefore what is earthly in you: fornication, impurity, passion, evil desire and covetousness, which is idolatry. On account of these the wrath of God is coming" (Col. 3:5). Paul felt a tremendous vulnerability as one who judged himself deserving of wrath because he was evil and base, and, if not evil in himself, then helplessly under the control of evil powers. "For I do not do what I want, but I do the very thing I hate" (Rom. 7:15). "So," Paul concluded, "I find it to be a law that when I want to do right, evil lies close at hand. For I delight in the law of God, in my inmost

112

self, but I see in my *members* another law at war with the law of my mind and making me captive to the law of sin which dwells in my *members*. Wretched man that I am!" (Rom. 7:21–24). Wretched man! A revealing cry of self-rejection. Wretched man, who served the law of sin "with my flesh" (Rom. 7:25). Wretched man who stood rejected, condemned. "Who will deliver me from this body of death?" (Rom. 7:24).

What I have done is to break Paul out of Scripture, to free him from those who would capture him inside the cult of an imposed holiness. I have let him speak for himself. He was a tortured man. His passion for perfection was in direct proportion to his torture. This was why he had advanced in Judaism beyond many of his own age. This was why he had been so extremely zealous for the traditions of his fathers. His pursuit of holiness through the Law was necessary to control a power and a reality that resided in his body and in his flesh and over which his mind had no control. The Law and pursuit of the life of righteousness were desired to control his uncontrollable passion. Without the structure of the Law, he was consumed with some inner desire. It was for Paul a loathsome desire, very probably connected in some way with sexuality, filled with evil and impurity. Any threat to the sanctity and power of the Law was a threat to Paul's control system, a threat to his fragile attempt "to possess his vessel in sanctification and honour, not in the lust of consuming concupiscence" (1 Thess. 4:5, KJV). I quote that text from the King James Version specifically because the Revised Standard Version changes the word *vessel* to the word *wife*—a translation that I believe misses Paul's point completely.

So it was that when the Christian movement appeared on the scene it seemed to Paul to undermine the Law, and if it undermined the Law, it undermined Paul's fragile security system. If Christianity prevailed, Paul would be destroyed, consumed by evil passions over which he had no control. Paul therefore hated Christianity. He hated it with a vehemence that was itself revelatory. Only something that shook the fragility of one's life support system could elicit the kind of killing hostility

113

that Paul exhibited toward the Christians. Religious anger is always revealing.

Paul, watching the first Jewish Christians decentralize the Law in favor of grace, was not unlike a fundamentalist watching his or her infallible Bible being replaced by an irresistible call into the insecurity of freedom. His response was rage. He wanted to kill, imprison, persecute. The Christians were agents of lawlessness, the devil incarnate. They must be stopped. This is not far from the kind of rage that emanates from the television evangelists when they are exposed, and the fragile control system that they have so laboriously constructed to keep their own passions in check begins to waver.

Powerful emotional commitments to a controlling religious system reveal not so much devotion and virtue but troubled waters that will not stay calm. Fears that reside deep in our being always seem to rise up to shake our world, our securities—fighting without, fears within. It is not surprising to me that time and time again the popular evangelistic preachers who speak so vehemently against the sins of the flesh wind up succumbing to the very fleshy sins they have condemned.

Paul was *not* free *not* to persecute the Christians, for if they survived, he knew that he would not. As a Jew he had been taught that "the study of the law diverted the mind from desire." The Fourth Book of Maccabees had stated that "by mental effort" all sexual desire can be overcome (4 Macc. 2:2). "The temperate mind can conquer the drives of the emotions and quench the flames of frenzied desires, it can overthrow bodily agonies even when they are extreme, and by nobility of reason spurn all domination by the emotions" (4 Macc. 3:17, 18). Paul counted on these assurances. With the Law as his ally, he tried daily to bank the flames of an uncontrolled and, in his mind, evil passion.

The "followers of the way," as the early Christians were called, were, in Paul's mind, seeking to invalidate the power of the Law, and therefore they elicited from Paul the reckless and uncontrollable rage of a persecutor, and an emotional and unstoppable persecutor he was. As he said, "You have heard of

114

my former life in Judaism, how I persecuted the church of God violently and tried to destroy it" (Gal. 1:13ff). Nothing about Paul was moderate. He was tightly drawn, passionately emotional, filled with enormous feelings of self-negativity, seeking to deal with those feelings in the time-honored way of external controls, unflagging religious zeal, and rigid discipline. He could not, however, master the passions that consumed him.

What were these passions? There is no doubt in my mind that they were sexual in nature, but what kind of sexual passions were they? Searching once again through the writings of Paul, some conclusions begin to emerge that startle and surprise the reader. Paul's passions seemed to be incapable of being relieved. Why was that? Paul himself had written that if one "could not exercise self-control" that person should marry. "For it is better to marry than to be aflame with passion" (1 Cor. 7:9). But we have no evidence from any source that Paul ever married. Indeed, he exhorts widows and the unmarried to "remain single as I do" (1 Cor. 7:8). A primary purpose of sexual activity in marriage, according to Paul, was to keep Satan from tempting people "through lack of self-control" (1 Cor. 7:5). Why, when Paul seemed to be so consumed with a passion he could not control, would he not take his own advice and alleviate that passion in marriage? He did write that marriage was an acceptable, if not ideal, way of life. "If you marry you do not sin" (1 Cor. 7:25). The reason he gave for his recommendation against marriage was the nearness of the apocalypse. "I think that in view of the present [or impending] distress it is well for a person to remain as he is. Are you bound to a wife? Do not seek to be free. Are you free from a wife? Do not seek marriage . . . the appointed time has grown very short" (1 Cor. 7:26ff). Yet toward the end of Paul's life when he wrote Colossians and Philippians, there was in Paul's mind a gradual waning of the immediacy of the second coming, and it was replaced by a growing hope of universalism. Still, however, marriage never seemed to loom for him as a possibility.

Paul has been perceived as basically negative toward women. He did write that "it is well for a man not to touch a woman" (1 Cor. 7:1). The passion that burned so deeply in Paul did not seem to be related to the desire for union with a woman. Why would that desire create such negativity in Paul, anyway? Marriage, married love, and married sexual desire were not thought to be evil or loathsome. Paul's sexual passions do not fit comfortably into this explanatory pattern. But what does?

Obviously there is no way to know for certain the cause of Paul's anxiety prior to that moment of final revelation in the Kingdom of Heaven. But that does not stop speculation. The value of speculation in this case comes when a theory is tested by assuming for a moment that it is correct and then reading Paul in the light of that theory. Sometimes one finds in this way the key that unlocks the hidden messages that are present in the text. Once unlocked, these messages not only cease to be hidden but they become obvious, glaring at the reader, who wonders why such obvious meanings had not been seen before.

Some have suggested that Paul was sexually impotent. This theory does not fit the data. Others have suggested that Paul may have been sexually abused in his childhood and thus was in deep conflict with the immobilizing twin emotions of fear and desire. This theory fits a little better, but it still leaves too many loose ends in the reconstruction.

Still others have suggested that Paul was plagued by homosexual fears. This is not a new idea, and yet until recent years, when homosexuality began to shed some of its negative connotations, it was an idea so repulsive to Christian people that it could not be breathed in official circles. This is not to say that our cultural homophobia has disappeared. It is still lethal and dwells in high places in the life of the Christian church, and it is a subject about which ecclesiastical figures are deeply dishonest, saying one thing publicly and acting another way privately. The prejudice, however, is fading slowly but surely. With the softening of that homophobic stance we might consider the hypothesis that Paul may have been a gay male. We might test that theory by assuming it for a moment as we read

116

Paul. When I did this for the first time, I was startled to see how much of Paul was unlocked and how deeply I could understand the power of the gospel that literally saved Paul's life.

When I suggest the possibility that Paul was a homosexual person, I do not mean to be salacious or titillating or even to suggest something that many would consider scandalous. I see no evidence to suggest that Paul ever acted out his sexual desires and passions. He lived in an age and among a people that cloaked the way he would have viewed this reality with layer after layer of condemnation. But for a moment assume the possibility that this theory is correct and look with me again at the writings of Paul and, more important, at the meaning of Christ, resurrection, and grace in the life of this foundational Christian.

Paul felt tremendous guilt and shame, which produced in him self-loathing. The presence of homosexuality would have created this response among Jewish people in that period of history. Nothing else, in my opinion, could account for Paul's self-judging rhetoric, his negative feeling toward his own body, and his sense of being controlled by something he had no power to change. The war that went on between what he desired with his mind and what he desired with his body, his drivenness to a legalistic religion of control, his fear when that system was threatened, his attitude toward women, his refusal to seek marriage as an outlet for his passion—nothing else accounts for this data as well as the possibility that Paul was a gay male.

Paul's religious tradition would clearly regard gay males as aberrant, distorted, evil, and depraved. When discovered, gay males were quite often executed. The Law stated: "You shall not lie with a man as with a woman; it is an abomination" (Lev. 18:22). Do not defile yourself by these things, the Torah continued, for God will cast out those who defile themselves. God will punish, promised the Law, and the land will vomit out those who are thus defiled (Lev. 18:24ff). To do these things is to be cut off from the people of Israel (Lev. 18:29). Later in the Torah death is called for as the penalty for homosexuality. "If a man lies with a man as with a woman, both of them have

117

committed an abomination; they shall be put to death" (Lev. 20:13).

Paul was a student of the Law. If homosexuality was his condition, he knew well that by that Law he stood condemned. His body was a body in which death reigned. He lived under that death sentence. What Paul knew himself to be, the people to whom he belonged and the Law to which he adhered called abominable, and Paul felt it to be beyond redemption. Is it not possible, even probable, that this was the inner source of his deep self-negativity, his inner turmoil, his self-rejection, his superhuman zeal for a perfection he could never achieve? Could this also be his thorn in the flesh, about which he wrote so plaintively? With this possibility in mind, listen once more to Paul's words: "And to help me keep from being too elated by the abundance of revelation, a thorn was given me in the flesh, a messenger of Satan, to harass me, to keep me from being too elated. Three times I sought the Lord about this, that it should leave me; but he said to me 'My grace is sufficient for you, for my power is made perfect in weakness' " (2 Cor. 12:7–9).

On another and perhaps earlier occasion, Paul had written, "You know it was because of a bodily ailment that I preached the gospel to you at first; and though my condition was a trial to you, you did not scorn or despise me but received me as an angel of God, as Christ Jesus" (Gal. 4:13). The word *angel* can also be translated *messenger*. Paul is the possessor of a condition that he believes to be incurable. It is a condition for which people might scorn or despise him. I have heard and read of commentators who suggested that this physical condition was some kind of chronic eye problem. This is based, I suspect, on Paul's words to the Galatians that they would have "plucked out their eyes and given them" to Paul (Gal. 4:15). But chronic eye problems do not normally bring scorn or the activity of despairing, and through the eye, which Paul called "the window of the body," life and beauty as well as death and pain enter the human experience. Paul, in these words to the Galatians, told them that he had now "become as they are," one in whom "Christ has been formed," and assured them that

118

they "did him no wrong" (Gal. 4:12, 19). That refers to an inner healing not an external healing.

Others have suggested that epilepsy was the condition from which he was not free. This appears to me a stronger possibility. Epilepsy was thought of as demon possession, but it was a periodic sense of being possessed by an alien spirit, not a constant malady. Also, in the biblical narrative the epileptic elicited a sense of pity, or at times fear, but seldom did it elicit despising or loathing. Epilepsy does not appear to me to account for the intensity of the feelings that Paul expressed. The realization that he was a homosexual male does. It is a hypothesis that makes sense of the data and accounts for the tone, the fear, the passion, and the behavior.

If this hypothesis is correct, it also illumines in powerful ways Paul's experience of conversion, his understanding of Jesus, his view of resurrection, and his move toward universalism. Furthermore, it provides us with a means to step into Christ as Paul did and to see the Christ experience outside the context of limited words and in the context of a universal human experience. It thus becomes for us a point of entry into a universal spirituality inaugurated by Christ that may endure into the unlimited future in a way that the narrow and brittle religious forms from our Christian past no longer seem capable of doing.

Listen once more to the rescued, converted, accepted Paul: "Forgetting what lies behind and straining forward to what lies ahead, I press on toward the goal for the prize of the upward call of God in Christ Jesus" (Phil. 3:13, 14). Paul believed that his personal unrighteousness had been replaced by the righteousness of God, and this gave him the hope of resurrection. He assured the Philippians that he had not obtained this gift or become perfect, but "I press on to make it my own, because Christ Jesus has made me his own" (Phil. 3:12).

Try to imagine the power present in these words if my thesis is anywhere near the truth. Paul, a God-fearing, strict Jew, a zealot for the Law, a Pharisee-to-be, being raised in Tarsus, slowly awakened to the fact that he was different. He did not understand his own feelings. Everything he knew, loved, and honored, from his parents to his synagogue to the sacred Law, told him that what he felt himself to be was evil, depraved, an abomination. The Law informed him that if one were zealous enough for the Law, all desire would be curbed. So with the frenzy of the desperate and the lost, he sought to master these disturbing and threatening desires by mastering the Law. He advanced beyond all those his age in zeal. He became before the Law blameless. But nothing worked. His condition was beyond his power to change. It was as if his body were possessed by an alien force over which he had no power. He felt as if there were a war going on in his members. With his mind he willed one thing, but with his body he felt another. He sought exoneration by blaming his affliction on something outside himself. "If my mind wills one thing and my body responds another way, it is not I but sin that dwells within me." More and more he tried by his passion for the Law to master the passions of his body. He became a rigid, externally controlled, religious, righteous man, with the resulting cold, hostile personality, who could lead a persecution movement to destroy utterly the movement within Judaism that revolved around the man named Jesus. To Paul Christianity weakened the Law that only by the most herculean efforts was holding Paul just above the abyss, so he struck back at that movement with the vengeance of a deeply threatened man. He killed, he hurled into prison, he sought to stamp out.

What Grace Did for Paul

One cannot persecute without drawing near to that which is the object of one's fury. Paul drew near to the Christ. It was for him a fatal attraction. In the midst of the fury that all but consumed him, he began to hear the gospel message of love— unconditional love, even love for one thought by himself to be loathsome, called by the sacred Law an abomination and condemned by society as a person with a depravity so complete as to be deserving of death. This Jesus could yet love this Paul. That was the gospel. The one who loved those who killed the love of God could also love this judged, driven, homosexually oriented Paul. Nothing Paul could do or be placed him outside the love of God present in Jesus the Christ. Somehow that message broke through on the hostile, hiding, vindictive, fearful Paul. It had all the force of an exploding, blinding light at midday. The scales fell, as it were, from his eyes. What the Law could not do, the grace of love had done. Paul was justified. Paul was loved. While still in his sin, Paul was accepted. Nothing could separate him from the love of God—nothing; not tribulation, distress, persecution, famine, not even nakedness, not even the secret of his unclothed body. Nothing could separate him from the love of God. Paul was now God's elect.

Who shall bring a charge against God's elect? It is God who justifies, accepts, loves. Who can condemn God's elect? It is Christ that died to make love known. Even the murderers of the Christ are not condemned; and if not they, so also not Paul. For God raised the righteous Jesus to his own right hand. This Jesus, loving the sinner, the outcast, the condemned abomination, has been vindicated by the Holy God. God is on the side of Jesus. God has raised him to the divine right hand. Jesus is the agent of God reconciling to God that which previously was thought to be irreconcilable. God has taken Jesus into the very selfhood of God.

Because this Christ loves me, I can now love myself. That was the way the gospel dawned on Paul. Because Christ accepts me, I can now accept myself. I do not have to become righteous by keeping the Law. God has declared me righteous as a gift of divine grace. God in Christ has reconciled me to God. Nothing will ever again separate me from this love—not death nor life, not angels nor principalities, not present things nor things to come, not powers over which we have no control, not heights, not depths. Nothing in all creation—not even that secret, unspeakable inner fear that possesses me and for which the world and the Law might well condemn me. Nothing shall separate me from the love of God. Nothing! Nothing! Nothing! (Rom. 8:31–39).

The being of Paul, a being he did not understand, a being he could not control, a being that all of the wisdom of his world and all of his sacred tradition condemned as worthy only of death, that being of Paul met the grace of God in the person of Jesus the Christ. It was for Paul as if a light from heaven appeared, and a doorway into God opened and Paul saw the Christ to be part of what God is. This was Christ risen—enthroned. Listen once more to Paul's words: "Jesus was raised for our justification" (Rom. 4:25). "Christ being raised from the dead will never die again; death no longer has dominion over him. The death he died he died to sin, once for all, but the life he lives he lives to God. So you also must consider yourselves dead to sin and alive to God in Christ Jesus" (Rom. 6:9). "Do not yield your *members* to sin as instruments of wickedness, but yield yourselves to God as men who have been brought from death to life, and your members to God as instruments of righteousness" (Rom. 6:12). "Just as you once yielded your *members* to impurity and a greater and greater iniquity, so now yield your *members* to righteousness for sanctification" (Rom. 6:19). "If Christ is in you, although your bodies are dead because of sin, your spirits are alive because of righteousness" (Rom. 8:10).

The righteousness was, of course, the righteousness of the Christ that had been given to Paul as a gift of grace. The Spirit that raised Jesus dwelt in Paul and gave life to Paul's dead mortal body. Christ is our wisdom and our righteousness, Paul asserted, because of the action of God in raising him to heaven (1 Cor. 1:30). Christ is now God's and I am now Christ's, Paul exclaimed (1 Cor. 3:23). "For the love of Christ controls us, because we are convinced that one has died for all . . . that those who live might live no longer for themselves but for him who for their sake died and was raised (2 Cor. 5:14). "The life that I now live in the flesh, I live by faith in the Son of God, who loved me and gave himself for me" (Gal. 2:20). "So have this mind in you which is yours in Christ Jesus; . . . and being found in human form he humbled himself and became obedient unto death, even death on a cross. Therefore, God has highly exalted him and bestowed on him the name which is above every name, that at the name of Jesus every knee should bow, in heaven and on earth and under the earth, and every tongue confess that Jesus Christ is Lord to the glory of God the Father" (Phil. 2:5–11).

Paul's Exalted Jesus

Who was Jesus for Paul? He was the reconciling agent for the grace of God. He was the image of the invisible God. He was the firstborn of all creation. He was a Jewish man who could be understood only in terms of the ultimate agent of God. He was identified with the son of man figure in Jewish mythology. He acted for God in creation. He held all things together and broke open the power of evil by being the firstborn from the dead. The fullness of God was pleased to dwell in him so that through him God could reconcile everything and make peace where there had been enmity. Paul could add that to those who "were estranged and hostile in mind, doing evil deeds, he has now reconciled in his body of flesh by his death" in order to present even Paul "holy and blameless and irreproachable before him" (Col. 1:21, 22).

Was Paul's Christ the God man of later Christian theology? Was this the Second Person of the divine Trinity? Would Paul have said, Jesus is God? Although he might not have denied the truth to which these words pointed, those forms of communication would never have occurred to the Jew from Tarsus. They were words a later generation of Christians who had lost their Jewish roots would develop to try to give rational form to their experience of Jesus. Jesus was for Paul God's "first creation." This is hardly an adequate Christology by later theological standards, but it served Paul well. For Paul, Jesus the Christ was a special human life through whom God had uniquely acted and in whom God was uniquely present. Jesus was for Paul a Jewish man so faithful to the meaning of God that when faithfulness cost him his life, God raised him to heaven in an act of vindication and as a way of saying that God is like what Jesus did and like who Jesus was.

When Paul speaks of the resurrection, he means the raising of the dead Jesus into heaven. The vindication of the life Jesus lived was proclaimed by God's exaltation of him. For Paul resurrection and ascension were not two actions, but one. It occurred not on the literal third day but on the eschatological third day, for it was beyond time and history. Above all, it was the act of God. Paul's consistent verb form for the resurrection is passive. He was raised by God. The action was God's action because it was God's vindication. The active verb, which suggested that Jesus did the rising himself, was in a very much later tradition. For Paul, witnesses to the resurrection were not people who conversed with a resuscitated Jesus in some earthly setting, as the later appearance stories would tend to indicate. The separation of the resurrection from the ascension is not reflective of primitive Christianity. Paul gave no narrative details of resurrection appearances, and he said his conversion, which clearly was a dawning, inbreaking vision of the now-heavenly Jesus, was different in no way from all other appearances, save that Paul's was last.

Mark, the earliest Gospel, also had no appearance stories and assumed that it would be the glorified, ascended Lord who would make himself known in Galilee at some later date (Mark 16:1ff). Matthew had the risen Lord meet the disciples only in the vision of the ascended Lord who appeared out of heaven to send the disciples into all the world (Matt. 28:1ff). John said that it was the ascended Lord who appeared to the disciples and breathed on them the gift of the Spirit (John 20:1ff). Only Luke clouded the witness by separating resurrection from ascension and making resurrection the action of Jesus and ascension the action of God. That was certainly a late-developing tradition, a concession, in my mind, to the need for literalizing the story of the breaking in to human consciousness of the meaning of the God of love and grace.

124

When Paul talked of resurrection, he used four verbs. Jesus died. He was buried. He has been raised. He has shown himself. The verb for "shown himself" is *ōphthē*—a technical term for this "paschal event," and it means God caused Jesus to be seen. For the apostles and other witnesses in Paul's list, Jesus had become "Epiphanous"; that is, they were all proclaiming that the crucified one had been raised and now the heavenly Jesus was at work in the missionaries. The apostles, including Paul, had been sent to proclaim this faith and none else. As the gospel moved from Jerusalem to Judea to Samaria, to the uttermost parts of the world, Jesus, the crucified one, became "Epiphanous" in wider and wider orbits. He drew, through love and grace, all people to himself as he restored them to themselves, building finally that inclusive community in which there is neither Jew nor gentile, bond nor free, male nor female. For all are one in Christ, whose love can embrace even the outcasts of society, even the one pronounced depraved and called an abomination, the one who by the mandate of the Law stood under the sentence of death.

This is the way my thesis would suggest that the gospel of Jesus Christ was experienced by Paul, the man from Tarsus. To me it is a beautiful idea that a homosexual male, scorned then as well as now, living with both the self-judgment and the social judgments that a fearful society has so often unknowingly pronounced upon the very being of some of its citizens, could nonetheless, not in spite of this but because of this, be the one who would define grace for Christian people. For two thousand years of Christian history this Pauline definition has been at the very core of the Christian experience. Grace was the love of God, an unconditional love, that loved Paul just as he was. A rigidly controlled gay male, I believe, taught the Christian church what the love of God means and what, therefore, Christ means as God's agent. Finally, it was a gay male, tortured and rejected, who came to understand what resurrection means as God's vindicating act. In the life and love of Jesus, who both expressed the love of God and bore in human history

125

the life of God, the ultimate meaning of God had been established. Because of Paul, no longer can we see Jesus in any way other than as the fullness of God.

When people consider scandalous this idea that a homosexual male might have made the grace of God clear to the church, I reply, "Yes, it is scandalous, but is that not precisely how the God of the Bible seems to work?" It is as scandalous as the idea that the Messiah could be crucified as a common criminal. It is as scandalous as the idea that a birth without acknowledged paternity could inaugurate the life that made known to us the love and grace of God. It also suggests that heterosexual people might be deeply indebted to homosexual people for many spiritual gifts that arise out of the very being of their unique life experience. Indeed, I have been the recipient of just that kind of gift from the gay and lesbian people who have shared with me their journeys with God through Christ.

What is the Word of God for us underneath the words of Paul? It is that each of us, no matter how dark our shadows, or how condemned we are made to feel, are nonetheless the objects of the infinite and graceful love of God. Each of us is called to live in the wholeness of that love as one who has been embraced by the giver of infinite value. Accepting that divine valuation, we are to find the courage to be the self God has created us to be, the self we are inside the graceful gift of the righteousness of Christ. For as the Epistle to the Ephesians, building on the gospel proclaimed by Paul, reminds us:

> Remember that you were at that time separated from Christ, alienated from the commonwealth of Israel, and strangers to the covenants of promise, having no hope and without God in the world. But now in Christ Jesus you who once were far off have been brought near in the blood of Christ. For he is our peace, who has made us both one, and has broken down the dividing wall of hostility, by abolishing in his flesh the law of commandments and ordinances, that he might create in himself one new man in place of the two, so making peace, and might reconcile us both to God in one body through the cross, thereby bringing the hostility to an end. (Eph. 2:12–17)

The Christian church thus becomes not an institution struggling for power, status, or even survival. Rather, it grows into being "a holy temple in the Lord" in whom each of us is built into being "a dwelling place of God the Spirit" (Eph. 2:21, 22).

I submit that this is a long way beyond a culturally conditioned denigration of women or affirmation of slavery that we find in only a literal reading of Paul. This is also beyond the common wisdom of the first century that believed things about Adam, Abraham, Moses, and David that biblical scholars can no longer affirm. Once we lay aside a commitment to the literal truth of the literal words of a biblical text, we discover that there is a way through these words to enter the timeless dimension of eternal love, graceful acceptance, and inclusive community. Beneath the words of the Bible is the living Word, acted out in the incarnate one, Jesus of Nazareth.

The ancient creed of the church that Jesus is Lord thus becomes a creed we modern folk can also shout with integrity, authenticity, and commitment. Moved by that creed we can begin anew the mission of the Christian church to proclaim love and grace to all who feel without love or apart from grace. And we will do so even when the proclamation of that gospel disturbs, convicts, and offends that institution that dares to call itself the church when it does not live out the meaning of being the accepting, loving, forgiving, affirming body of Christ.

9

Mark:
Beyond Mythology to Reality

Do demonic spirits exist? Do they speak? In what language? Do they discern supernatural power in others? Are they responsible for wind and storm? Do they grapple with people and throw them to the ground in violent seizures? Are these demonic forces present in injuries, accidents, and even moral blindness? Is history to be understood in terms of the titanic struggle between God the creator and the demon spirits who have taken over that creation? Does the divine nature of Jesus reside primarily in his ability to cast out these demonic forces, to break their power over human life? Was the crucifixion of Jesus accomplished through a counterattack of these demonic powers against the power of the inbreaking God? Is that why the death of Jesus was marked with the violent tearing of the curtain in the temple? Was that magic? Can a citizen of the twentieth or twenty-first century respond in a meaningful way to this pre-scientific analysis of reality? Can such a narrative be literalized and still make any sense to anyone outside that ancient period of history?

These questions, with their implied assertions about what is real, would have been answered with a resounding affirmation by the writer of the Second Gospel, known to us as "Kata Marcus" or "According to Mark." Indeed, it would never have occurred to Mark to doubt these conclusions that he assumed in his narrative. This was the common, unquestioned, popular wisdom of the world of first-century Judaism. Mark, who was not a scholar, was, however, a citizen of that world. He grasped neither the great philosophical thought processes of his day nor the nuances that lay behind the popular mythology. He simply accepted the street version of this mythology without question. He shared without demurrer in the popular conclusions of that time regarding not only demons but also the certainty that the earth was flat, the conviction that God dwelt just above the blue canopy of the sky, and that the sun rose and set as it circled the earth. The earth, for Mark, was not just the center of the universe, it was also the very extent of all that God had made. To the author Mark there was no reality beyond that which could be seen, and thus no explanations were necessary beyond the supernatural one that explained quite adequately for that time and place what a pre-scientific world could readily observe. They could not imagine that sickness could be caused by germs or viruses, since those agents of distress would not be known for hundreds of years. A microscopic examination of that part of the world which lay beneath the range of the unaided human eye was beyond conception. So also was a telescopic examination of those realities that found a home in the vast reaches of space.

Inevitably, therefore, any event that occurred in this period of history would be explained in terms of this worldview, for there was no other. Jesus of Nazareth was an event in the history of the Jewish world in the first century. He was born, grew to adulthood in the Galilean town of Nazareth, exercised the trade of a carpenter, and somewhere around the thirtieth year of his life launched a career as an itinerant teacher and preacher of some considerable power and renown. Stories began to circulate around him. Tales of miraculous power were attributed to him. The farther away from him the tale originated, the more fantastic it seemed to be. It is noteworthy to observe that even Mark's Gospel suggested that those who knew Jesus best and who observed him most closely said that they had never seen the miraculous things that others described so vividly. Unbelief seemed to mark both the members of his family and his neighbors in Nazareth. To explain this, the Gospel writer said that because of their lack of faith it was impossible for Jesus to do any mighty works in Nazareth (Mark 6:5).

From afar, however, came stories asserting that Jesus had stilled a storm, calming both the wind and the sea (Mark 4:35–41). Since the storm was thought to have been stirred up by supernatural demonic forces, to calm the storm was to demonstrate a power superior to that possessed by the demonic forces. That such power could only belong to God was the inevitable conclusion.

It was also said that Jesus restored the mind of a village wild man who lived among the tombs and howled at the moon at night. This creature, so obviously possessed by demonic forces, could not be restrained. The people had tried to control him with cords and chains, which was thought to be the proper way to treat mental patients in first-century Palestine. It fitted well with their understanding of the causes of mental illness. But this possessed creature seemed to have been given by his demonic visitors enormous power that enabled him, like Samson of old, to break his fetters as if they were threads. But, according to the word-of-mouth reports, these demonic powers met their match in the teacher from Nazareth. The host of demons recognized Jesus. Adversaries in the supernatural struggle for dominance over the earth seemed to know each other. "What have you to do with me?" the demon-possessed man was said to have asked. So compelling was Jesus' power that the demented man was pictured as running to Jesus and worshiping him, something no human being had yet thought it proper to do. The demon also called him by the name "Son of the Most High God" (Mark 5:7).

Jesus spoke with this demon. The dialogue in Mark moved swiftly. "What is your name?" Jesus asked. "Legion," the demon responded, "for we are many." Then the disturbed man, thought by Mark still to be but the mouthpiece of the spirits who lived within him, begged Jesus "not to send 'them' out of the country." This demonic host recognized that Jesus possessed a power greater than theirs. Then plea-bargaining ensued. The host of demons spotted a herd of swine feeding on the hillside. Mark had been careful to note that this episode took place in gentile territory in the country of the Gerasenes. Pigs were not animals that Jews would raise, since the Law of Moses called the flesh of swine unclean and forbade its use as food (Lev. 11:7, 8). The demons appealed to Jesus' Jewish aversion to swine and begged, "Send us to the swine, let us enter them." It was a fitting habitat for demonic spirits. Unclean spirits would invade unclean animals. So, said Mark, "Jesus gave them leave and the unclean spirits came out and entered the swine, and the herd, numbering about two thousand, rushed down the steep bank into the sea and were drowned in the sea" (Mark 5:9–13). It did not seem to occur to Mark that the swine represented someone's livelihood, indeed, probably a person's entire fortune. Nor was it helpful, as one wag observed, to suggest that from this story we get deviled ham!

For Mark this was a description of the reality that he believed was at work in his world. The power of these demonic forces was being challenged in Jesus of Nazareth. In the actions of this Jesus and most especially in his constant victories over these same demonic forces, Mark thought Jesus' status as God's special emissary was established beyond reasonable doubt. In the life of this Jesus the cataclysmic conflict between good and evil, God and Satan, was being waged. No other possible explanation was conceivable for this author. If this frame of reference is not grasped by the contemporary reader, the Gospel of Mark makes no sense. But if this frame of reference is literalized by those who assert that the Bible is the inerrant Word of God, it becomes a bit of fantastic first-century folklore and mythology that is neither believable nor intelligible.

To the degree that the life of Jesus of Nazareth has been captured for us inside this worldview and explanation of reality, this Jesus is rendered increasingly impotent as a relevant force in our life today. This is the critical issue that Christians face in the battle to rescue the Bible from fundamentalists. Unless the truth of the Bible is lifted out of the literalistic framework that captured it some two thousand years ago, that truth can have for modern women and men no meaning, no credibility, and no appeal. The end of such a warped version of biblical truth is surely death, and with that death will come the end of all of those values that derive from the Bible, including in large measure historic Christianity. This is no exaggeration. The people of this twentieth- and twenty-first-century world of science and technology will not long take seriously a faith story that is proclaimed inside the fantastic symbols of a premodern world, especially if the popular voices of that faith story insist on a literalistic acceptance and interpretation of those symbols. When the religious liberals whose voices might reject that literalism are so mired in an overwhelming biblical ignorance and see no compelling reason to dispel that ignorance, the alternatives facing the modern Christian pilgrim are bleak.

Christianity has in our time increasingly divided itself into these two sterile camps, neither of which gives hope of having the ability to revive this ancient faith system. The fundamentalists will appeal to the need for emotional security by trafficking in religious certainty. The system they create will survive momentarily—it might even flourish for a time—but it will not endure. Delusions can be immensely satisfying. For short periods of time people seem to enjoy turning off their brains and listening to those who assure them that all is well.

The anger, however, that is present in this premodern religious revival reveals its own vulnerability. Anger cannot dispel doubt. Suggested enemies—liberals, secular humanists, false prophets, whatever the nomenclature—cannot finally be blamed for the unbelievability of nonsensical words. Fundamentalism is both an expression of and an assisting cause in the terminal sickness that hangs over religious life today. When the depth of that sickness becomes obvious, it will leave in its wake disillusionment, despair, and pain. No seeds of renewal are contained in a literalism that is itself afraid of truth.

The other sterile camp confronting institutionalized religion today is an empty postmodern secularity that has infected both the mainline churches and the society at large. It expresses itself in the shallow life dedicated to the search for material pleasure conducted within a vast spiritual vacuum. It is revealed in the lives of those for whom God has died and fate has become the final arbiter of meaning. Frequently this attitude is not so much articulated as it is lived. It is a response even of those who, because of the habits of a lifetime, still relate to religious institutions at nominal levels, even though they find no real sustenance there. Membership in such an institution does not finally affect their life, and ultimately it is so tangential to their being that they will not pass on to their children a living religious heritage. No seeds of renewal will be found for the church in those who either consciously or unconsciously take up citizenship in the secular city.

The church that does not face this dilemma seriously either does not understand the problem or does not know how to address it. Such a church drifts aimlessly, replacing faith with fellowship, avoiding the tough issues of life, standing for less and less for fear another part of its family will be offended and depart, knowing full well that the church's drawing power is declining day by day. There is no future for Christianity unless the essence of Christian truth can be extracted from the phenomenalistic framework of the ancient past. There is no better place to pose the issue in all of its searing power than by opening to readers in a new way the Gospel According to Mark. For this is the issue with which this Gospel confronts a modern-day reader.

The Story from Mark's Point of View

Mark was the first of the canonical Gospels to be written. This literary work was identified quickly with the city of Rome and may well have been written there. It was also associated with the Apostle Peter and early in the second century came to be regarded as the Petrine Gospel. The second-century Bishop of Hierapolis (ca. 130), a man named Papias, wrote that Mark was the interpreter of Peter. He wrote accurately, said Papias, but not in order. Mark had neither heard the Lord nor been his personal follower, but he had followed Peter. According to Papias, Peter adapted his teaching to the needs of his hearers, but he did not give a connected account. What Mark learned of Jesus, however, he learned from Peter.[1] This assumption, whether accurate or not, surrounded Mark's Gospel with the aura of apostolic authenticity, for Peter was widely regarded in the Christian tradition as the first among equals in the apostolic band.

When this fact was combined with a connection to the city of Rome, it added up to enormous power for this messenger. Rome was already beginning to assert the same primacy in ecclesiastical matters that the capital city possessed in political matters. Mark's Gospel did carry with it such apparently inside stories involving Peter as the healing of his mother-in-law (Mark 1:29–39), the Gethsemane narrative (Mark 14:32ff), and the account of Peter's denial (Mark 14:66–72), which served to strengthen its Petrine claim.

The Gospel as a whole, however, reflected not so much the thought of a single author as the narration of the accumulation of a whole community's faith tradition. That tradition seemed to be aimed at conditions that marked the city of Rome during the time of Emperor Nero. Roman Christians were struggling with unpopularity, persecution, and even death. To strengthen those so threatened, the text of this Gospel emphasized such things as the sufferings of Jesus, the warnings of Jesus that following him would involve sharing his suffering, and the promise of great rewards to those who endured without the loss of their faith. It was clearly a message designed to communicate with and to arm for faithfulness those facing the reality of martyrdom (see Mark 8:34–38; 10:28–30).

The suffering of Jesus was preordained, this Gospel asserted. It was a suffering that lay in the innermost counsels of God. For Mark the innocent suffering of the righteous emissary of God was the way of atonement, and the one whose life accomplished this feat was marked with clear messianic overtones. Beyond that, identifying with the innocent victim in his suffering promoted the possibility of receiving the ultimate gift of forgiveness, which carried with it the promise of a heavenly reward.

Yet the behavior of Peter and all the other disciples during Jesus' lifetime had not been marked with either courage or integrity. Such memories as betrayal, denial, and abandonment were so real and so vivid that they could not be expunged from the record even after the passage of thirty to forty years. So they had to be explained. Mark accomplished this with the device known as the messianic secret. All during Jesus' life he had urged secrecy on those who glimpsed his power. That power was to be hidden until the revelatory moment of Easter. Even the chosen twelve were kept in doubt, as their behavior clearly revealed (Mark 1:25, 34, 44; 5:43; 7:36). All they could do was question: "Who then is this?" (Mark 4:41), and Jesus could be heard saying to them, "Do you not yet understand?" (Mark 8:21). Even when a story was told in which Jesus raised from death to life the daughter of Jairus, the possibility of something less than a supernatural presence was stated by Jesus himself. "The child is not dead but sleeping," he said (Mark 5:39). So those whose hearts were hardened always had a rational explanation, an alternative to faith, and the disciples had room to doubt, which made their treatment of Jesus understandable even if not admirable. Mark was writing at a time when that revelatory moment of Easter had removed the blinders, but the memory of the blindness lingered, and for it an explanation had to be offered.

The idle curiosity of modern people about the biographical details of Jesus' life did not seem to interest Mark at all. He tells us nothing about Jesus' appearance, his physique, his health, or his personality. We know that his mother's name was Mary only because one of his critics could not explain his power and wondered how it was that the "son of Mary" could do these things (Mark 6:3). The name of Jesus' presumed father, Joseph, was never mentioned, adding speculation to the early whispers that Jesus was illegitimate, for designation of one as "son of Mary" was not done normally unless the name of the father was unknown. This same critic also asserted that Jesus was a carpenter. The Christian community had trouble with this concept. Perhaps it proved to be far too human and therefore too derogatory an image. In Matthew's Gospel, written fifteen to twenty years later, this biographical note was changed to suggest that Jesus was not the carpenter but "the carpenter's son" (Matt. 13:55). In one stroke Matthew removed the absence of Jesus' father and the human-sounding trade of being a carpenter. The power of the myth was growing.

In Mark there is no reference as to whether Jesus was married, no definite length of his public ministry, no age at the moment of death, no instance from his earlier environment, and no development of his outlooks and beliefs. Indeed, everything that Mark suggested that Jesus said and did could be accomplished in no more than four weeks. Biography was clearly not his purpose.

Mark assumed that in the community for which he wrote they already knew this Jesus. This community had been, with Mark, the accumulators of the tradition that fed his manuscript. He had no need to introduce his subject to them. Indeed, he did not even explain who John the Baptist, Herod, or Pilate were (Mark 1:4; 6:14; 15:1), nor did he act as if anyone would fail to know what he meant when he referred to "the wilderness" (Mark 1:12) or the Jordan (Mark 1:9). Mark's task was to commit the faith of his community to writing. Perhaps the impulse for this was the suggestion in the tradition that Peter had been put to death as a martyr under Nero, and that therefore the story so deeply shaped by Peter had to achieve the permanency of the written word while it was still fresh. This is part of the speculative argument that would date this Gospel no earlier than 65 c.e. and no later than the early 70s.

Mark had only the embryo of a narrative. He started with the baptism and brought his story slowly but irrevocably from its Galilean origins to its Jerusalem climax. In the first half of his book, the emphasis was on the miraculous deeds of Jesus that caused the crowds to wonder. His teaching was directed toward those crowds. The burden of his message had to do with the inbreaking of the Kingdom of God. The first words Mark put into the mouth of Jesus were "The time is fulfilled, and the Kingdom of God is at hand; repent, and believe in the gospel" (Mark 1:15). It was a message consistent with the mythological framework in which Mark and the early Christians understood the meaning of Jesus. Only by getting our minds inside that framework can the literal nuances of the Markan narrative begin to be understandable. Even that process, however, will not make those words believable. It is nonetheless the first step that one who seeks the Bible's truth must take.

For Mark and the early Christians the universe, no matter how limited their understanding of it was, had nonetheless been brought into being by a single creative act of God. God had a purpose for the created world. It was to be the arena in which the divine will was done on earth as it was in heaven. Throughout history God had exerted pressure to bring the world into conformity with that purpose—a process that explained both the Law and the Prophets. God's problem was that various powers opposed to God roamed this earth under the direction of their satanic leader, causing the world to diverge widely from the divine intention. Plans were set for a decisive divine intervention that would set up the ultimate struggle between good and evil. Some thought that intervention would be by direct action. Others thought God would act through an intermediary. Some thought the final state would be the Kingdom of God on earth. Others thought it would require the creation of a new heaven and a new earth for the redeemed. Still others combined the two—a state of salvation here and eternity in the new age.

The powers of evil would not give up this world without a struggle, so the suffering of the final days would be intense. "For in those days there will be such tribulation as has not been from the beginning of the creation which God created until now, and never will be" (Mark 13:19). This struggle would affect the whole universe: "the sun will be darkened, and the moon will not give its light, and the stars will be falling from heaven, and the powers in the heavens will be shaken" (Mark 13:24, 25). These words are part of Mark's prelude and preamble to the story of the passion of Jesus of Nazareth.

This man Jesus was seen as nothing less than the divine emissary. The *bar nasha* of Jewish mythology was a term translated "son of man" in the biblical text, but it more accurately meant simply "the man" and referred to a godlike, transcendent figure sent from heaven, where he had once existed at God's side. "The man" would possess, Mark assumed, the divine power to work supernaturally. The demons would know him and quake before him. In episode after episode he would exorcise them as a public sign of his power. He would control the forces of nature. He walked on water (Mark 6:48) and commanded the wind (Mark 4:41).

Finally the struggle reached its climax. Jesus came to Jerusalem in a visible claim of messianic status (Mark 11:1–10). People recognized him and shouted that he came "in the name of the Lord." They cried, "Hosannah in the highest" (Mark 11:10). He viewed God's temple as clearly in the hands of the enemy (Mark 11:11). He cursed a fig tree for not bearing fruit (Mark 11:13ff). It was not the season for figs, but this was the agent of God's creation to whom the whole creation must be responsive. Then he claimed the temple in a violent prophetic act (Mark 11:15ff). Shortly thereafter he told a parable about those who beat and killed various emissaries of the one who owned the vineyard. Finally, when the owner sent his own son, they murdered him and claimed the vineyard for themselves. The lord of the vineyard would, however, finally prevail. The tenants

139

would be banished. The vineyard would be given to those worthy to inherit it (Mark 12:1–9).

The drama heightened. The power of Caesar was invoked against him (Mark 12:14ff). The tradition of the Jews was invoked against him (Mark 12:18ff). The interpretations of the Torah were invoked against him (Mark 12:28ff). Then came the power of nature reflecting the mortal struggle (Mark 13). Finally one of Jesus' own became the betrayer. Mark simply said, "Then Judas Iscariot, who was one of the twelve, went to the chief priests in order to betray him to them. And when they heard it they were glad" (Mark 14:10). Luke, writing a generation or so later, sought to make sure his readers did not misunderstand that this act of treachery was also part of the final struggle between God, the source of light, and Satan, the prince of darkness; for Luke wrote, "Then Satan entered into Judas" and the act of betrayal was set (Luke 22:3). John observed that when Judas left the table fellowship that fateful evening, "it was night" (John 13:30). The power of darkness was about to extinguish the light. In the darkness of that night Jesus sat with his disciples to give them a foretaste of the messianic banquet that would inaugurate the Kingdom of God (Mark 14:22ff). He knew that they would all be scattered, and he said so. He knew Peter would fail, and he told him so openly. This would enable them to believe that they, too, fell for a moment under the sway of the powers of evil.

The drama proceeded until the powers of evil had their day. When Jesus was arrested, Luke changed Mark's words by adding "This is your hour, and the power of darkness" (Luke 22:53). When the son of man was being killed, darkness, said both Matthew and Luke, engulfed the whole earth (Matt. 17:45; Luke 23:44). Mark had the centurion standing watch on the hill called Calvary exclaim, "Truly this man was the Son of God!" (Mark 15:39). This is one of only five occasions when Mark used this title. Exactly what it meant to him is not clear. It is only clear that this evangelist attached great significance to it. On that fateful Friday, in the minds of the followers of Jesus, darkness had prevailed and Satan was victorious. Hope was gone.

140

The disciples were scattered. Evil reigned supreme. It was against this background that the moment called Easter dawned for Mark.

For this Gospel writer Easter did not mean a resuscitation back to life. There was in Mark no story of something we might call a resurrection appearance. There was only an empty tomb, an angelic proclamation, and some startled women. There was the hint of an epiphanous manifestation that would occur in the future, for the messenger said, "Tell his disciples and Peter that he [Jesus] is going before you to Galilee; there you will see him, as he told you" (Mark 16:7). The presence of an angelic messenger would argue to Mark's readers that the power of darkness was not able to achieve a total victory.

The sheep that Jesus said would be scattered (Mark 14:37) would now, the angelic hint suggested, be gathered once more behind their victorious shepherd. He would then lead the reconstituted community into Galilee, just as Mark had portrayed him earlier as saying he would do (Mark 14:28). Galilee had for Jesus and his earliest followers a special status as a holy place. Jerusalem, by contrast, was the source of opposition and unbelief. It was in Galilee that they believed the inbreaking of the Kingdom, called the Parousia, would take place. The disciples in Galilee would behold him in the splendor of his Parousia appearance. The women who received this instruction, however, according to Mark, "fled from the tomb; for trembling and astonishment had come upon them" (Mark 16:8). Far from carrying out the angelic instruction, according to Mark, the women "said nothing to any one" (Mark 16:8).

In the Greek the emphatic note in these words cannot be dismissed. D. E. Nineham argues that "the women's profound emotion is described in order to bring out the overwhelming and sheerly supernatural character of that to which it was a response."[2] This was a device Mark had used when he concluded the story in which Jesus stilled both wind and wave. "And they were filled with awe, and said to one another, 'Who then is this'" (Mark 4:41). Mark used it again when he narrated the story of Jesus walking on the water. "They thought it was

141

a ghost, and cried out; for they all saw him, and were terrified" (Mark 6:49, 50).

Is it not conceivable that within Mark's worldview he had led his reader to the same stance and was suggesting that if the reader could come to understand the full significance of what had occurred, a similar response of amazement and godly fear would be forthcoming? For what had flowed from this moment his readers knew full well. Indeed, they still waited anxiously for that final return. Mark has said earlier:

> And then they will see the Son of man coming in clouds with great power and glory. And then he will send out the angels, and gather his elect from the four winds, from the ends of the earth to the ends of heaven. . . . Truly, I say to you, this generation will not pass away before all these things take place. Heaven and earth will pass away, but my words will not pass away. But of that day or that hour no one knows, not even the angels in heaven, nor the Son, but only the Father. Take heed, watch; for you do not know when the time will come. . . . And what I say to you I say to all: Watch. (Mark 13:26–37)

Mark took his readers through the battle between demonic forces and God's emissary. The evil powers seemed to prevail, but the tomb was empty. The angelic messenger proclaimed that the crucified one had been raised. God had restored him to heaven to the right hand of divine power. From there he would come in triumph; so stand in awe and tremble in fear, and he will lead you into Galilee, and there the end of time, the Kingdom of God, will enter history. Those who were among God's elect, those who knew the Messiah, would enter that Kingdom.

How Should We Interpret Mark?

That is Mark's story. That is Mark's Gospel. That is Mark's understanding of the one he calls Lord and Christ. Most especially, that is the faith tradition and corporate understanding of a community of Christians, probably in Rome, who were en-

142

during the rigors of a persecution and martyrdom that had recently claimed their revered leader Peter.

But where does that leave us? The mythology that Mark believed so fervently is hardly believable in our day. But within that mythology Mark has captured, explained, and distorted the Jesus of history. Can we ever meet this Jesus apart from this mythology? Is there a Jesus to meet beyond the interpretive framework of the first century? We understand what causes wind and wave, epilepsy and deaf muteness in ways that involve no appeal to supernatural forces. If we use the phrase *darkness at noon* it would have for us only poetic, not supernatural, connotations. Does the mythology of the first century possess a truth we can recover, a power we can meet? Can the Christ who had such an awesome, life-changing reality for those who met him through this mythology still meet us even if it must be apart from this mythology? Can we stand figuratively with the women before that empty tomb and say, "I believe," even if we have to add "help thou my unbelief" (Mark 9:24)?

Was Jesus in touch with an ultimate meaning that is eternal and life giving? Can he be for us a way into that meaning, a way into God that will change our lives? In the Johannine words, which I will examine in a subsequent chapter, can Jesus be for us the way, the truth, and the life without religious delusion or hysterical religious claims? These are the questions that the Gospel of Mark raises for me and perhaps for my generation. The literalization of the Scriptures is worse than no answer. It clothes God in ignorance, prejudice, and irrationality. Not to use the Scriptures as a guide, however, is to dismiss our one link to this powerful figure, Jesus of Nazareth, who may be worthy of our deepest exploration. This Jesus of Nazareth may well be, as many millions have claimed for him, our doorway into the love and meaning that we call God and that each of us in myriads of ways seeks.

"There are," as New Testament scholar Edward Schillebeeckx asserts, "no ghosts or gods wandering around in our human history; only people."[3] Yet this Jesus made many aware that through his life God was at work within him. Somehow Jesus had the power to touch off a religious movement that became a world religion, asserting that this Jesus was the revelation of God in the very intensity of his personal life. He triggered in his own day responses so powerful that some professed unconditional faith and others aggressive unbelief. It is easy to understand in the light of such a range of responses how people could have interpreted his very being in terms of the ultimate and supernatural battle between life and death, God and Satan, light and darkness.

But we need to recognize that it was the movement brought into being by this Jesus that has preserved for us any portrait whatsoever of the Jesus of history. No matter how deeply distorted the various interpretations of him have been, it is only because his was a life that demanded interpretation then and demands it still that he remains alive for us. He is, because of this ongoing and living tradition, still available to our touch and perhaps even to our grasp. Like the disciples, we, too, are led to ask, Who is this man that people could believe that the wind and waves obeyed him, that water was his to walk on, that fig trees existed to feed him even when figs were not in season, and that even death could not contain him?

The New Testament is nothing less than the deposit of that Jesus movement. The movement was the reality that forced the narratives to be written. It was Jesus' life that created the movement, and the Christian response to Jesus has not yet been concluded, not even by the freezing of the story in the various forms represented in the canon of Scripture. He has been many things to many people in many ages—all of them different, most of them not mutually exclusive. The response has run between the poles of fully human and truly divine. What manner of human being is this about which the human response has been so intense?

There is no starting place for this inquiry other than the New Testament. It is the church's charter or foundation document. It is not to be ignored, because there is no substitute for the Scriptures. But it is beyond and beneath its words that we must journey. One cannot, however, journey beyond and beneath its words unless one knows those words deeply, fully, and in the spirit created by those words. For the early Christians spirit and the recollection of Jesus were a single reality. The spirit was that which brought all things to remembrance. Jesus left a movement that remembers. He left a people conscious of being new. His legacy was the intense human hope that a universal shalom could be created that would enable the world to say that the Kingdom of God has come, that our God reigns.

It is inside that movement that modern Christians are called to journey today. We journey as those seeking to discover our own identities. We journey as men and women in search of wholeness for ourselves and one another, for freedom from the distortions of our prejudices, fears, threats, angers. We look at those things that both define us and limit us: sex, family, tribe, and religion. We look at the arenas of our competition in the never-ending struggle to survive. We see those things that affirm our being in the face of the ultimate threat of nonbeing, and we call those holy. We even call those things God. We plumb the depths of our own humanity until we touch our limits, and then we seek ways to transcend those limits. Enhanced consciousness does it, deepened humanity does it, an infinite and eternal love does it.

Is God, that once we pictured as dwelling in the sky external to us, now to be seen as the holy presence that is met at the edges of our own transcendence? Do we find God in the call to live and love and be, the call to openness, to heightened consciousness, and to the willingness to risk for the sake of gaining these treasures? Can God be found in these moments for us, and if God can be found there, is there any longer any wonder that our forebears in this Christian journey found God in the person of Jesus? He was alive, loving, forgiving, inclusive, open, and universal. The primary mark of this movement that stemmed from him was that barriers faded. In Christ there is neither Jew nor Greek, bond nor free, male nor female (Gal. 3:28), and, dare we add with the knowledge of our day,

145

homosexual person or heterosexual person. In the Christ spirit, the barrier of language disappeared and a holy community took its place where the universal language of love marked the fellowship (Acts 2:5ff).

Is not the primary message of the Easter narratives that even the barrier of death must not deter us in our quest for life and love? Even at the point of death our faith tradition asserts that darkness can be pushed aside by the power of the Life-Giver. These are the symbols that must be resurrected and made real for our time. Then we can walk in the company of Christians like Mark, whose yearning and whose experience was quite similar to our own but whose words and concepts came out of another time, another world, another frame of reference. We can read his words not as portraying those symbols that have captured truth but as opening those symbols that point to truth. Then we modern Christians can travel with his pointers and, discovering his reality, can know that it is in touch with our reality. Then Mark's words, called Holy Scripture, can become for us living words once more.

This is my hope and my longing. That is also the primary reason that I seek to rescue the Bible from fundamentalism. I want Mark to point me beyond his angels and devils, beyond his nature miracles and miraculous healings, beyond the darkness at noon and the empty tombs to discover that living Lord who made God real for Mark and for his community of people. Then I also can begin to find the life that makes God real for me. I can then proclaim with Mark that I stand as he did at "the beginning of the Gospel of Jesus, Messiah, the Son of God" (Mark 1:1).

10

Matthew:
The Story of Jesus
from a Hebrew Perspective

Many preachers, it is said, first have a sermon to deliver and only then, as a matter of second importance, do they seek a text to give that sermon biblical authenticity. In many ways the author of the Gospel of Matthew follows this procedure. Both these anonymous preachers and the author of Matthew sometimes stretch the biblical text beyond its original meaning and not infrequently even beyond recognition.

Who Was Matthew?

The author of this Gospel was a Jew living in perilous times. The city of Jerusalem had been destroyed by the Romans more than a decade earlier. The temple, the symbol of Jewish religious life, had been razed. The cohesive center of Jewish identity was no more. There was among the Jewish people, including those Jews who had come to acclaim Jesus of Nazareth as Messiah, a sense of devastation and irrevocable loss. They had both consciously and unconsciously defined themselves in terms of Jerusalem. They were the Jews of the Diaspora, the dispersed Jews, who knew from whence they were dispersed. Now that the symbol of their unity was gone, they would need to define themselves in a new way or perish as a people of history.

For Jewish Christians this dilemma was even more intense. As Christians they were subjected to the abuse of the pagan gentile government of Rome. The persecutions under Emperor Nero were seared into their memories. Important first-generation Jewish Christian leaders, like Peter and Paul, had perished in that hostile wave. In addition to this, however, the Jewish Christians also felt the lash of hostility from their Jewish brothers and sisters. By opening themselves to the messianic claims made on behalf of Jesus of Nazareth, these Jewish Christians had broken ranks with orthodox Judaism. They had moved beyond the strict observance of the Law. The Christian day of resurrection had begun to compete with the Jewish Sabbath day observance as the primary holy day for worship. Table fellowship with non-Jews, a practice anathema to strict Jewish observance, was part of the very worship life of the Christian community.

Christians gathered weekly on the Lord's day to share the bread and wine of the Eucharist. At this point in history that eucharistic act had not yet been so refined liturgically that the original form of a common meal was not still obvious. Sometimes the Eucharist was even part of a larger banquet called the agape or love feast. Certainly this practice threw down the gauntlet to those who felt that the radical exclusiveness of their Jewishness forbade table fellowship with non-Jews. For over five hundred years, or since the Babylonian exile, Jewishness had been preserved by a tradition of radical separatism. Now this seemed threatened by the Christian sect within Judaism called the followers of the way. With threat comes fear, hostility, and, not infrequently, overt acts of violence. So it was that Jewish Christians felt vulnerable on both the gentile and the Jewish sides of their lives.

148

The author of Matthew's Gospel almost certainly lived in this double-edged vulnerability. He was a Jew of the Diaspora, deeply familiar with and deeply devoted to this religious tradition. More than any other Christian writer he identified with his Jewishness. Matthew had no desire to abandon his faith, but he had every desire to stretch it toward inclusiveness. There is at least the possibility that he left one autobiographical note in the text of his Gospel itself when he wrote, "Every scribe who has been trained for the Kingdom of Heaven is like a householder who brings out of his treasure what is new and what is old" (Matt. 13:52), for bringing both the value of the old and the freshness of the new out of Scripture is exactly what he did in the Gospel we call Matthew.

An analysis of the internal nuances of this book make it evident that the author of Matthew was a conservative-minded Jew, one who was trained in the legal disciplines, and one who followed the methods and interests popular among the Levites. He related Jesus to Jewish ideals, expectations, and heroes. He reflected a consuming interest in Israel as the chosen people and in Jesus as the embodiment of a new Israel.

Where in the empire this Gospel was written has never been finally established. Antioch is the favorite. It was, scholars are certain, written beyond the physical boundaries of Palestine, the holy land, but not beyond a passionate desire to affirm the traditions and priorities of Palestinian Judaism, even as that tradition and those priorities were opened to new dimensions by a Jewish Messiah named Jesus. This narrative was finally designed to compel people to go into all the world.

This was a story that only a Jewish-Christian scribe could tell. It burned within him so intensely that he read all the Jewish Scriptures and looked at all the Jewish traditions in the light of that one revelatory truth he had come to acknowledge in Jesus of Nazareth. Inevitably, like many preachers whose zeal is greater than their research, Matthew's use of these Jewish texts to prove his case left much to be desired. By modern standards of biblical scholarship, Matthew was something of a disaster. This, for the biblical literalists, creates some insurmountable problems.

Matthew was not perfect. On many occasions he was not even correct. Matthew's Jesus was portrayed as saying things that are not believable unless rationality itself is suspended. Such problems are not unique to Matthew. They are discoverable and present in almost every part of the Bible, as we have seen in previous chapters and will see again in succeeding chapters.

Matthew's Sources and Story

Matthew knew of the Gospel of Mark and used it extensively. Mark had been circulating among the various Christian communities for fifteen to twenty years. Matthew had no difficulty with the framework of demonic powers that was assumed by the First Gospel. That was the unquestioned wisdom of the day. But he also did not regard Mark as either Holy Scripture or as literally inerrant, for Matthew altered Mark's text frequently to suit his agenda, his writing task, his audience, and his theological perspective. Because Matthew wrote after Mark, the need to define Jesus had had more time to develop, had more challenges to meet and more false ideas to confront. The way Matthew changed the Markan text made this clear.

Mark raised the question about authority in the treatment of the Sabbath day issue and had Jesus say, "The sabbath was made for man, not man for the sabbath; so the Son of man is lord even of the sabbath" (Mark 2:27, 28). Matthew heightened the impact of this debate by omitting the first part of this saying and by proclaiming rather polemically that something greater than the temple and all the religious traditions of Israel was present in him. Only then does he claim for himself lordship over the Sabbath (Matt. 12:6–8).

Mark was far more hesitant to make the specific identification of Jesus with the Son of man (Mark 8:38) than Matthew was (Matt. 16:24–28). It was a slight shift, but Matthew wanted to make overt what Mark seemed to claim somewhat covertly. This pattern was repeated in another episode in which Matthew both corrected and enhanced Mark's record. In Mark (10:17–18) a man addressed Jesus saying, "Good teacher, what must I do to inherit eternal life?" to which Mark had Jesus respond, "Why do you call me good? No one is good but God alone." The relationship between Jesus and God was not worked out very well at this early stage, represented by Mark. Recall that Mark seemed to know nothing about a supernatural birth tradition or a resurrection appearance tradition. The divinity of Christ claim was evidently not offended by Mark's Jesus declining to be called "good," reserving that designation for God alone.

By the time Matthew wrote, however, the Christ claim to be uniquely related to God had been established. Matthew changed Mark's narrative thus: "One came up to him [Jesus] saying 'Teacher, what good deed must I do to have eternal life?' And he [Jesus] said to him, 'Why do you ask me about what is good? One there is who is good" (Matt. 19:16–17). Matthew's apologetic need is obvious in the way he altered the Markan text. For Matthew's version implies that Jesus himself is the Good One. This Evangelist Jesus was not just the herald of God's saving act, he had become the principal, the restorer, the agent through which God had acted. This point of view was enhanced when Matthew had Jesus say to his disciples, "He who receives you receives me, and he who receives me receives him who sent me" (Matt. 10:40); when Jesus said, "Whoever receives one such child in my name receives me" (Matt. 18:5); and finally when the Matthean Christ said, "Where two or three are gathered in my name, there am I in the midst of them" (Matt. 18:20).

Recall that this closer identification of Jesus with God appeared in Matthew's birth narrative, when Joseph was informed in the dream that this child will "be called Emmanuel (which means God with us)" (Matt. 1:23), and was repeated in Matthew's resurrection narrative, when the exalted Christ promised, "Lo, I am with you always, to the close of the age" (Matt. 28:20). Matthew's conception of who Jesus was had clearly gone beyond the view that he received from Mark. Furthermore, the permanence of Jesus' relationship to the Christian community in Matthew drove him to enhance in a similar fashion the permanence of Jesus' relationship to God. Jesus was the Son of man so "every one who acknowledges me [Jesus] before men [and women], I will also acknowledge before my Father who is in heaven; but whoever denies me before men [and women], I also will deny before my Father who is in heaven" (Matt. 10:32–33). This claim, which sounds only slightly threatening in this Matthean passage, became overtly vengeful later when Matthew had Jesus say, "For the Son of man is to come with his angels in the glory of his Father, and then he will repay every man [person] for what he [she] has done" (Matt. 16:27).

As the Messiah Jesus was for Matthew sent to the lost sheep of the house of Israel (Matt. 10:6; 15:24). As the risen Lord he had been given authority over heaven and earth (Matt. 28:18). As the Son of man he would judge the earth and separate the sheep from the goats, sending one group to bliss, the other to torment (Matt. 25:31ff). The figure of the Christ was significantly enhanced for Matthew, and because of this, he changed, edited, and added to Mark in his story to make these heightened claims unmistakable to his readers. In Mark's story about the stilling of the storm, the disciples addressed Jesus as "teacher" (Mark 4:38), but when Matthew included that story in his narrative, he changed "teacher" to "Lord" (Matt. 8:25). In the transfiguration narrative, Mark had Peter address Jesus as "Master" (Mark 9:5). Matthew in his Gospel also changed that to "Lord" (Matt. 17:4). Mark had James and John, the sons of Zebedee, come to Jesus seeking the personal honor of sitting on his right and left in glory. They addressed him as "teacher" (Mark 10:35). Matthew, perhaps unable to put these disciples in so bad a light, changed his story so that it was the mother of James and John, rather than the disciples themselves, who made this request. She did not address Jesus by any title but rather knelt before him to beg him for this honor for her sons (Matt. 20:20–21). The context and the debate about who Jesus was and is had moved by the time of Matthew to a new level—a level that Mark did not even need to understand. This simple fact alone makes it all but nonsensical to claim that somehow such contradictory differences can still be the literal, inerrant work of God.

Matthew was also given to heightening the miraculous. Miracle and magic were part of the world in which he lived. It was Matthew alone who said that the birth of Jesus was marked by a star that wandered through the heavens (Matt. 2:1–2). It was Matthew alone who had Jesus suggest that Simon Peter should pay his taxes with the money that he would find in the mouth of the first fish he caught when he went down to the sea (Matt. 17:24–27). This strange story is generally avoided by fundamentalist preachers. It was Matthew who expanded dramatically Mark's list of wonders at the time of Jesus' crucifixion. Mark told us only that "the veil of the temple was torn in two, from top to bottom" (Mark 15:38). Matthew added that "the earth shook, and the rocks were split; the tombs also were opened, and many bodies of the saints who had fallen asleep were raised, and coming out of the tombs after his resurrection they went into the holy city and appeared to many"(Matt. 27:51–53). It is strange that no one else ever mentioned such weird and awesome phenomena. The only explanation is that these events did not happen but were a figment of Matthew's fertile imagination. Once again, this is a text embarrassing to literalists and generally ignored by fundamentalists.

Matthew's penchant for heightening the miraculous also colored his story of the resurrection. To Mark's narrative Matthew added an earthquake and a descending "angel of the Lord" to explain how the tomb was opened (Matt. 28:2). The supernatural aspects of the angel were enhanced by such words as "his appearance was like lightning and his raiment white as snow" (Matt. 28:3). This in turn accounted for the ineptitude of the guards who had been posted at the tomb. These supernatural wonders, Matthew asserted, caused them "to tremble" and to become "as dead men" (Matt. 28:4). Matthew also added a resurrection appearance of Jesus to the women in the garden that Mark had not suggested at all. Matthew's narrative here, however, was cumbersome and gives the impression of being contrived. The risen Christ in this text was not very original. For example, he repeated almost verbatim the earlier message of the angel to the women (Matt. 28:9, 10). Finally Matthew countered the obvious criticism that had begun to arise in Jewish circles that suggested that the disciples had stolen the body. It was, he offered, a lie begun by the chief priests, who bribed the soldiers to perpetuate this "official version," which, said Matthew, "has been spread among the Jews to this day" (Matt. 28:15).

Beyond his affinity for heightening and exaggerating the miraculous, Matthew also made some obvious mistakes. Like Mark, he assumed the Davidic authorship of the Psalms (Matt. 22:43). More obviously, in the genealogy that opens Matthew's Gospel, there are gross inaccuracies. Matthew left out some things in order to make operative his miraculous scheme of exactly fourteen generations from Abraham to David, David to the exile, and the exile to Jesus (Matt. 1:1–17).[1] There are those who have suggested in jest that Matthew could not count very well.

Counting seemed to have been a problem for Matthew's Jesus also. Matthew had Jesus say, "For as Jonah was three days and three nights in the belly of the whale, so will the Son of man be three days and three nights in the heart of the earth" (Matt. 12:40). We are so accustomed to the creedal phrase "on the third day" that we slide unthinkingly over this strange text. Jesus, however, even according to Matthew, was not three days and three nights in the heart of the earth between Good Friday and Easter. He was buried after his death, which occurred about 3:00 P.M. (the ninth hour) (Matt. 27:45, 46) on Friday. He had escaped the tomb before dawn on the first day of

154

the week (Matt. 28:1). This is not three days and three nights. It is one day and two nights or thirty-six hours, not seventy-two hours.

Matthew also had a strange fascination with hell, gnashing of teeth, weeping and wailing, burning pits, and eternal punishment. Indeed, if Matthew could be deleted from the Christian writings, about 90 percent of the references to the fires of hell would be eliminated from the Christian tradition. Hell was not a Matthean invention. It was, however, a Matthean emphasis. Indeed, his was an overemphasis when compared with other Christian writings. Hell is a favorite theme in the evangelistic preaching of the literalists, of course, where behavior control by means of reward and punishment is prominent. To portray a God who would inflict eternal suffering and pain on those whose evil no matter how gross was nonetheless not eternal is itself a strange concept. But the contrast between fiery pits with distorted creatures who could but weep and wail for eternity and the life of bliss where the good were united with their loved ones in a land flowing with milk and honey and possessing golden lampstands was powerful indeed. In a world of premodern unsophistication, such images were literally believed. They still are believed, but by a smaller and smaller number of people, who appear incapable of thinking outside concrete images. For those whose minds can escape into the realm of the abstract, these images long ago lost their power.

These accumulated weaknesses that are apparent in Matthew's Gospel render the literal understanding of this Gospel to be both inept and incapable of being sustained. But that is to judge this ancient work by modern critical standards. In fairness, it must be stated that neither the author of Matthew nor the original readers of this Gospel would have been aware of or distressed by this list of weaknesses. It is relevant only for those who want to freeze the Bible into literalism and must therefore, in the service of that distorting straitjacket, impose the framework of centuries ago upon the modern believer as a prerequisite to faith.

155

To explore the truth in Matthew's Gospel one needs to take seriously Matthew's Jewishness and one needs to be conversant with the living tradition that fed the practice of Judaism in the first century. Apart from these things, the meaning of the New Testament in general and Matthew's Gospel in particular will be lost to modern minds. Matthew wanted to call the Christian movement in this critical moment of its history to a genuine and deep appreciation of its Jewish heritage, and then he wanted to call Jew and gentile alike to an inclusive community in which the God of the Jews could be worshiped by the gentiles. Matthew worked primarily, however, on the Jewish side of that equation. As we shall observe in the next chapter, Luke worked primarily on the gentile side of that equation. This is the significant difference between these two particular evangelists, who had so much besides their personal angle of vision in common, sharing as they did an enormous amount of common data.

The Gospel of Matthew was an early attempt in a Hebrew context to answer the question, Who is this Jesus? It appealed constantly to the Hebrew Scriptures. It viewed that Scripture overwhelmingly as pointing in word and symbol to Jesus of Nazareth. It suggested that the covenant people of God called the *ecclesia* must relive the Hebrew experience. The prologue to Matthew's story, known as the birth narrative, proclaimed that Jesus was the son of Abraham, the son of David, and the son of God. All three designations were important to Jews (Matt. 1:1).

The Bethlehem birth story was fashioned around the words of the Hebrew prophet Micah (Matt. 2:1–6; Mic. 5:2). The escape into Egypt by the holy family fleeing the clutches of Herod relived the Egyptian phase of Hebrew history (Matt. 2:13ff; Gen. 46). The slaughter of the innocents (Matt. 2:16) retold the story of Moses' escape at his birth from the wrath of Pharaoh (Exod. 21:1ff). Rachel weeping for her children echoed the exile

(Matt. 2:18; Jer. 31:15; Gen. 35:16–20). Moses, the one who led the children of Israel out of the bondage of slavery in Egypt, would inevitably color the account of the new and greater Moses who would lead the world out of the bondage of sin and into the promised land of the Kingdom of God. Israel's Red Sea experience was present in the story of Jesus' baptism (Matt. 3:1ff; Exod. 14:21ff). In both episodes identity was secured first as a nation and second as a messianic figure. Both the national identity of Israel and the personal identity of Jesus as messiah were, however, the by-products of a unique relationship to the Holy God. The heavenly words heard at the baptism (Matt. 3:17) echo the words of Isaiah (Isa. 42:1), where the faithful servant, portrayed as the ideal Jew, first walked the earth's stage.

Israel wandered in the wilderness for forty years, says the history of these people. In the wilderness they tested their vocation, they received the Law at Sinai (Exod. 19ff), and they were fed by their God with heavenly food, called manna (Exod. 16:4ff). The messianic figure, it was widely believed in Jewish circles, must repeat that history; so the period of Jesus' life that had been spent in the desert was transformed into forty days of temptation and testing (Matt. 4:1ff). Various modes of living out the messianic role played in Jesus' mind. All of them were to be rejected. He would not be the miraculous feeder of the hungry, as a way to gain attention and power, for "man [woman] does not live by bread alone" (Matt. 4:4). He would not accumulate the wealth and status of the world to accomplish his purpose, for "you shall not tempt the Lord your God" (Matt. 4:7). He would not surround himself with the things and accoutrements of worship by acting out religious miracles, for "you shall worship the Lord your God and Him only shall you serve" (Matt. 4:10).

Matthew's Jesus emerged from the wilderness and went to a mountaintop to teach the crowds the meaning of the New Covenant. This symbol was not missed by Matthew's readers. Moses had gone to a mountaintop to get the Law, so the new and greater Moses must do likewise. The Mosaic Law began with the short, pithy, easy-to-remember rules we call the Ten Commandments. The New Covenant also began with short, pithy, easy-to-remember statements that we call the Beatitudes. In both series there were really only nine statements. However, because ten is the number of fingers on both hands, the commandments have always been recorded as being ten in number.[2]

Still to come in Matthew's Gospel was the account of Jesus feeding the multitude in the wilderness (Matt. 14:13–21), yet another reference colored by the memory of Moses. By the time this narrative was written, whatever the historic event was had been lost and what was left was a highly stylized narrative with obvious eucharistic and liturgical nuances. The historic words of the liturgy of the Last Supper were used. Jesus *took* the bread, *blessed* it, *broke* it, and *gave* it (Matt. 14:19). Matthew followed Mark here and recorded two feeding miracles. One miracle was for Jews with five loaves and two fish; the other was for gentiles with seven loaves and a few fish (Matt. 15:32–39). On the Jewish side of the lake, five thousand men were fed (plus women and children—in patriarchal society women and children really do not count), and twelve baskets of fragments were gathered afterward. On the gentile side of the lake, four thousand men were fed (plus women and children), and seven baskets of fragments were collected.

It is certain that the Gospel tradition was moving inexorably toward that understanding of Jesus as the Bread of Life that became overtly stated in the Gospel of John, but in Matthew's time it had not quite arrived. What Matthew did see and did communicate was the portrait of the one who fed his people in the wilderness just as the Holy God had done long ago. Beyond that, Matthew was claiming for this Jesus a sufficiency to feed both Jew and gentile with the heavenly food that would not pass away. As Matthew said, "Those who hunger and thirst for righteousness shall be satisfied" (Matt. 5:6). The heavenly banquet, so much a part of the messianic expectation of the Jews, had in these narratives been dramatically acted out.

158

When the recapitulation of Israel's history had been described in such high and clear relief, when Jesus had been portrayed as compelling the people to return to the fundamental inner meaning of the Law, Matthew was ready to introduce the next image that would enhance the understanding of Jesus, which was his purpose in writing. The term Matthew employed for this image is usually translated "the Son of man." These words, so deep in Israel's folklore, meant the one who acted both as God's agent and with God's authority. It was the Son of man who gave divine pardon. To the paralytic he said, "Take heart my son; your sins are forgiven" (Matt. 9:2). When this apparently blasphemous statement was challenged by the scribes, Jesus responded, "Which is easier, to say, 'Your sins are forgiven,' or to say, 'Rise and walk'? But that you may know that the Son of man has authority on earth to forgive sins—he then said to the paralytic—Rise, take up your bed and go home" (Matt. 9:2–6). Later he elicited charges of being in league with Satan. "It is only by Beelzebul, the prince of demons, that this man casts out demons" (Matt. 12:24). Those who expected Jesus to fulfill their messianic expectations were driven to acknowledge his power even if they had to explain it in terms of demon possession.

From the middle of the twelfth chapter of Matthew forward (Matt. 12:38ff), Jesus reinterpreted the covenant with Israel to be inclusive in many ways. First there was a series of parables: the sower, the mustard seed, and the leaven. Each called the hearers to judge this movement not by the insignificance of the present moment but by the results in the future. The mission of the servant continued to be misunderstood by the disciples. Peter could not walk on the water (Matt. 14:28ff). Those for whom the Kingdom had been prepared were not yet worthy. The daughter of the Syro-Phoenician woman—a startling event in a Jewish context—a non-Jew, became the recipient of divine healing (Matt. 15:21–28). While still in the gentile territory around Tyre and Sidon, Jesus cured "the lame, the maimed, the blind, the dumb and many others" (Matt. 15:30). The people seeing this, even though they were gentiles, said Matthew, "glorified the God of Israel." Inclusiveness was dawning. The priority was recognized even as the promises to Israel were opened to include gentiles.

The drama intensified when Peter finally made the confession "You are the Christ, the Son of the living God" (Matt. 16:13–20), and for his insights he was rewarded with the promise that he would be the rock upon which the church was built. But when the work of the Christ was spelled out in terms of the passion, Peter's rocklike substance turned to putty, and he received the rebuke of Jesus and was told that he was identified with Satan (Matt. 16:21ff). There was work yet to be done to create the new Israel.

Then came the transfiguration, where Peter, James, and John got to see the true nature of this Jesus. Moses had been transfigured by his mountaintop experience, and his face had shined so brightly that it had to be covered (Exod. 34:29–35). When Peter failed to understand this revelation, the heavenly voice repeated the baptism formula: "This is my beloved son" (Matt. 17:5). Surely truth must dawn soon in Peter. To assist that dawning Jesus began to teach about what it meant to participate in the inbreaking Kingdom. This was the theme that Matthew employed to move his drama toward its climax on the cross, which would be for him the ultimate revelation.

At every step along the way Matthew had fashioned his narrative and shaped his story by appeals to the Jewish tradition and to the Jewish Scriptures. Some appeals are overt and easily recognized; others are lost, especially on those of us who do not share the knowledge of the Hebrew heritage that Matthew's Jewish readers would have shared. We do not easily recognize, for example, that Matthew divided his work into five books in a deliberate attempt to model the form of the five books of the Jewish Torah. This fact would not generally be recognized by those of us who do not understand the Torah's power in Jewish thinking. In addition, Matthew had Jesus use a rabbinical device of numbers in his teaching. It was not just an accident or a coincidence that there were three temptations (Matthew 4), three examples of righteousness (6:1–18), three prohibitions (6:19; 7:6), three injunctions (7:7–20), three healings together (8:1–15), three miracles demonstrating the authority of Jesus (8:23; 9:8), three restorations (9:18–34), three "fear nots" (10:26, 28, 31), three types of persons unworthy of Jesus (10:37, 38), three sayings about "little ones" (18:6, 10, 14), three parables on sowing (13:1–22), three parables of warning (24:43–25:30), three prophetic parables (21:28–22:14), three questions in the passion narrative (22:15–40), three prayers in Gethsemane (26:36–46), three denials of Peter (26:57–75), and three questions of Pilate (27:15–26).

Seven was another favorite number in rabbinic teaching, so Matthew had seven woes (23:13), said that a man cleansed of one demon might be repossessed by seven (12:43–45), asked a seventy-times-sevenfold pardon (18:21–22), referred to seven brethren (22:25), seven loaves (15:34), and seven baskets of fragments (15:37). These familiar number passages made teaching easier.

But above all Matthew was a Jewish Scripture quoter: "This took place to fulfill what the Lord had spoken by the prophet" (Matt. 1:22). This was his constant theme. Matthew thought the virgin status of Mary fulfilled Isa. 7:14. Jesus' birthplace in Bethlehem fulfilled words from Micah (5:2). Jesus' flight to Egypt fulfilled Hos. 11:1. The destruction of the innocent children by Herod fulfilled Jer. 31:15. Jesus' home in Nazareth fulfilled Isa. 11:1.[3] John the Baptist lived out the words of Isa. 40:3, and his appearance was drawn deliberately to resemble the Hebrew prophets of old (see 2 Kings 1:8; Zech. 13:4). Jesus responded to the various temptations by quoting Hebrew Scriptures (Deut. 6:16; 8:3). The setting in the wilderness reflected Jeremiah 31. In the Sermon on the Mount there was the constant refrain "You have heard that it was said to the men [and women] of old. . . . But I say to you . . ." (Matt. 5:21, 27, 31, 33, 38, 43). In this manner the Hebrew tradition was reinterpreted so that its original intention was recalled.

Matthew's Jesus treated the Jewish Law with an authenticity that was found in few other places in the Christian writings. It was Matthew who recorded Jesus as saying, "Think not that

I have come to abolish the law and the prophets; I have come not to abolish them but to fulfill them. . . . Whoever then relaxes one of the least of these commandments and teaches men [and women] so, shall be called least in the kingdom of heaven" (Matt. 5:17–19). When Jesus healed the leper, Matthew portrayed him as instructing the now-clean man to "go, show yourself to the priest, and offer the gift that Moses commanded" (Matt. 8:4). When Jesus, in the house of Peter, healed many, including Peter's mother-in-law, Matthew added that this was done "to fulfill what was spoken by the prophet Isaiah. He took our infirmities and bore our diseases" (Matt. 8:17). His healing ministry was his possession because he was the servant of whom Isaiah spoke (Isa. 42:1–4). He was the one in whom God had placed the divine spirit. The inability of Jesus' critics to respond properly was to fulfill Isaiah's words that some hear but never understand (Isa. 6:9–10). Echoes of Daniel (12:3) were heard in Jesus' words "Then the righteous will shine like the sun in the Kingdom of their father" (Matt. 13:43).

When the story of the passion arrived, passages from Isaiah (40–55) and Zechariah (9) coalesced in Matthew's mind to give the narrative its shape. Both sources drove the meaning of Jesus' life and death beyond the boundaries of Israel. God's act in Jesus gathered the dispersed of Israel but at the same time reminded the people of Israel that there were others, not of this fold, who must yet be gathered. Davidic messiahship was not enough. It was too confining. Even David called the messiah Lord. How can he be David's son, the Christ asked, as the David symbol was broken open (Matt. 22:43). They will come from north and south, east and west and sit down atthe table of Abraham in the Kingdom (Matt. 8:11, 12). That was the promise of Israel's messiah as Matthew understood him. Jesus had fulfilled the Jewish tradition that was the first half of Matthew's truth. Jesus had opened that Jewish tradition to a radical inclusiveness that was the equal second half of Matthew's truth.

The drama was brought to its climax on the cross, where the words of Psalm 22 shaped the narrative. Jesus quoted from that psalm (22:1). His garments were divided by the casting of lots (Matt. 27:35; Ps. 22:18). The derision of the crowd (Matt. 27:39) reflected Ps. 22:7–8, as well as Ps. 109:25. Even the details of crucifixion leaned on Psalm 22: "My bones are out of joint—my strength is dried up . . . my tongue cleaves to my jaws . . . thou dost lay me in the dust of death . . . they pierced my hands and feet" (Ps. 22:14ff). He was crucified with robbers and buried by Joseph of Arimathea, a well-to-do man, said Matthew. These assertions made vivid the words of Is. 53:9— "And they made his grave with the wicked and with a rich man in his death."

Then came Easter. More will be said about this event in chapter 13, but the risen Christ for Matthew was clothed with the unmistakable authority of the Son of man. Now there could be no wavering of doubt, not even by Peter. A text from Daniel (7:14) was quoted to say that to this man was given all authority in heaven and on earth. Jesus, the son of Abraham and the son of David, was now the exalted Son, the agent through whom salvation had come. He had been lifted into heaven to sit at God's right hand, and out of heaven he now appeared in resurrected glory to send the disciples into all the world. Their task was to build the inclusive community so that through this Christ the promise to Abraham could be fulfilled that in and through the father of the Jewish people all the nations of the earth would be blessed. There Matthew ended his story.

Matthew's Gospel was and is a brilliant and moving piece of work. It was a time-conditioned piece that offered its deepest secrets only to those who could get inside the Jewish context for which it was written. Much of the meaning and power of this Gospel was lost when the heritage of the Hebrews was lost. Unfortunately this is the case with so many who might read Matthew today.

For the literalists this book is a nightmare, for in Matthew's eagerness to fashion his story to his Jewish audience, he violated

163

the meaning of his Hebrew text time after time. The enigmatic text in Isa. 11:1, for instance, that referred to a branch out of Jesse could hardly be used to undergird the fact that Jesus went to live in Nazareth, yet that appears to be the way Matthew used it. That word that is translated "branch" in Hebrew is *Nazir*. It can mean a number of things, but to make it refer to a citizen of the town of Nazareth is not one of them. Nor can the Hebrew holy man, called a Nazirite (Num. 6:2, 6–8; Judges 13:5, 7, 16:17), and defined as one who did not cut his hair or drink wine, be related to living in Nazareth. The details of the crucifixion and burial were not predicted by Psalm 22 so much as they were deliberately shaped by that psalm. The servant passage of Isaiah, the son of man passages of Ezekiel and Daniel, the triumphant passage from Zechariah, the shepherd and Bethlehem passage from Micah all became vital and valuable tools for understanding and interpreting Jesus in the Jewish context. In each instance Matthew altered the original meanings of these texts to suit his own needs. His zeal overwhelmed his rationality.

The more Jewish the audience, the more these ancient narratives were brought into play. If Jewish people believed Moses to be the greatest religious leader in history, it must be in terms of Moses that the story of Jesus was told. Matthew wanted his readers to understand that one greater than Moses had come (chaps. 5, 6, 7). If Jewish people believed Solomon's wisdom to be the greatest wisdom in history, then it must be in terms of Solomon that the story of Jesus was told. Matthew wanted his readers to understand that one greater than Solomon had come (Matt. 12:42). If the Jews believed the temple to be the place where God made the divine presence known in Jewish history, then the story of Jesus in whom God has been experienced as uniquely present must be told in terms of the temple. Matthew wanted his readers to understand that one greater than the temple had come (Matt. 12:6). If Jonah stood in the Hebrew folklore for one who died and returned to life again through his experience in the innards of a great fish, then the story of Jesus who entered death and conquered it must be told in terms of

Jonah. Matthew wanted his readers to know that one greater than Jonah had come (Matt. 12:41).

If in your enthusiasm as an author, you overstep your boundaries, claim too much, ignore the context of Scripture in order to claim a particular text for your purposes, it does not invalidate the truth of your experience; it only calls into question your competence as a scholar. Only when hundreds of years later someone claims for your literal words what you would never have claimed yourself—namely, that they possess infallibility or inerrancy—do the mistakes of your enthusiasm become hurtful to your cause and glaring to your critics.

The author of Matthew was a sensitive, passionate man, who made his case to his audience well. He did not possess the levels of scholarship available to us today. He did not seem to know the original Hebrew language. He did not appear to have a sense of history when it came to plucking proof texts out of the past. He did, however, understand that he had experienced God in Jesus of Nazareth and that this God had called him into a journey that would finally take him beyond every barrier, beyond every definition, and beyond every security system he had ever known. He knew that his ethnic values must be opened. His religious traditions must be made inclusive. A universal community in Christ must be built. That was what God in Christ meant to him, for Matthew understood that only beyond human limits does one find the fullness of life, the reality of God, and the meaning of community. This was Matthew's message. This was why he brought gentile stargazers to worship the Christ child at the beginning of his story. This was why he concluded his narrative with a picture of the cosmic Christ sending the disciples "into all the world."

Beneath Matthew's literal details, some of which are so gauche as to be embarrassing, the voice of God can still be heard calling us all to discover the One in whom Jew and gentile can reside as one. If Jew and gentile can reside as one, then white and black, Asian and Caucasian, Protestant and Catholic, male and female, gay and straight, rich and poor, Moslem, Buddhist, and Hindu can also meet in the body of Christ. Then and only then will that body be "one, holy, catholic and apostolic."

This was Matthew's vision. When we get beneath the literal words of Matthew's text, it becomes our hope, our dream, and our promise that someday through Christ we will all dwell in the Shalom of God.

11

Luke:
The Story of Jesus
from a Gentile Perspective

Luke, the Third Gospel in the Christian canon of Scripture, poses a mighty challenge for those who claim to be biblical literalists. His opening segment is the very beautiful and familiar Christmas story. This narrative is worthy of the fuller treatment it will receive in chapter 13, but suffice it to say in this instance that its narrative cannot be harmonized with the birth story of Matthew. These two accounts of Jesus' birth are mutually exclusive and mutually contradictory, as we shall see. Only the Christmas card industry can blend these two accounts together adequately, and they do so by falsifying what they do understand and ignoring what they do not understand.

On the other end of Luke's Gospel, his account of the resurrection tradition also sets him apart sharply from Matthew and Mark on one set of issues and makes him incompatible with John on another set of issues. Luke locates all of Jesus' resurrection appearance stories in the Jerusalem area and spreads the Easter moment over a period of fifty days. Once again, these issues will be pursued in detail in chapter 13. I file them here almost by title.

Beyond these rather glaring inconsistencies, Luke still gives no support to those who would treat his words literally. Luke's version of the parable of the talents is such a strange narrative that very few people even know about it. Luke's account of this story is by and large ignored by the preachers of history in favor of Matthew's more familiar version (Luke 19:11–27; Matt. 25:14–30). Luke's parable has the nobleman who gave his servants the talents conclude the story by saying, "But as for these enemies of mine, who did not want me to reign over them, bring them here and slay them before me" (Luke 19:27). This hardly sounds like "the Word of the Lord"! At the very least, a Lord who acted like that would not be worthy of worship.

Despite these problems, Luke's Gospel remains the bearer of some of the more incredibly rich traditions of early Christianity that flowed together to create our biblical heritage. Luke alone, for example, has preserved for us the stories of the widow's son at Nain (7:11–17), the mission of the seventy (10:1–12), the account of Mary and Martha (10:38–42), the healing of ten lepers (19:11–19), the account of Zacchaeus (19:1–10), the account of Easter in the village of Emmaus (24:13–25), and the content of both the ascension narrative (Acts 1) and the Pentecost narrative (Acts 2). It is to Luke alone that we are also indebted for the parables of the good samaritan (Luke 10:29–37), the prodigal son (15:11–32), the rich fool (12:13–21), the lost sheep (15:3–7), the lost coin (15:8–10), the unjust steward (16:1–9), Lazarus and the rich man (16:19–31), the Pharisee and the publican (18:9–14), and the unjust judge (18:1–8). How poor and bereft the Christian tradition would be had not Luke decided that "inasmuch as many have undertaken to compile a narrative of the things which have been accomplished among us, just as they were delivered to us by those who from the beginning were eyewitnesses and ministers of the word, it seemed good to me also, having followed all things closely for some time past to write an orderly account to you most excellent Theophilus, that you may know the truth concerning the things of which you have been informed" (Luke 1:1–4).

Who was Luke? Why did he write? To whom did he write? How did who he was and who his audience was shape his message? These are the questions that we will now pursue in our quest to be led far beyond the level of literalism and into the heart of the gospel message. These questions will also make us aware that time and place, language and circumstances inevitably color objective truth. There may well be an eternal objective truth beyond all of our words, but the minute that truth is spoken by a human being who is a subject, it ceases to be either eternal or objective. It becomes then truth compromised by time, concept, vocabulary, history, and prejudice.

Both the sacred Scriptures and the creeds of the Christian church can point to but they can never finally capture eternal truth. The attempt to make either Bible or tradition "infallible" is an attempt to shore up ecclesiastical power and control. It is never an attempt to preserve truth. Indeed, those who would freeze truth in any words, concepts, or creed will guarantee a time warp that will finally doom that truth to extinction. Only truth that is freed from its captivity to time and words and allowed to float in the sea of relativity will survive the ravages of subjectivity. Only truth that can constantly call out new words capable of lifting yesterday's experience into today's mind-set will finally survive.

The formulations of today or tomorrow will be no more eternal than the formulations of first-century people. This is not a plea to give up inadequate ancient words for ultimately inadequate modern words. It is to force upon us the realization that all words are, in the last analysis, inadequate. Truth is never finally found in words. Truth is always beyond words. Yet there can be no truth for human beings unless we use words first to understand it and second to convey it. So we mortals live with our subjective truth in the constant anxiety of relativity. That is all we can do and that realization strikes a mortal blow at the traditional excessive claims of all religious systems.

Religion almost inevitably tries to take our anxiety away from us by claiming that which religion can never deliver—absolute certainty. If religious systems succeed in giving us certainty, they have surely become idolatrous, for the ultimate mystery and wonder of God cannot be reduced to a particular language or captured in the concepts of any human being. The Christianity that I advocate and follow does not rob me of my humanity by making claims of either inerrancy for Scripture or infallibility for papacy or sacred tradition. My religion does not reduce God to an idol of its own creation. It does not give me certainty or even security. Rather, in my religious system I meet a God in Jesus who calls me deeper and deeper into my humanity—part of which is a constant quest and journey into truth.

That journey in time always becomes for me a journey into God. In this journey I find the courage to live by faith as I think the Bible understands that word. It also provides me with the integrity of honesty as I live in the midst of religious uncertainty and insecurity. This kind of Christianity does not affirm those whose deepest need is to know that they are right, that in their religious tradition they possess the truth. My understanding and knowledge of the history of religious systems convinces me that whenever a group of religious folk begin to believe that they possess God's truth, almost inevitably they become those who in the name of their version of that truth persecute, excommunicate, purge, burn at the stake, or justify cruel religious wars against any who will not salute their tradition or acknowledge their rightness in things religious.

It is not coincidental that the angriest mail I receive comes from those who claim to be the most religious and who think they speak with the very voice of God. Indeed, some of these letter writers even state that their hostile missives do not contain their own fallible words but the divine words spoken directly by God to me through them. I am always surprised at how vindictive God has become. I suppose these people need some authority beyond themselves to give them permission to be so angry.

170

In more sophisticated but no less inadequate ways, this infallible mentality feeds the activity that mainline churches call "evangelism" and "foreign missions." Both movements assume that truth lies with those who do the evangelizing and the missionary work. The history of both activities is rife with insensitivity, the brutalization of local customs and traditions, religious and political imperialism, and even the violation of human rights. It is no wonder that when churches begin to talk about "a decade of evangelism," Jewish people begin to lock their doors and secure their windows. Foreign missions has in our day become far more rhetoric than reality. Christians continue to talk about the process. Very few in fact engage in it significantly, for after two thousand years Christianity, even allied with the world's most powerful political, social, economic, and military systems, has still failed to penetrate the non-Western world save in the most minuscule way. The time has come, in my opinion, for all religious systems, including Christianity, to look at the truth that lies beneath the words of every great world religion, to respect that truth, to learn from that truth, and to spend its "missionary" efforts only on those lives that have no sense of the holy, no experience of a transcendent wonder. Most of the people who fit that description, I might add, live in the secularized Western world.

In the attempt to remove imperialism from Christianity, to become humble before the infinite mystery of God, a proper starting place for me is in facing the subjectivity of all religious words, including the words of Holy Scripture. The subjectivity of the Gospel of Luke can serve as a perfect doorway into this understanding.

Luke's Story and Its Setting

When Luke wrote his story, he had before him and was significantly aware of the Gospel of Mark. About half of Mark was incorporated into this Third Gospel, but Mark was not sufficiently adequate for Luke's purposes. The world had moved significantly in the fifteen- to twenty-year period since

Mark's Gospel had achieved written form. A Jewish rebellion had brought disaster on the holy land. In the ensuing warfare, Judea had been conquered and Jerusalem destroyed. Christianity thus lost its Jewish center, and by this time most of the first generation of Christian leaders, all of whom had been Jewish, had died. Chief among these leaders were Peter, Paul, and James. John, who might well have been the youngest of the twelve, may also have lived the longest. At least this was the tradition of the early church, which seemed to need to explain his death in a particular way (John 21:23). Christianity by this time was becoming more and more a gentile movement. For this gentile world a Gospel nuanced to their lives and concerns was increasingly needed. It was to meet that special and peculiar need that Luke felt called to take up the task of being a Gospel-writing evangelist.

Luke was a gentile. This is the conclusion of most of the world of New Testament scholarship. There are those who still maintain that Luke was a hellenized Jew, but they are a minority. In some sense it does not matter, for the more thoroughly hellenized a Jew became, the more the barrier that separated Jew from gentile blurred and faded. In my opinion, Luke was more a Jewish-influenced gentile than he was a gentile-influenced Jew, but where this line crosses is relatively insignificant.

In the ancient Mediterranean world near the end of the first century of this common era, the gods of the Olympus were dead. No viable unifying religious system had risen to take their place, creating a vacuum at the religious heart of life. That vacuum spawned a wide variety of cults, mystery religions, and superstitions. In that environment many gentiles found themselves drawn to the God of the Jewish tradition. The synagogues had galleries for those gentiles who were attracted to the ethical monotheism that marked Jewish worship. These gentile worshipers, however, seldom became converts. They were not drawn to what might be called cultic Judaism with its dietary regulations, the requirement of circumcision, and the Sabbath day regulations. This was an eclectic time, and people felt free to pick and choose those aspects of the various religious systems that appealed to them.

Gentiles who worshiped regularly at synagogues—known officially among Jewish people as "proselytes"—did, however, become familiar with the great stories of the Jewish Scriptures. These Scriptures had been translated into Greek in an official version, called the Septuagint, between 250 and 130 B.C.E. The Jews' enslavement in Egypt, the deliverance under Moses at the Red Sea, the account of the giving of the Law at Sinai, the conquest of the holy land under Joshua, the figures of David and Solomon, the defeat of Judah and the subsequent exile into Babylon—all became familiar history to gentile worshipers. Perhaps most important and to the gentiles the most appealing part of Jewish Scripture was found in the writings of the prophets—that peculiar and unique Jewish gift to the world. The prophets addressed their messages to such universal themes as justice, peace, and future hope.

When one reads the Book of Acts—also written by Luke, the author of the Third Gospel, as the second volume of his story—it becomes clear that among these gentile proselytes Paul found his most enthusiastic response. Regularly the Book of Acts told the story of the rejection of Paul's message by the Jewish leaders and his subsequent turning to the gentiles. Paul's understanding of the gospel had the effect of driving a wedge between worship and the various cultic practices that marked traditional Judaism. It was the same wedge that he drove between grace and law.

Thus Christianity, as people like Paul interpreted it, found itself increasingly capable of fully welcoming gentile converts without placing onto them the cultic requirements of the Jewish Law. This created an enormous discomfort in the early church between those Jews who found in Christ the fulfillment of Judaism to which they were committed and those gentiles who found in Christ a way to separate faith from cultic practice. The first great battle in Christian history, as we have noted earlier, was between these two elements, and the issue was how much of the Jewish Law must be imposed upon gentiles when they, by baptism, entered Christianity. The issue was more intense before 70, for before this date Christianity was primarily a Jewish movement. However, with Jerusalem's fall the Jewishness of Christianity began to recede and the gentile identity of the movement began to predominate.

The story of Peter's conversion told in the Book of Acts (Acts 10:9ff) was a significant transition point in this conflict. It is interesting to me to note how much more familiar people are with the Book of Acts' version of Paul's conversion than they are with Acts' version of Peter's conversion. In Peter's conversion narrative he was asleep on a rooftop in Joppa when he had a dream. In that dream a sheet was let down from heaven containing all sorts of "animals and reptiles and birds of the air" (Acts 10:12) that violated the Jewish dietary laws. A voice from heaven said, " 'Rise, Peter; kill and eat.' But Peter said, 'No Lord; for I have never eaten anything that is common or unclean.' And the voice spoke a second time and said, 'Peter, What God has cleansed, you must not call common' " (Acts 10:13, 14). Rising from this dream, Peter went to the home of Cornelius, a gentile, baptized him, and said, "Truly I perceive that God shows no partiality, but in every nation any one who fears God and does what is right is acceptable to God" (Acts 10:34, 35).

The barrier dividing Jew from gentile had been transgressed. Peter, himself the leader of the Jewish movement, walked across it. For our purposes we need to remember that these words and this account were written by Luke, who was in all probability one of these gentile proselytes who had responded to Paul's gospel and who now, in the ninth decade of the Christian era, needed to tell the story of Jesus in this new worldwide context. He wanted to show Christianity projected to the stage of the world. He wanted to show how its center had shifted from Jerusalem, the capital of Judea, to Rome, the capital of the world. Above all he wanted to show how gentiles like himself had come to be included in this Jewish religion.

Luke also wrote at a time of tension in the empire and in a rising fever of persecution. When Rome had burned while

Nero, the mad emperor, had fiddled (64 C.E.), a scapegoat was needed. The Christians had filled that role nicely for Nero. There were laws against starting new religions in the empire. Judaism was a recognized and protected religious system. Christianity was not so recognized nor was it protected. There were rumors about the Christians that excited the fears of the populace and provided justification for those who launched the official persecution. Black magic and cannibalism were two of the charges frequently leveled against the Christians. This strange sect, it was said, through its prayers and incantations produced magic power that could be malevolent. Such power could even result in the burning of Rome. When these Christians got together to worship, it was alleged, they ate the body and drank the blood of the one they worshiped. Such orgies were repugnant, and these rumors, to most people then as now, were more a cause to believe the gossip than they were a call to seek the facts. A wedge was thus driven between Jews and Christians in the minds of typical Roman citizens that left the Christians vulnerable to blame and persecution. That persecution under Nero was fierce and resulted in the deaths of many Christians. Some Christians were crucified, some were torched to provide light for Nero's garden parties. In time this fervor subsided, as always happens, but the threat of its renewal was ever present.

About the year 80 C.E. the Emperor Diocletian came to power, ruling until the year 96. With his ascent to the throne, the fires of persecution began to be stoked once again. It was in this context that Luke decided the time had come to write a public document addressed to a Roman official he called "most excellent Theophilus" to counter, if he could, the rising tide of hostility. It was Luke's task to show that Christianity, far from being subversive, was a natural development within a recognized and respected Jewish religious tradition. Christianity, Luke was asserting, had simply grown past the Jewish limits and had become a worldwide religion. Luke's gentile status and the circumstances of his world dramatically shaped his message.

In the birth narrative of this Jesus, Luke had a heavenly host in the sky herald, for all the world to see, the arrival of this child. The old priest, Simeon, announced that this child would be "a light for revelation to the Gentiles" as well as "for glory to thy people Israel" (Luke 2:32). In the genealogy of this Jesus, Luke had traced his heritage not back to Abraham, the father of the Jewish nation, as Matthew had done, but to Adam, the father of the entire human race. In the "seed" of Adam, gentiles as well as Jews were present. In his narrative Luke constantly fought against limiting prejudices that would rule some group out. Perhaps this is why only Luke made a hero out of a good Samaritan and only Luke told the story in which a Samaritan leper, alone out of the ten cleansed, returned to give Jesus thanks.

Because Luke was arguing for official Roman recognition of the Christian movement, he treated Roman officials kindly in his narrative. Christ was pronounced innocent by the Roman procurator, Pontius Pilate. Pilate acquiesced in Jesus' execution only to placate the religious leaders of Judaism, who placed extreme religious and political pressure upon him. In Luke it was Herod's soldiers, not Roman soldiers, who scourged Jesus, while a Roman soldier, a centurion, at the cross pronounced Jesus the Son of God. It was only in Luke's Gospel that we are told to render to Caesar the things that are Caesar's. The Christ about whom Luke would write had turned his back on political revolution in favor of a revolution of the spirit. The Kingdom this Christ proclaimed was "not of this world." There was no threat here to the political establishment, Luke was arguing, and there was therefore no need for persecution.

Similarly Luke showed Paul protected by such Roman officials as Felix, Festus, and Agrippa and even delivered from hostile mobs and Jewish imprisonment by his Roman citizenship. The fact that Paul was put to death under the Roman Emperor Nero was never mentioned in the Book of Acts. That book closed with the words "And he [Paul] lived there [in Rome] two whole years at his own expense, and welcomed all who came to him, preaching the kingdom of God and teaching about the Lord Jesus Christ quite openly and unhindered" (Acts 28:30, 31).

Before Luke could make clear to the Roman officials his universal claim for the Christian religion, he had to present Jesus as the fulfillment of Judaism. This meant that, like all the Evangelists, he had to draw deeply on the Jewish heritage. Matthew had done that well in his attempt to address a Jewish world. Luke must do it equally well in his attempt to address his gentile audience. Matthew had leaned particularly on the figure of Moses, who was the dominant personality in the Jewish religion. He had presented Jesus as the new and greater Moses. As the giver of the Law, Moses stood at the apex of that inward-looking tradition of Judaism. The law defined internally the life of the Jewish people. Moses was a figure in Luke's background also but not as the lawgiver so much as he was the one who led Israel from bondage to freedom, from Egypt to the promised land. When Luke wrote the journey segment of his Gospel (Luke 9:51–18:14) that would carry Jesus and the disciples from Galilee to Jerusalem, the figure of Moses could be discerned in the background as Jesus led his followers from the bondage of sin into the Kingdom of God.

A second Hebrew image that resided powerfully in the background of Luke's story was the suffering servant portrait of Second Isaiah. The servant role was born only when the exiled people returned from captivity in Babylon to discover that their holy city was a broken and abandoned town surrounded by the weeds of neglect and the once-proud temple was a pile of rubble. Upon these hard facts the delusions of greatness, fanned by the national dreams of the ages, were broken. Israel would never again be great or powerful or influential in any worldly sense. What then did it mean to be the elect of God, the chosen people?

The unknown prophet whose postexilic work was added to the scroll of the preexilic prophet Isaiah, thus acquiring the name Second Isaiah, addressed this question quite specifically. His answer was to propose a new role for the people of God—not power but servanthood, not grandeur but a willingness to be abused for the sake of revealing the presence of God. The role of Israel or the role of the ideal Israelite was for Second Isaiah the role of vicarious suffering for the sake of the world. This servant figure lodged in the Jewish tradition as a minority report and was a primary means through which the early Christians came to understand Jesus of Nazareth.

The echoes of Second Isaiah are present throughout the New Testament, but they are heard most consistently in Luke. In Simeon's song, which we call the Nunc Dimittis (Luke 2:29–32), there were three overt references to the words of Second Isaiah (Isa. 42:6; 49:6; 52:10). At the baptism of Jesus the heavenly words "Thou art my beloved son; with thee I am well pleased" (Luke 3:22) were echoes of Isa. 42:1. In Jesus' sermon in the synagogue at Nazareth that inaugurated his public ministry, the scroll from which he read was Second Isaiah: "The Spirit of the Lord is upon me, because he has anointed me to preach good news to the poor. He has sent me to proclaim release to the captives and recovering of sight to the blind, to set at liberty those who are oppressed, to proclaim the acceptable year of the Lord" (Luke 4:18–19; Isa. 2; 58:6; 61:1).[1] The words of the servant had become the words of the Christ. When the temple was cleansed during the last week of Jesus' life, the words of Jesus "My house shall be a house of prayer; but you have made it a den of robbers" (Luke 19:46) were in fact a quotation from Second Isaiah (56:7). Finally, in the Emmaus road story, Luke had the risen Christ "open the scriptures" to Cleopas and his friend so that they understood that it was "necessary that the Christ should suffer these things and enter into his glory" (Luke 24:26). No scriptural portrait of salvation through suffering was more powerfully developed than in the servant passages of Second Isaiah. For Luke this was an important image, and he leaned upon it heavily. The servant was also a universal figure who served well the universal thrust of Luke's message.

There was another Hebrew figure, however, that was for Luke a means to show that Jesus fulfilled the Hebrew tradition even as he transcended it, making it capable of including gentiles. This figure was little known outside Judaism, but he was generally regarded in the Jewish tradition as the founder of that prophetic tradition that drove Judaism beyond its limits and onto the stage of the world. Luke lifted him out of his Jewish setting and made him, I believe, the primary model by which Jesus of Nazareth was understood as the exalted and universal Christ of heaven and earth. The name of this Jewish figure was Elijah.

Luke was careful in his Gospel not to give the Elijah role to John the Baptist, as both Mark and Matthew had done. Luke did not clothe John in the garments of Elijah, specifically omitting Mark's reference to camel's hair and a leather girdle. For Luke, John the Baptist was only "the voice of one crying in the wilderness," preparing the way of the Lord (Luke 3:4ff; Isa. 40:1ff). John was one who came in the "spirit and power of Elijah" (Luke 1:17), but for Luke he was not Elijah. The reason for this subtle shift in the tradition becomes clear as Luke's story unfolds, for Luke wanted to see and to portray Jesus as the new and greater Elijah.

Elijah emerged overtly in Luke's narrative in the story of the transfiguration. Upon the twin towers of the Jewish religion, the Law, symbolized by Moses, and the prophets, symbolized by Elijah, were thought to hang all the sacred traditions. So Luke chose Elijah upon whom to pattern his portrait of Jesus for the gentiles. From the transfiguration onward the Elijah theme rose in Luke's story until it reached a crescendo in the climax of this Gospel.

At the turning point of Luke's Gospel, this Evangelist had Jesus "set his face to go to Jerusalem" (Luke 9:51). He sent messengers ahead to Samaritan villages to make ready for him. The Samaritans, however, would not receive him "because his face was set towards Jerusalem" (Luke 9:53). This prompted the disciples James and John to request permission to call down fire from heaven to consume the Samaritans. Jesus rebuked James and John and went on to the next village. Those people who knew the biblical tradition knew that the power to call down fire from heaven was the Elijah power. In Elijah's showdown with the prophets of Baal on Mount Carmel, the contest was over whether Elijah or the prophets of Baal could call down fire from heaven. "The God who answers by fire, he is God" (1 Kings 18:24). Elijah won this competition, for when he prayed, "the fire of the Lord fell" (1 Kings 18:38). Later in the Hebrew Scripture, when King Ahab's son Ahaziah sent messengers to Elijah, Elijah called down fire from heaven to consume the captain and his fifty men. A second captain and his fifty men were sent, and they likewise were consumed with Elijah's fire. Only when a third captain and his fifty-man company were sent did Elijah relent and go to see the king (2 Kings 1:9ff). The power of a consuming fire was forever afterward associated with the power of Elijah. If Jesus was the new and greater Elijah, thought James and John, he would allow us to call for heavenly fire to consume the unresponsive Samaritans. For their insight they received only the rebuke of Jesus. The new and greater Elijah would not use Elijah's fire power to destroy but to expand, to open, to refine, and to save. The disciples did not understand, and so Luke's story moved on.

The journey of Jesus and his disciples continued until they reached the gates of Jerusalem. Then, to the accompaniment of palm branches, Jesus entered the holy city. He accepted the shouts of hosannah and the enthusiasm of the crowd blessing the one who came in the name of the Lord. In quick succession the events of holy week transpired: the betrayal, arrest, denial, trial, sentence, scourging, crucifixion, death, burial, and resurrection. Unlike the other Gospels, however, the resurrection was not the climax to Luke's Gospel. The resurrection was for Luke but the prelude to the ascension and to the day of Pentecost.

As we noted earlier, only Luke gave us a narrative of the ascension and only Luke gave us a narrative of the day of Pentecost. These two events have been so deeply burned into the consciousness of Christians through the celebration of the liturgical year that we find it difficult to imagine that they hang by the thread of only one Gospel. Only Luke separated the events of Easter, ascension, and Pentecost into three separate narratives. Why he did that has been a perennial question in New Testament scholarship. The answer is found, I am convinced, in the figure of Elijah and in Luke's desire to present Jesus in terms of the Elijah portrait. First, however, one must know the Elijah story or one might be tempted to be literal about details that Luke surely did not intend to be literalized.

Was Jesus' ascension a literal description of a physical reality? We have already observed that when the narrative is literalized, it is tied to a flat earth and to the location of heaven as just beyond the blue canopy of the sky. That may have made sense in terms of the understanding of the cosmos available to people living in the first century, but it makes no sense at all to space-age people. It would be refreshing to realize that Luke never intended that story to be literalized in the first place. Even Luke knew he was writing in a symbolic way. He was, in fact, retelling the story of Elijah as the vehicle through which to lead his gentile audience to see a Jewish Jesus who had become the universal Christ.

Recall the last days of Elijah. He gathered to himself his spiritual heir and single disciple, a man named Elisha. When Elijah's days drew to an end, the sacred story said that "the Lord was about to take Elijah up to heaven by a whirlwind" (2 Kings 2:1). Elijah was aware of this and with Elisha he journeyed to meet his destiny. Elisha pleaded with his master not to send him away, and twice Elisha promised that he would never abandon his master. The sons of the prophets told Elisha that "today the Lord will take away your master from over you" (2 Kings 2:5). Elisha answered, "Yes, I know it." When the moment of departure came, Elijah asked Elisha what he would like from him as his final request. Elisha requested a double portion of Elijah's spirit. It was a difficult request to fill. Elijah's spirit was an enormous human spirit. Nonetheless, Elijah responded, "If you see me as I am being taken from you, it shall be so for you; but if you do not see me, it shall not be so" (2 Kings 2:10).

Then as they talked, according to the story, a chariot of fire led by horses of fire separated the two men. Elijah went up into heaven in a whirlwind. Elisha saw the departure, and he cried out until he saw Elijah no more (2 Kings 2:12). Because Elisha saw, a double portion of Elijah's spirit was his possession. He took up Elijah's mantle and found himself capable of doing extraordinary things with it. The sons of the prophets also saw this, and they said, "The spirit of Elijah rests upon Elisha," and they bowed in reverence before Elisha, acknowledging him as the new leader of the prophetic movement (2 Kings 2:15ff). Elisha now acted with Elijah's power. This was the story of Elijah. It was known to all those who had even the slightest familiarity with the Hebrew Scriptures.

Luke intended to present to his gentile audience a portrait of Jesus patterned at least in part on this Elijah narrative. He wanted his readers to see Jesus as the new and greater Elijah, the heir to that outward-looking Jewish prophetic tradition. On the model of Elijah, therefore, he constructed his portrait. Like Elijah, Jesus set his face to walk toward his final earthly destiny. He journeyed toward Jerusalem and Calvary. Just as Elijah's disciple Elisha had accompanied him, so Jesus' disciples accompanied Jesus. Elisha was tenaciously faithful, however, and would not be deterred from the disciple role, while Jesus' followers all fell away, leaving Jesus dramatically alone to endure torture, crucifixion, and the grave. But Easter reconstituted this frail group and gave them a second chance. Then came the climax to Luke's story, rooted as it was not in Easter but in the narratives of the ascension and Pentecost. Like Elijah, Jesus was taken up to heaven. He did not need a fiery chariot and fiery horses; he rose to heaven on his own. Jesus was greater than Elijah. That was Luke's constant message.

Jesus' disciples, like Elisha, beheld his ascension. It occurred, said Luke, "while the disciples were gazing into heaven" (Acts 1:10). The reward for seeing the exaltation of the hero was that the disciples became the recipients of the hero's spirit. Elisha, Elijah's single disciple, had received a double portion of the immense but nonetheless human spirit of Elijah. But Jesus was greater than Elijah, so, Luke asserted, the disciples received from Jesus the infinite power of God's Holy Spirit. It came not just to one lone disciple but was poured on the entire assembled host of disciples.

When that gift was received, the fire of God's spirit was pictured as resting upon their foreheads like vibrant and leaping flames. The fire of God's spirit differed markedly from the fire of Elijah. It did not consume or destroy. This fire of God was designed to purge, to open, to cleanse, to ignite, to fill life full. When life was filled to its fullness, the fire of the spirit bound human beings together in a holy fellowship. Elisha, indwelt by the spirit of Elijah, began to act with Elijah's power. The disciples, when indwelt by the Holy Spirit, began to act with the power of the Christ, and in these "acts of the Apostles" the church of Jesus Christ was born. The primary mark of that church was to enable all human barriers to fall in the power of the divine spirit. In Luke's account we can see the barriers falling in the Pentecost story.

Luke's Meaning for Us

The Christian life was portrayed by Luke as a barrier-free life beyond language, race, sex, nationality, and economics. When the spirit came and the tongues of fire danced on the foreheads of the Christians, they found they could speak to each other across any barrier. They spoke, said Luke, in whatever tongue the hearer understood. In the power of the Christ Spirit, all separations were overcome. All of this, Luke was arguing, was the gift of the one who took the symbols of Elijah and expanded them a thousandfold. Because one greater than Elijah had come, through this Christ the door had been opened for God to dwell in the midst of God's people and for God's people to be at one with each other. In Christ, Luke was saying, and in those people who had received the Christ Spirit, the human touched the divine; and when that occurred, the depth and beauty of the human could at last be seen, ignited, revealed, and experienced. To meet Jesus was thus for Luke to enter God, and to enter God was to be at one with all human life. This was the Gospel of Luke that was to be found underneath the symbols of the Hebrew heritage and, most especially, underneath the conscious use of the symbol of Elijah.

The ascension of Jesus was not about space travel or moon shots. It was not to be literalized in terms of a first-century cosmology. The Pentecost story did not mean that ignorant fishermen like Peter and Andrew suddenly were able to speak Chinese, German, or Swedish. To literalize the Lukan narrative would be to destroy it irrevocably. The task of the modern Christian is to learn how to read this story with an open heart, to hear it beneath the level of a narrow surface literalism. The task of the modern Christian is to have the living Word that moves beneath the literal words of the Bible erupt to call people into life and into the task of building an inclusive community where Christ is seen in all persons, where those in Christ can begin to respect the dignity of every human being, and where all people can begin to respond to the presence of God that is over, under, around, and through all of life.

God was and is an omnipresent God. Yet this God was seen with burning intensity in the full humanity of the one we call Jesus of Nazareth. This God calls those who have been divinely created in this God's image to be the persons God created them to be, for in the fullness of humanity the presence of God can still be experienced. A literal view of Holy Scripture will never lead one to this vision. Saint Luke knew this, and so it was that through his masterful use of symbols he called us beyond his words to a place where we might engage the living Word.

Fundamentalism is so limited. This is surely why Paul wrote that "the written code kills, but the Spirit gives life" (2 Cor. 3:6).

12

The Fourth Gospel:
In the Beginning—I Am

The Fourth Gospel, called by the name John, is in many ways the Bible's most profound book. Biblical scholars have made the study of this book the crown of their academic lives. Its magnificent lines are quoted perhaps more than any other part of Holy Scripture. It is read frequently at funeral services: "Let not your hearts be troubled; believe in God, believe also in me. In my Father's house are many rooms; if it were not so, would I have told you that I go to prepare a place for you?" (John 14:1–2). Most people have heard these words enough to be familiar with them even if they cannot tell you their source.

John's Gospel contains what is probably the Bible's best-known verse, "For God so loved the world that he gave his only Son, that whoever believes in him should not perish but have eternal life" (3:16). It also lays claim to the answer of the trivia question, What is the shortest verse in the Bible? The answer is "Jesus wept" (John 11:35), and it comes from John's narrative about the raising of Lazarus. The prologue of John's Gospel was once read as the final blessing at every Roman Catholic Mass and at many Anglican services in the Anglo-Catholic movement and became quite familiar in those liturgical traditions.

185

Among biblical fundamentalists the Fourth Gospel also ranks as a favorite. Verses supporting the divinity of Christ are readily available in the text of this book. John the Baptist proclaims Jesus the "Son of God" in chapter 1 (v. 34). The Samaritans acclaim Jesus the "Saviour of the world" in chapter 4 (v. 42). The disciples call Jesus "the Holy One of God" in chapter 6 (v. 69). Jesus himself announces that "I and the Father are one" (John 10:30) and "I am the Son of God" (John 10:36). In this narrative the humanity of Jesus is significantly muted. There is no temptation in the wilderness for John, no agony in the garden of Gethsemane, and no anguished cry of "my God, my God why hast thou forsaken me" from the cross.

John's Challenge to Literalists

Yet this book offers the fundamentalists some very serious problems. The words of Jesus, coming as they do in elaborate discourses, show evidence of long theological development and cannot possibly have been the literal words of the historic Jesus. In what is called the great high priestly prayer (chap. 17), for example, Jesus reportedly says "that they may know thee, the only true God and Jesus Christ whom thou hast sent." Strange it would be indeed if Jesus of Nazareth had talked about himself in the third person and in theological terms that did not emerge until the latter part of the first century. In the synoptic tradition, Jesus enjoined silence upon those who would broadcast his divine origin or his secret identity. In the Fourth Gospel, however, this identity was all but shouted from the rooftops. The synoptics suggested a public ministry for Jesus that lasted but one year, and in their narratives Jesus came to Jerusalem only for the climax of his life at holy week and Easter. John, however, had Jesus involved in three Passover celebrations, which would imply a two- to three-year public ministry, and he had Jesus go to Jerusalem on several occasions. Indeed, as we have noted earlier, the cleansing of the temple occurred in John at the beginning, not at the conclusion, of Jesus's public ministry (John 2:13ff), in direct opposition to the synoptic tradition. For fundamentalists to suggest that there were two temple cleansing experiences is too farfetched to be taken seriously.

John disagreed with Matthew, Mark, and Luke about whether the Last Supper was the Passover meal. For John it was a preparation meal eaten on the eve of the Passover. Interestingly enough, the content of the Last Supper is significantly absent from this Gospel. One must also wonder, as I have done in a previous book,[1] whether the Johannine narrative about the raising of Lazarus (John 11:43) was anything more than this author's meditation on the parable of Lazarus and the rich man that Luke alone of the synoptic Gospels records (Luke 16:20ff). But I will save the explanation of that for the chapter on resurrection.

Quite apart from its discrepancies with other Gospel narratives, the Fourth Gospel seemed to delight in poking fun at those who would literalize Jesus' words. To take the words of the Johannine Christ literally was clearly to miss Jesus' meaning. Nicodemus, who possessed a fundamentalist mentality that insisted on literalism, illustrates this. Jesus said to Nicodemus, "Truly I say to you, unless one is born anew he cannot see the Kingdom of God" (John 3:3). To this Nicodemus responded, "How can a man be born when he is old? Can he enter a second time into his mother's womb and be born?" (John 3:4). The response quite simply misses the point, but this is how a literalistic mind works, John seemed to be saying.

The Samaritan woman at the well was also a literalist. Jesus asked her for a drink. She responded with a debate about the state of relationship between Jews and Samaritans. Jesus cut through that dialogue by saying, "If you knew the gift of God, and who it is that is saying to you 'Give me a drink,' you would have asked him, and he would have given you living water" (John 4:10). The astonished woman responded, "Sir, you have nothing to draw with, and the well is deep; where do you get that living water?" (John 4:11). This was the painful naïveté of literalism captured by this author.

187

Not to be outdone by the literal gullibility of others, the disciples themselves entered the fray in a similar manner. Jesus began to say to this sometimes insensitive group, "I have food to eat of which you do not know" (John 4:33). Incredulously the disciples said to one another, "Has anyone brought him food?" (John 4:33). This literalistic attitude persisted after the story of the feeding of the multitude, when Jesus said, "The bread of God is that which comes down from heaven and gives life to the world." To which the disciples responded, "Lord, give us this bread always" (John 6:33, 34). When he continued to identify himself in this Gospel with the bread that came down from heaven, his critics countered by recounting his known human origins. "Is this not Jesus, the son of Joseph, whose father and mother we know? How does he now say, 'I have come down from heaven'?" (John 6:42). Later this literalistic attitude continued as his critics asked, "How can this man give us his flesh to eat?" (John 6:52). Finally Jesus began to tell the crowds that where he was going "they cannot come." The text of John said that the Jews responded to this by asking, "Where does this man intend to go that we shall not find him? Does he intend to go to the Dispersion among the Greeks and teach the Greeks?" (John 7:33ff). Later, still speculating, they asked, "Will he kill himself?" (John 8:22).

Those who would literalize the biblical text have still further problems with John. This Gospel had John the Baptist preparing the way for Jesus before either of them was born (John 1:6ff). This author had John say of Jesus the first time he saw him, "Behold, the lamb of God" (John 1:29). Only by postulating direct revelation from God could one explain the Baptist's insight.

Perhaps most distressing of all, taken literally this Gospel had fed the dark side of religious bigotry more than any other part of the Christian Scriptures. On most occasions when the words "the Jews" were used in the Fourth Gospel the connotation was evil. The Jews are "from below," the Johannine Jesus asserted (John 8:23). "You [the Jews] are of your father the devil, and your will is to do your father's desires," Jesus declared (John 8:44). For Jesus to call Jews "children of Satan" is out of character to the divine nature, but because it is in Scripture it has served to justify religious bigotry for ages. If Jesus could insult Jews, how much permission do his disciples need to go and do likewise? Is it conceivable that the Jesus of history could have actually said such things? Hardly! Can this portrait of Jesus be reconciled with the portrait in Matthew, where the primacy of the Jews in salvation history was assured and asserted time after time? Of course not. Is it consistent with that other part of the Christian heritage that has Jesus say, "Love your enemies and pray for those who persecute you" (Matt. 5:44)? Obviously not! Is, therefore, a literal understanding of Scripture a viable alternative for anyone? Not if the literalists bother to read the Bible at all. Does this mean that the Bible in general and John's Gospel in particular are to be abandoned? This is the issue when fundamentalists make assertions that cannot be sustained and when no other possibilities are known or available to be explored.

Appreciating the Essence of John's Gospel

John's Gospel is so profound, so poetic, so skillfully crafted, so dependent on images and concepts out of the Jewish past that it is worthy of the study of a lifetime that so many biblical scholars have given to it. But it is distorted, trivialized, and made almost contemptible by those who cannot escape their commitment to the shallowness of only literal truth. I am convinced that there is an ancient and primitive historic tradition that lies behind the Fourth Gospel. I am all but certain that this primitive tradition was traceable to and associated with John Zebedee, who was, I believe at least in his own mind, "the disciple whom Jesus loved." I also believe that this Gospel captured better than any other the essence of Jesus as the church had come to understand that essence, and therefore its words

189

and phrases must be taken seriously if not literally by modern Christians. With all its literal shortcomings, the Fourth Gospel still looms for me as the mountain peak of Christian writing, the holy of holies in the New Testament. To portray that essence freed from the distortion of literalism is my ambitious aim and goal for this chapter.

As I have noted in this book in my analysis of other writings, the starting place for all biblical study must be the context in which the biblical narrative was originally written. No one writes, thinks, or communicates in a vacuum. Every written work is but one half of a dialogue. Unless we recover some sense of the other half of the dialogue, we will never understand the nuances, accents, or, in many cases, even the words that the biblical writer has used. If one is content to believe that there is some literal, objective, unchanging reality about the words of Scripture that defies the normal distortions of antiquity, then the probability of misunderstanding the text is close to 100 percent.

I remember meeting a Moslem child in the airport at Tel Aviv some years ago. I was dressed in my clerical collar with the bishop's cross around my neck. On my particular cross at the center are the letters YHWH, written in Hebrew. I designed that cross quite literally to affirm the Jewishness of Jesus, to whom I like to refer as "This Hebrew Lord." This child, intrigued by these letters, asked me why I had Jewish writing on my cross. "That is my way," I responded, "of reminding people that the Jesus we Christians worship was Jewish and was a gift of Judaism to the world." The child looked puzzled. "Jesus was Jewish?" she asked. "Yes," I responded. "Does that upset you?" "No", she answered, "but I thought Jesus was Catholic!"

Most people today have such a narrow view of history that they cannot even understand themselves. It was inconceivable to this Moslem child that "Jewish" could mean historically something different from what it meant in her world. Modern prejudices tend to get read back to eras in which they did not exist. Ancient origins are forgotten. Biblical ignorance is one of the manifestations of a loss of historic memory and historic context. Nowhere is this truth more apparent than in a study of John's Gospel.

The experience of Jesus in the first century was a powerful, life-changing experience. It had to be processed, understood, and communicated. It was at its beginning a Jewish experience. It occurred in a Jewish world. Its first adherents were Jewish people. It was inevitable that the Jewish world would provide the means, the concepts, and even the vocabulary for articulating the meaning people found in Jesus. It was also inevitable that the Jewish Scriptures would be searched in the quest for clues to illumine their understanding of what had happened to these first believers, who, in the words of the most primitive Christian creed, proclaimed, "Jesus is Lord." This original affirmation would then have to be explained and defended, and thus creedal theology began its journey through time as all traditions do. In that process the tradition would be modified, altered, amended, and it would grow. In time it would also be translated. At every step along that way literalism would be compromised.

When the tradition was finally reduced to written words, two things occurred. First, the written word reflected, more than even the author suspected, the period of history in which the final writing was done. Second, the written text froze these words of Scripture at that point in history, rendering those words increasingly brittle as the world moved to newer and newer agendas. The modern expositor of a sacred story must probe the historic words in quest for the underlying experience and then seek ways to bring that experience forward in time so that its truth might be known again even in our generation.

The Gospel of John may well represent the richest mine for spiritual excavation that is found in the Christian tradition, but it surely is also the least literal, least objective piece of Christian writing in the Bible. I do not believe I can make a case for a single word attributed to Jesus in the Fourth Gospel to be a literal word actually spoken by the historic Jesus. Yet I also believe that this Gospel writer understood Jesus and his ultimate meaning better than any other. Aware of that provocative

191

conclusion, I now invite my readers to enter with me into the mind of the one we call John.

The Authorship of the Gospel

Some sixty to seventy years had passed since the life of Jesus before John's Gospel became available to the Christian community. The tradition reflected in this Gospel was born, as all traditions are, in the impact of that life. One of Jesus' disciples was John Zebedee, a fisherman. He, along with his brother James, had left his nets and his father to follow this teacher. In the synoptic narratives the sons of Zebedee were usually listed as "James and John," which would tend to indicate that James was the older and John the younger of the two (Matt. 4:21; 10:2; Mark 1:19; Luke 5:10). Interesting also is the fact that James is never mentioned in the Fourth Gospel. There is even some possibility that James and John were cousins of Jesus, the children of Salome, who may have been the sister of Mary (John 19:25). If this could be proved, it would help account for the commitment by Jesus of Mary, his mother, to the care of the beloved disciple at the time of the crucifixion—a story that only the Fourth Gospel recorded (John 20:26ff). Mary, Jesus' mother, also may have had priestly connections, as she was related, according to Luke (1:5, 36), to Elizabeth, who was a daughter of Aaron. That might account for the fact that John, her nephew, could get Peter into the courtyard of the high priest on the night of the arrest (John 18:15, 16).

In any event, Peter, James, and John became the inner circle, according to the synoptic tradition, and shared with Jesus such events as the transfiguration and the garden of Gethsemane. James, according to the narrative in Acts, became the first of the apostles to be martyred (Acts 12:2), but John continued to exercise a powerful role of leadership in the Christian community, being listed by Paul in his letter to the Galatians (ca. 49–52) as one of the "pillars of the church" (Gal. 2:9). The Book of Acts confirmed that John was active in Jerusalem and Palestine (Acts 3:1; 8:14). Since Mark's Gospel had the authority of Peter behind it and as such greatly influenced Matthew and Luke to create the synoptic tradition, it could hardly have been challenged by a tradition that did not itself carry apostolic authority of an equal rank.

Yet the Fourth Gospel challenged the synoptic tradition at several key points. Its "author" had to be authoritative and highly respected. John, the son of Zebedee, was the only figure who could fit such a description. Does that mean that John Zebedee was the author of the Fourth Gospel in the way we understand authorship today? I know of no one in the ranks of biblical scholarship that would argue for that today. The book was written in Greek near the end of the first century and carried within it a very obvious reference to the death of John Zebedee (John 21:23).[2] Each of these facts alone would serve to make the actual authorship by John Zebedee more than problematic. Together they are all but conclusive. That the authority of John Zebedee was the authority behind this work and that it reflected a tradition that reached back to this man is itself, however, a high probability. In the ancient world the "author" was not necessarily the writer but the person upon whose authority the book rested.

Iranaeus, early in the second century, in his treatise against heretics (*Adv. Haer* III, 1:1) said that John "the disciple of the Lord who reclined on his bosom" published his Gospel in Ephesus. This tradition was corroborated by Eusebius, the fourth-century church historian, who said he was quoting earlier documents by such authorities as Clement of Alexandria. Justin, writing from Ephesus about 135, did mention John as being in that city. Papias, writing about 130, referred to two Johns, the disciple and one known as the elder or the presbyter, both of whom later writers located in Ephesus. Eusebius even referred to two tombs at Ephesus that bore the name John (*Church History* III, 39:6), and Dionysius was reported by Eusebius to have suggested literary activity for this John (*Church History* III, 25:6–16), attributing to him the Book of Revelation and the second and third Johannine epistles.

There was also a "memory" in the early church that was alluded to not infrequently suggesting that there was a group of disciples who gathered around John Zebedee in Ephesus and formed what might be called a Johannine center or school of thought. Clement said, "John was encouraged by his disciples and companions." The preface to the Latin Vulgate, written near the end of the fourth century, said John called together his disciples in Ephesus before he died. The Latin anti-Marcionite prologue, also written in the fourth century, spoke of Papias writing the Gospel at John's dictation. In a fifth-century work called the Acts of John, Prochorus claimed to have been the scribe to whom John dictated his Gospel at Patmos. None of these allusions can finally be documented as historically accurate, but when taken together they seem to point to the tradition that disciples of John contributed significantly to the writings that bore his name. When one analyzes the five books in the New Testament that are attributed to John (the Gospel, the Revelation, and Epistles 1, 2, and 3), one finds similarity in content and values but wide variety in style and vocabulary— facts that could be accounted for if they were products of a Johannine school but authored by different individuals. If the primary writer of the Gospel did turn out to be John the Elder, who was a disciple of John Zebedee and who may have written this Gospel based on material that had been gathered, that had served as the basis for meditation, that had been discussed, preached about, and treasured by the school of disciples that gathered around John Zebedee in Ephesus, then much of the Gospel would be opened to new understanding. I am convinced that some such process did, in fact, occur.

There is no reason to doubt the long-standing tradition of longevity that was associated with John Zebedee. As he became the sole surviving apostolic figure, there is also no reason to question the fact that this circumstance enhanced his prestige, his status, and his authority. His experience with Jesus and his remembered words of Jesus were surely shared with his disciples. This was the content upon which their minds played. The accuracy in the details of both events and places in and around Jerusalem that appear in the Fourth Gospel argue for a primary and trustworthy early tradition. The long discourses and the unique way in which words were placed onto the lips of Jesus that made him express advanced theological ideas about himself as the "Light," "Tabernacle," "Temple," "Messiah," "Servant of Yahweh," "King of Israel," "dispenser of eternal life" — all argue for a long period of development.

There was obviously a theological giant in this process somewhere, a genius of rare spiritual depth who could weave together this profound narrative. This person must have regarded that revered figure who served him as mentor as Jesus' beloved disciple and, probably true to the style of life that this person had known of his mentor, portrayed John Zebedee as a self-effacing one who would be nameless and who would do such things as step aside so that Peter could enter the tomb first (John 20:5). He would also be likely to insist on the authenticity of his master's eyewitness account, as the author of the Fourth Gospel did on two occasions, even suggesting that "we know his testimony is true" (John 19:35; 21:24), as if to say that a second generation was actually recording it.

John's Appropriation of Hebrew Scripture

The Johannine material revealed, as all early Christian material did, a dependence on the Hebrew Scriptures. By the time the Gospels were written, the Old Testament had been culled again and again, looking for treasures of interpretation and hints that might prefigure the Christ. A common body of material had emerged. Micah's suggestion that Bethlehem was to be the birthplace of the Messiah lodged in the Fourth Gospel not in a birth narrative, as it had done for Matthew, but in the voices of Jesus' critics who challenged him because of his place of origin (John 7:42ff). It must be noted that the Micah reference could not for John appear in a birth narrative, for the Fourth Gospel specifically omitted any birth material. John did refer to

Psalm 22 in his account of the crucifixion (John 19:24, 36), but he deliberately omitted the opening verse of this Psalm that both Mark and Matthew placed onto the lips of Jesus. The servant passages of Isaiah (53:9) were clearly present in John's narrative of the cross (John 19:18, 37, 38ff). The uniquely human cry "I thirst," which John alone mentioned, rested upon Psalm 62:21.

There were, however, other less obvious references to Hebrew sacred writings that colored significantly the Johannine material. Echoes of the patriarchs could be heard in the text time and again (Abraham, 8:31ff; Isaac, 3:16; Jacob, 4:5ff). Moses and the Exodus, while not as dominant as it was in Matthew, was nonetheless present in John. God enabled Moses to give Israel water from the rock and manna from heaven. John's Jesus provided his people with the living water and bread of life that he maintained were present in himself. Moses gave the Law, said John, while "grace and truth came through Jesus Christ" (John 1:17). "If you believed Moses," Jesus argued in John, "you would believe me" (John 5:46). Under the skill of John's pen, the bronze serpent that Moses lifted up to stop the plague of serpents (Num. 21:9) became a prefiguring reference to Jesus, who would also be lifted up to become the source of life. There are those who see parallels in the speeches of Moses in Deuteronomy and the composition of the Johannine discourses of Jesus in the Fourth Gospel. Both took traditional material and reworked it into the format of a discourse. If a modern reader is either unfamiliar with these points of reference or unaware of them, many of the nuances of the biblical story will simply be lost.

This author had also, through his life's experiences, found a unique way to tell his Christ story that contrasted his work sharply with and separated it from the other Gospel traditions. The most decisive influence on both the form and style of the Fourth Gospel came from the wisdom literature tradition of late Judaism, by which I mean such canonical books of the Bible as Proverbs and such apocryphal books as Ecclesiasticus (Sirach), the wisdom of Solomon, Baruch, and the Book of Enoch. In the wisdom tradition was found the primary place where the thought forms of Greek philosophy had entered Judaism and the Jewish Bible. Lady Wisdom (in Hebrew wisdom was always feminine) was with God before there was an earth or a creation (Prov. 8:22, 23; Sir. 24:9; Wisd. 6:22). It came out from God in divine emanations.[3]

These concepts provided the analogy by which John understood Jesus as "the Word." Wisdom was a pure pouring forth of the glory of the Almighty (Wisd. 7:25). For the Fourth Gospel Jesus possessed the Father's glory, which he made manifest (John 1:14; 8:50; 11:4; 17:5, 22, 24). Wisdom was a reflection of the everlasting light of God and was to be preferred to any natural light that might illumine one in life (Wisd. 7:26). For John, Jesus, who came forth from God, was the light of the world and of human beings. Wisdom descended from heaven to dwell with the human family (Prov. 8:31; Sir. 24:8; Bar. 31:37; Wisd. 9:10). Jesus was portrayed by John as the Son of Man who had descended from heaven to earth (John 1:14; 3:31; 6:38; 16:28). The ultimate return of wisdom to heaven offered John a parallel for understanding the exaltation of Jesus to his heavenly throne, which John called both his glorification and his ascension (John 17:1, 22, 24; 20:17). The function of wisdom was to teach the things that are above (Wisd. 9:16–18). In numerous Johannine passages the function of Jesus was to reveal divine truth (John 17:6ff). Wisdom roamed the streets seeking a dwelling place in human life and specifically in the human heart (Prov. 1:20–21; 8:1–4; Wisd. 6:16), so Jesus, as John portrayed him, walked alone encountering those who would follow him (John 5:14; 9:36) and crying out his message in public places (John 7:28, 37; 12:44). Wisdom instructed disciples who were called her children (Prov. 8:32–33; Sir. 4:11; 6:18). John called the disciples of Jesus his children (John 13:33; 21:5).

Wisdom, like the Johannine Christ, tested her disciples and formed them until they loved her and thus became the friends of God (Sir. 6:20–26; Prov. 8:17; Wisd. 6:17, 18). Peter was the striking Johannine figure who after being tested and failing was confronted three times with the question, "Do you love me?" (John 21:15, 16, 17). Jesus also informed his disciples that they had become, after being purified and sanctified, his beloved friends (John 15:15; 16:27). Those who encountered wisdom were forced to make a decision. Some would seek and find, others would not, and when they changed their minds, it would be too late (Prov. 8:17; Sir. 6:27; Wisd. 6:12). Jesus, said John, forced the same response. They must decide while they had the opportunity, for they could not come to where Jesus had gone once that chance was missed (John 7:34; 8:21; 13:33).

Finally the power of wisdom was that she pervaded and penetrated all things. She was a breath of the power of God, a pure emanation of the divine glory (Wisd. 7:24, 25). In the same fashion the Johannine Jesus inhabited those who believed in him (John 14:23; 15:10; 17:8), and the risen Christ breathed the Holy Spirit upon his disciples (John 20:22). John saw in the Old Testament an apocryphal concept of wisdom, a primary analogy by which he would understand and present his Christ. What Moses was for Matthew and what Elijah was for Luke, wisdom was for John—a major interpretive clue. The linking of wisdom to the Word occurred, I believe, in the Johannine school long before the final version of the Gospel was written, and this analogy colored dramatically the meditations and prayers that marked that primary community, and it grew in influence 'as time passed.

What was it that caused a member of this community to take that which had been the richness of their internal meditative life and turn it, with all its profundity, into a Gospel narrative? What caused that narrative to be so infected with a hostile passion toward a group of people called "the Jews"? What caused this Gospel writer to make the extravagant claims he made for Jesus of Nazareth using, as we shall demonstrate, two additional major aspects of the Jewish tradition to validate his case? That story also opens, illumines, and focuses the Johannine narrative.

How Did This Gospel Come to Be Written?

In the years between the life of Jesus and the writing of the Fourth Gospel, the Christian movement had been successfully launched. It began in Jerusalem and then spread primarily among the Jews of the Dispersion. In the fifth and sixth decades of the common era Christianity began to make inroads into the gentile world, primarily as the result of Paul's work. But even after Paul's death in 64, Christianity remained mostly a Jewish movement until the city of Jerusalem fell to the Roman army in 70. The loss of this Jewish center dealt a significant blow to the centrality of the Jewishness of the Christian religion. Without the Jerusalem anchor gentile Christianity began to grow quite apart from the previous Jewishness that had kept the daughter religion faithful to her Jewish heritage. The tension that divided Jew and gentile in this period of history also divided Jewish Christian and gentile Christian. Because Jewish Christians were by definition those who could watch their faith tradition grow in new directions, it also drove a wedge between them and the strict and more orthodox Jewish adherents. None of these tensions was helped by the frequent assertion heard in gentile Christian circles that the fall of Jerusalem was God's judgment and punishment upon all Jews for their rejection of Jesus.

In times of high anxiety and stress, religious systems always seem to narrow their focus and become more rigidly orthodox. This is a survival technique. It has happened many times before and will certainly happen again. Indeed, the various fundamentalistic revivals in our time, including both Moslem Iran and Christian America (in both its Protestant and Catholic forms), are illustrative of this principle. Judaism in the latter years of the first century was no exception. The temple was gone—razed to the ground, save for the wailing wall, by the forces under the Roman general Titus. With the destruction of the temple went the sacrifices and the guardians of Jewish orthodoxy. The devotion to the Law was all that the Jews had left that identified them with their past. The Law alone

199

held the dispersed Jews together in some sense of unity. In this traumatic moment of their religious history those Jews who believed in Jesus were looked upon as a subversive force of heterodoxy in their midst. As these passions grew they found expression throughout the 80s in sporadic but increasingly hostile attempts on the part of the orthodox Jews to force Jewish Christians out of the synagogues. Even at this late date, Jewish Christians remained as practicing synagogue worshipers inside the Jewish communities of the Dispersion.

In the midst of this rising tension one of the chief prayers prayed in the synagogue was reformulated. It was called the Shemoneh Esreh and consisted of a series of beatitudes and anathemas. In the reformulation (we would call it a revision of the prayer book) the twelfth beatitude was changed into a curse against heretics and especially those heretics who insisted on attributing to a human being too close a connection with the Holy God. It was not ambivalent in its aim at those Jews who called Jesus Lord. Between the mid-80s and the mid-90s this revised prayer slowly made its way into common usage in the synagogues, where it had to be recited in the corporate liturgy. This meant that a Jew who believed in Jesus was forced to curse himself or herself or, by refusing to recite this curse, admit publicly his or her belief in Jesus and face the religious hostility of the defenders of Jewish orthodoxy. In the 90s the use of formal excommunication grew more frequent as a weapon designed to be used against dissenters.

This was the setting, the background in history that caused a member of the Johannine school to take pen in hand to fashion a Gospel based upon the material gathered and treasured by John's disciples in the Ephesus community. Perhaps this Gospel writer was that revered older man known as John the Elder, who had been John Zebedee's most significant disciple, but we cannot be sure. We do know that this author drew on material that had been accumulating for years. We know that this material had the quality of a series of meditations far more than biography. We know that this writer was a competent and significant theologian and that when he turned a word of Jesus into a discourse, he achieved a profound synthesis. We know that this material was aimed not at Palestinian Jews so much as at the Jews of the Dispersion, for it was originally written in Greek, not Hebrew, and it constantly explained Jewish terms like rabbi, messiah, Siloam, and the relationship of Jews to Samaritans, all of which would have been unnecessary in a Palestinian setting.

The audience for whom this material was written may well have been identified when the author had Jesus' critics say, "Does he [Jesus] intend to go to the Dispersion among the Greeks and teach the Greeks?" (John 7:35). As the screws of Jewish orthodoxy were tightened, John made his appeal to those Jews who were torn between their faith in Jesus and their deep emotional desire not to leave Judaism. The heavy emphasis in the Fourth Gospel on Jesus as the Messiah, Jesus as the Temple not made with hands, Jesus as the new meaning for Jewish feasts was all designed to encourage those who might be forced to withdraw or be expelled from the synagogues. It suggested again and again that those who had Jesus would miss nothing of Judaism when they were expelled. On four occasions this Gospel spoke of excommunication from the synagogues (John 9:22, 34; 12:42; 16:2). On two occasions this author referred to those who believed in Jesus but who did not have the courage to confess that faith publicly (John 12:42, 43; 19:38). John posed as a hero, a man who came to believe in Jesus even at the cost of excommunication (John 9). When this author referred to the Jews, it was clear that his primary reference was to those rigid defenders of orthodox Judaism who were making life miserable for those who had found in the Jewish Messiah Jesus, the light and the life of God. He did know other Jews that he did not condemn. Indeed, he called one of them "an Israelite indeed in whom there is no guile" (John 1:47). For these Jewish Christians this Gospel was written and to them John issued his most powerful appeals.

Only when the context is understood do the most dramatic aspects of the Fourth Gospel begin to make sense. Beyond the influence of the wisdom literature, this Gospel was most noted

201

for two things—the dramatic opening of the narrative and the strange series of words attributed to Jesus that involve the verb "to be," known as the "I Am" sayings.

John struck back at the rejecting Jews by making a polemical appeal to the very heart of the Jewish understanding of God as the only means through which Jesus could be acknowledged as Lord, Messiah, King, and Son of God. He took the Jewish Scriptures and fashioned his opening statement, known as "the prologue," on the analogy of the creation story that was, as chapter 1 of Genesis, the prologue to the Jewish sacred story. "In the beginning God created the heavens and the earth," thundered the first words of the Jewish Bible (Gen. 1:1). "In the beginning God" meant that before the earth was formed, before there was time or space, God was present in solitary, uncompromised, originating otherness. John deliberately alluded to these words from the creation story and in the process made a radical, some might say blasphemous, claim for Jesus, but a claim that would appeal mightily to Jewish Christians. "In the beginning," countered John, there was not just God but "the Word." The Word, like wisdom, was part of the essence of God. "The Word was with God, and the Word was God. He was in the beginning with God; all things were made through him, and without him was not anything made that was made. . . . And the Word became flesh and dwelt among us" (John 1:1ff). This was a powerful Christian polemical claim to those Jews who sought to purge Jews who were believing Christians from the ranks of the synagogues.

The God whom Jews believed to have created all things in fact created through his Word, John was asserting. That Word became flesh and was present in human history uniquely in the person of Jesus Christ. That Word possessed life and light. Those who came to him would know that life and they would never walk in darkness. But when this life came into the world, the very world the Word had created still did not know him. He came to his own people, those who said they believed in God, and his own people did not receive him. In him the very glory of God had been revealed or manifested but they (the

Jews) were not able to see. Notable biblical scholars, such as Raymond E. Brown, have suggested that this prologue is based on an early Christian hymn, but, whatever its origin, the author of John chose it as the way to open his narrative and to fling his Christ claim boldly out to those who in the name of God were exiling Jewish Christians from the faith traditions of their mothers and fathers.

Even as profound as that Christ claim was, this author had still another, even more intense, claim to make for this Jesus. Once again it was a claim based upon the Hebrew Scripture's understanding of God. His appeal to Jewish holy concepts was part of his attempt to root Jesus in Judaism so deeply that those Jews who sought to expel Jesus from their life or to excommunicate those Jews committed to Jesus from the synagogues would discover that they were expelling something absolutely essential to their own faith story. Jesus was the very essence of their Jewish life, the meaning of their God without whom they could no longer even claim to be the elect people of God.

Unless this context of a battle between two groups of Jewish people is seen as the source of the aroused passions present in this theological work of art, the Fourth Gospel can become, as indeed it has become, the source of the ugliest antisemitism and religious bigotry known in human history—a bigotry that has plagued Christianity to its shame, creating that dark tradition that has compromised Christian integrity for two thousand years.

Jesus the I Am

In the Book of Exodus God had confronted Moses in the wilderness while he was tending the flocks of Jethro, his father-in-law. In that narrative God's presence was manifested in a bush that burned without being consumed (Exodus 3). God called Moses in that moment to be the divine agent to free the Hebrew people from their enslavement in Egypt. Moses argued, demurred, and twisted in the wind in a vain attempt to escape this demand. In one of his escape attempts, Moses demanded to know God's name (Exod. 3:13ff). If I go down to Egypt and seek Israel's freedom on the direct orders of God, they will say, "Who is this God? What is the divine name?" If I cannot answer that I will be the laughingstock of Israel. What, God, is your name? In this ancient story God responded with a very enigmatic Hebrew phrase that was and is difficult to translate. The suggested translations are: "I am that I am" or "I will be what I will be" or "I am the one who causes everything that is to be." The Hebrew name Yahweh is our modern attempt to capture this essence and to pronounce what is, in fact, an unpronounceable set of letters.

The name of God was in some way related to the verb "to be." This was the message of Exodus revealed in the call of Moses. God was being, the ground of being, the fullness of being, the sum of being, being itself. God is. Of this God it could be said that "the eternal and complete 'I' shares, undergirds, and affirms the eternal and complete world that is." "I Am" was their way of saying this, of describing the indescribable. "I Am" was God's name. The voice of the burning bush said to Moses, tell them "I am" sent you.

The author of the Fourth Gospel took that story of the name of God and made it another key to his interpretation of Jesus. In the face of the Jewish Christians' rejection and excommunication from the synagogues, John portrayed Jesus as part of that very Jewish definition of God. Jesus was to be understood as part of the great "I Am" of God. It was a startling, provocative, polemical claim.

Even the translators do not always catch the profundity of this claim, for frequently they would add a subject to that startling verb form even when there was no subject in the Greek text. The best example of this is in the eighth chapter, where John had Jesus say, "when you have lifted up the Son of Man then you will know that I am he" (v. 28). What the Greek actually says is "when you have lifted up the Son of Man then you will know I Am." You will know "I Am" when you see the glorified Christ. The lifting up was not a reference to the cross, as I long thought, but rather it referred to the lifting up to glory. Paul would call that the exaltation; Luke would call it the ascension; John would call it the glorification. Jesus lifted up would reveal the glory of the God, Yahweh, I Am, a glory, John asserted, that Jesus shared before the foundation of the world.

In case John's readers missed this point, he reemphasized this insight a few verses later (8:57–59), still in that chapter dedicated to Jesus' identity. Jesus had said to them, "Abraham rejoiced that he was to see my day; he saw it and was glad." The religious authorities who heard this were dumbfounded. "You are not yet fifty years old," they shouted with incredulity "and have you seen Abraham?" To this Jesus responded, "Before Abraham was, I Am." That verse cannot be mistranslated. Jesus' hearers knew it. He had claimed for himself, according to John's text, the sacred name of God. They responded by taking up stones to stone him to death. That was the fitting punishment for blasphemy. But if this claim were true, as John was suggesting, it made the rejection of Jesus and the rejection of those Jews who believed in Jesus nothing less than the rejection of God by the Jews themselves. Those who sought to preserve God from being compromised by a changing revelation of truth in fact were banishing God's truth from their midst.

The "I Am" claim for Jesus was carried by this author throughout the entire text of his Gospel. When John portrayed Jesus as the one who could feed a multitude in the wilderness, he had Jesus say, "*I am* the bread of life" (6:35). When his enemies wanted to debate his origins, John had his Jesus respond by saying, "*I am* the light of the world" (8:32). To those who were thirsting after an ultimate truth, John had his Jesus assert, "*I am* the living water" (7:37). To those who might be lost in a human wilderness where no one cared, John's Jesus was made to say, "*I am* the door to the sheepfold" (10:7) and "*I am* the good shepherd" (10:11). To those who were uncertain about their ultimate destiny, John had his Jesus claim, "*I am* the way, the truth, and the life" (14:6). To those who felt a radical sense of disconnectedness when they were banished from the synagogue, John's Jesus was heard to say, "*I am* the vine. . . . Abide in me" (15:1). To those facing the specter of death, the

Christ of the Fourth Gospel was pictured as saying, "*I am* the resurrection" (11:25). "I Am" was the constant claim of the Johannine Christ. The Word who was with God in the beginning, the Word who was made flesh and dwelt among us, in the "I Am" sayings of this Gospel laid claim for this Jesus to the very name of God.

No other Gospel writer recorded these sayings of Jesus because the Jesus of history obviously did not say them. They would be ludicrous and out of place in Mark, where the divine secret of Jesus' identity was to be preserved until its ultimate revelation in the cross and resurrection of the Christ. Are these sayings then not true? They were and are true to the experience of Christ in the hearts of believers. Christ has been and is bread to the hungry, water to the thirsty, caring for the alienated, the vine for the rejected, life for the dying. Truth is so much deeper than literal truth. The testimony of faith affirms the profundity of the Fourth Gospel. Requiring that the Fourth Gospel undergo the test of literalism would rob it of that very profundity.

Jesus, said this profound piece of Christian writing to those Jewish Christians being banished from the traditions of their own faith because of their openness to Jesus, was himself part of the secret of divine being incapable of being separated from the God worshiped by the Jews. Over and over Jesus was portrayed as laying claim to the divine name. If you know Jesus, you will know the Father, for the Father and Jesus were one. They were inseparable. To be called into the life of this Christ was to be called into the very being of God. That is the message of the Fourth Gospel.

In the midst of a painful religious controversy, the Gospel of John made these bold claims. By exploring the divine power present in the Christ, John carried his reader far beneath the level of the literal words and even the historic deeds of Jesus' life. Those who looked only at the literal level would be as absurd as Nicodemus or the Samaritan woman by the well. Jesus was inviting the world to allow the essence of God to be born in them. The Johannine message was not to be literalized, it was to be lived. How can one worship the source of being, the great "I Am," except by having the courage to be the self God created each of us to be? The Christian is the one called so deeply into life, into love, and into being that he or she can say with a Christlike integrity, I AM!

This Fourth Gospel, born out of decades of contemplation and meditation on the meaning of Jesus, was at one and the same time the least literal and the most accurate. The way it is used by literalistic Christian people today reveals the most profound biblical ignorance and the least understanding of the depth of Scripture. These things are written, this author said in conclusion, "that you may believe that Jesus is the Christ and believing you may have life in his name" (John 20:31). Literalize John and you will lose this Gospel. For that which is literalized becomes nonsense, while truth that is approached through sign and symbol becomes the very doorway into God. It is a pity that those who seek to defend biblical truth so often fail to comprehend its message.

13

Christmas and Easter: Ultimate Truth and Literal Nonsense

Christmas and Easter are Christian holidays still celebrated in a secular society. They are based on biblical narratives that have transcended the narrow religious base of their origins. In some way and to some degree even those persons who have never been inside a Christian church are familiar with some parts of this Christian story. Yet even here there is a confusion and an almost blatant unwillingness on the part of believing Christians committed to a literal Bible to face the irreconcilable contradictions found in these narratives.

In the four chapters of the Bible (Matthew 1 and 2, Luke 1 and 2) that purport to tell the story of Jesus' birth and in the six chapters of the Bible (Matthew 28, Mark 16, Luke 24, John 20, 21, 1 Corinthians 15) that purport to tell the story of Jesus' resurrection, there are striking details, mutually exclusive traditions, historic errors, and blatant exaggerations that can be easily and quickly identified. If the test of literalism is applied to this part of Scripture, it is impossible to ignore the fact that mutually contradictory details are present. At the very least, mutual contradiction means that someone is wrong, and it opens the possibility that perhaps none of the Gospel writers is correct in the literalness of their assertions.

We look first at the Christmas story. It is the most familiar part of the Bible. Scenes from the narratives of this event adorn store windows and Christmas cards so extensively that they are inescapable. Christmas carols pour forth during the holiday season from radio stations, television Christmas specials, and through speaker systems in crowded shopping malls. High school bands, with high-stepping majorettes, march in Christmas parades across this land to the tunes of "O Come, All Ye Faithful" and "Hark! the Herald Angels Sing." Because of the popularity of these tunes, the content slips, by osmosis, into our subconscious minds. We know of Bethlehem, a star in the east, angelic choruses, shepherds, and wise men. If we attend church at all, we usually make it to the annual Christmas pageant. At some point in our lives most of us have been actors on that holiday stage. Despite this background we remain either blissfully unaware or blatantly ignorant of the enormous problems presented by these narratives if a literal interpretation is required.

What kind of understanding of cosmology is presented in these narratives? Is not the assumption present in these stories that the blue sky separates God's dwelling place in heaven from the human habitat on earth? What other meaning could there be to mysterious new stars that appear in the sky or to bright lights and angelic choruses that brighten the darkness of night for hillside shepherds? Does our understanding of astronomy allow us to literalize tales of a wandering star that guided oriental astrologers to the birthplace of a new king? Once we drop the romance of poetry and pageantry, is any part of this tale believable to twentieth-century people? Do we believe in angels? Can they sing? In what language?

Bethlehem was a little town and, as such, full of small-town gossip. If it literally occurred that a star led three exotic eastern magi on their camels to the door of that little house, where they dismounted and presented to an infant gifts of gold, frankincense, and myrrh, would not that house have been indelibly marked in the minds of everyone for miles around? Why then was Matthew the only Gospel writer to relate such an account? Even more peculiar was Matthew's later story that Herod did not seem to know either the location of the house or the identity of the infant, and so he indiscriminately killed all the Jewish male babies up to two years of age in order to remove the newborn king. Yet no official records of King Herod made a reference to this act. No other biblical source seems to be aware of this act. Interestingly enough, this account of the murder of the innocent children is never dramatized in a pageant, even though it is as much a part of the wise men story as the familiar star in the east or the gifts of gold, frankincense, and myrrh.

In the shepherd story in Luke, the shepherds journey into Bethlehem and somehow find the holy family in the stable. How did they manage that needle-in-a-haystack feat? Our common wisdom tells us that they were led by a star, but Luke does not know anything about a star. That star is only in Matthew, and Matthew does not appear to know anything about any shepherds. All Luke tells us is that the shepherds went to Bethlehem and found the child. Remarkable! Biblical literalists must postulate supernatural miracle after supernatural miracle to keep their fundamentalism intact. God has to hang a star in the air and let it roam through the sky.

Remember that when the Bible was written, no one had ever flown, the solar system was unknown, no one knew that stars were suns or that our sun was what we call a star. The common belief at that time was that God dwelt just beyond the sky, which was not too far above the earth. We since have flown in airplanes many thousands of feet above the earth. Human beings have journeyed to the moon, and human technology has devised the means by which we have viewed with dramatic closeness every planet that rotates around our sun. If a supernatural deity performed in a literal way all of the supernatural events that are described in the birth narratives of the Bible, this deity seems to have been limited by a Ptolemaic worldview. The inescapable conclusion is that God was bound at the time of Jesus' birth to a view of the universe that is today

211

abandoned by every literate human being. God not only had to act in a supernatural fashion but this God had to assume in those supernatural acts a view of the universe that is today universally dismissed. How believable is that? Is God all knowing or is God bound by the human intelligence of any given age? Even if these serious questions could be answered satisfactorily, a literalistic view of the birth narratives has other equally grave problems to overcome.

I mentioned earlier that Matthew did not seem to know anything about shepherds, but it could also be stated that Luke did not know anything about wise men. The traditional church Christmas pageant normally follows Luke's story line of annunciation, journey to Bethlehem, birth, angels, shepherds, and concludes with the shepherds kneeling before the crèche within the stable. If Matthew is used at all, the story of the wise men is simply tacked on as the final scene. This produces the visual fallacy of the wise men presenting their gifts to the baby in the manger, which may be romantic, but it is biblical nonsense. There was no manger in Matthew's story of the wise men, there was no stable, and there was no journey by Joseph and Mary from Nazareth to Bethlehem for a taxation enrollment. In Matthew's Gospel Mary and Joseph lived in a house in Bethlehem over which a star could stop. They were not travelers to that city from a distant place. The holy family went to live in Nazareth, according to Matthew, only because Herod's brother Archelaus had taken his brother's place on the throne in Judea and might continue his brother's murderous vendetta to destroy the newborn king. Luke said quite specifically that Mary and Joseph lived in Nazareth before they journeyed to Bethlehem. Someone was wrong.

This discrepancy is not an example of paradox, as one theologian tried to maintain in a review of one of my books.[1] A paradox is a profound truth that embraces contradictions that can neither be reconciled nor dismissed, so they have to be held in tension. These narratives involve, I believe, simple facts that are contradictory and irreconcilable. Joseph and Mary either lived in Nazareth, as Luke asserted, or they lived in Bethlehem,

212

as Matthew believed. They either returned to their home in Nazareth, as Luke informs us, or they by chance happened upon Nazareth in fulfillment of divine prophecy, as Matthew has related. Both Evangelists may be wrong on these facts, but both Evangelists cannot be right. If one is right, the other is wrong. Biblical inerrancy is once again a casualty of a mutually exclusive contradiction.

The pain of literalism does not stop here. Luke tells us that on the eighth day of his life Jesus was circumcised (Luke 2:21) and that on the fortieth day of his life Jesus was presented in the temple in Jerusalem. Only then, when this family group in faithful Jewish obedience had accomplished in a rather leisurely fashion all of these things required by the Law, did they return into Galilee "to their own city Nazareth" (Luke 2:39). While these liturgical acts were being performed in Jerusalem and while they were returning peacefully to their home in Nazareth, according to Luke, Matthew said that Mary, Joseph, and Jesus were fleeing for their lives into Egypt, and only after the death of Herod were they able to risk returning to their Bethlehem home and even felt that to be too dangerous, so they journeyed on into Galilee to settle in Nazareth. One cannot be in Jerusalem and in Galilee and in Egypt at the same time. Someone is wrong. Maybe both Evangelists are wrong, but certainly both of them cannot be right. Biblical inerrancy, no matter what the television evangelists proclaim, is a logical impossibility.

It has been mentioned earlier but it bears repeating in this context that the genealogies in Matthew (chap. 1) and Luke (chap. 3) are not capable of being reconciled. They disagree in many details, not the least of which is the number of generations (Luke said it was seventy-six; Matthew said forty-two), the son of David who carried the messianic line (Solomon, said Matthew; Nathan, said Luke), or even the name of Jesus' grandfather (Jacob, said Matthew; Heli or Eli, said Luke).

There are still more facts that render a literalization of these birth narratives strange and bizarre. Matthew quoted a text from Isaiah to prove the virgin birth tradition. Fortunately for

213

Matthew's integrity, he quoted that Hebrew text in Greek, where the connotation of "virgin" is present in the Greek word *parthenos*. However, if he had gone to the original Hebrew, he would have discovered that the connotation of virginity was not present in the original text of Isaiah. The Hebrew word for "virgin" was *betulah*. The word used in Isaiah is *'almah*, which means young woman. It does not mean virgin in any Hebrew text in the entire Bible in which it is used. Furthermore, the context of Isaiah (7:14) where the supposed virgin text is found renders Matthew's use of that text strange indeed. The prophet Isaiah was going to give King Ahaz of Judah a sign from God that the siege of Jerusalem being carried on at that moment by the armies of Syria and the northern kingdom of Israel would not be successful. A child born some seven hundred years later could hardly accomplish that purpose. Literalism dies whenever the Bible is studied seriously. Even the familiar birth narratives that feed our Christmas traditions fall apart when analyzed. Whatever their ultimate meaning might happen to be, if literalized they cannot survive the light of day.

Biblical scholars have today uncovered many signs that point to the composition of these narratives as deliberate attempts to retell stories in the Hebrew tradition. The story of the wise men in Matthew seems to have been crafted on the basis of the Hebrew account of Balaam (22–24). The shepherd narrative in Luke may well have been composed on the basis of Micah (4, 5). The Bethlehem story was created to fuel a messianic expectation based on Micah (5:2), and the reputation of Nazareth as a fit place out of which anything good, and most especially a messiah, might come seems to have created problems for the early Christians. Herod's murder of the innocent children was a retelling of the Pharaoh-Moses infancy story, where once before a wicked king had sought to destroy God's chosen deliverer. Even the star in the east has been found in some later Hebrew midrash (ongoing rabbinic interpretation of the Torah) to have been a phenomenon that marked the birth of Isaac, the child of promise, in Jewish folklore. Finally, the character of Joseph to whom God spoke frequently in dreams

214

was clearly patterned on the model of the patriarch Joseph from the Book of Genesis, to whom God frequently spoke in dreams and who, like his Matthean counterpart, saved God's elect by taking them down into Egypt.

Am I suggesting that these stories of the virgin birth are not literally true? The answer is a simple and direct "Yes." Of course these narratives are not literally true. Stars do not wander, angels do not sing, virgins do not give birth, magi do not travel to a distant land to present gifts to a baby, and shepherds do not go in search of a newborn savior. I know of no reputable biblical scholar in the world today who takes these birth narratives literally. Does that mean that the virgin birth story is not literally true? Let me answer this categorically. The virgin birth tradition of the New Testament is not literally true. It should not be literally believed. Should we then purge the Bible of these stories? Absolutely not! These birth narratives are not only among the most beautiful parts of Scripture but they are among the most profound. It is the beast of literalism that must be purged so that the depth of truth contained in these narratives can be rescued and heard in our generation.

It is not my intention here to analyze deeply the birth narratives. My purpose here is to see the truth to which these narratives point. Birth narratives tell us nothing about the birth of the person who is featured in those narratives. They do tell us a great deal, however, about the adult life of the one whose birth is being narrated. No one waits outside a hospital room for a great person to be born. This is not the way human life works. A person becomes great in his or her adult years, and the significance of that life is celebrated in tales that gather around the moment in which that powerful adult figure entered history. We celebrate the birthdays of George Washington, Abraham Lincoln, and Martin Luther King, Jr., only because those lives in their adult years became turning points in our history, and so the day on which they were born is noted as a significant day in our history.

It was not different with Jesus of Nazareth. It was his adult life, his adult power, the experience of God that women and men had in his presence, his crucifixion, his resurrection, and the outpouring of God's spirit through him that caused stories of his birth to begin to circulate. Underneath the level of the fanciful, literal details the message of the birth narratives was and is simple. This was the early church's way of saying, "What we have met and experienced in Jesus the Christ we do not believe human life alone is capable of creating. He must be of God. If God can be met, engaged, and embraced in and through the adult life, the death, and the resurrection of Jesus, then surely God had to be in this Jesus. So there must have been a time when God entered him or else we could not have met God so completely through him that we have come to believe that God and Jesus are, in some unique way, one and the same. We cannot meet Jesus without experiencing God. We cannot envision God without seeing Jesus." That was the Christian experience, and it is the bedrock of the Christian faith.

In the words of Paul, "God was in Christ reconciling." How God got into this Jesus became a later debate, and four different theories are incorporated into Holy Scripture itself. They are not completely mutually exclusive, but they are not mutually compatible either. Paul, the earliest biblical writer, said that Jesus was "declared to be the Son of God by the spirit of holiness at the resurrection from the dead" (Rom. 1:4). Mark, the first Gospel writer, suggested that the Holy Spirit descended upon this Jesus when the heavens opened at his baptism (Mark 1:10, 11). That was the moment for Mark when Jesus was declared Son of God. Between Paul and Mark that moment had moved from Easter to baptism, but in both instances it was the work of the Spirit.

Matthew and Luke continue to employ the Spirit, but in their unique and incompatible ways they move the moment back from baptism to conception. It remains for the Fourth Gospel to suggest that even conception was not soon enough—that Jesus was the preexistent Word of God that became enfleshed in the life of Jesus the Christ. From resurrection to baptism to conception to preexistence—that was the pathway that the ex-

216

planation of Jesus traveled in a uniquely human attempt to explain the origins of the reality of God that was their experience in and through this life.

When fundamentalists suggest that if the literal virgin birth concept is surrendered, the divinity of Christ can no longer be supported, they are once again victimized by their own biblical ignorance. Paul, Mark, and John seem to have had no notion at all of a virgin birth tradition. Yet their understanding of the Christ is perhaps the most profound in all of Holy Scripture. It is literalism that finally is at risk, not the divine nature of the Christ. When that point is clear, a major retreat from the literalization of Scripture will be inevitable.

Discovering the True Easter Story

When we turn to look with scholarly eyes at the resurrection narratives of the New Testament, the anxiety of the fundamentalists rises perceptibly. The birth narratives may be important to the literalistic Christians, but they could abandon this outpost of their creed more easily and quickly than they could abandon the resurrection, by which they normally mean the physical, bodily resurrection of Jesus. Fundamentalist people like to quote Paul, that if Jesus be not risen "your faith is in vain" (1 Cor. 15:17). Risen to them means physical rising and bodily resuscitation. The birth accounts may be important to the Christian story, but the events of Easter are absolutely crucial. There can be no compromise here, no watering down of the essential details. Once again, it is helpful to fundamentalists not to read the Bible, for only in this way can their illusions be preserved.

What does physical, bodily resurrection mean? The Bible tells us of a risen Christ that can appear and disappear as if out of or into thin air (Luke 24:15, 31). Is that physical or bodily? The Bible tells us that the risen Christ appeared in a room where the doors were shut "for fear of the Jews" (John 20:19). Can a physical body walk through a door? The Fourth Gospel in one instance had the risen Christ say to Mary Magdalene, "Touch me not for I have not yet descended to my Father" (John 20:17), and in another instance he said to Thomas, "Reach here your finger and touch my wounds and take your hand and thrust it into my side" (John 20:27). That would seem to indicate that in the mind of the Johannine writer the unascended Lord was not touchable but the ascended Lord was. It is a strange image, not easily understood and certainly not capable of being literalized. How can something be real and yet not physical? Paul wrestled with that and coined the phrase "spiritual body" to embrace it. Paul was quite sure that "flesh and blood could not inherit the Kingdom of God" (1 Cor. 15:50). Did Paul believe in the physical resurrection or the bodily resurrection? Until one defines those terms no one can say. He did suggest that the risen Christ could never die again (Rom. 6:9). Somehow that phrase calls my mind beyond physical, bodily categories.

This debate, exciting and ingenious as it is, is not the chief problem biblical literalists have with the resurrection narratives of the New Testament. That problem comes rather with the knowledge that the details in the narratives of the various Gospels are simply incapable of being reconciled one with another. Here in the central primary moment of the Christian story there is significant discrepancy in vital details. Literalism is battered when the resurrection narratives are compared.

Who went to the tomb at dawn on the first day of the week? Paul said nothing about anyone going. Mark said that Mary Magdalene, Mary the mother of James, and Salome went (chap. 16). Luke said that Mary Magdalene, Mary the mother of James, Joanna, and some other women went (24:10). Matthew said Mary Magdalene and the other Mary only went (1:28). John said that Mary Magdalene alone went (20:11). This is not an important detail unless you claim inerrancy for every word of Scripture. If that claim is made, even minor disagreements become catastrophic.

What did the women find at the tomb? Since Paul made no reference to a tomb visit, he has nothing further to contribute to this section of the narrative. Mark, however, said that the women found a young man dressed in white garments who gave the resurrection message. Luke said it was two men clothed in dazzling apparel. Matthew said it was nothing less than "an angel of the Lord" who descended in an earthquake, put the armed guard to sleep, rolled back the stone, and gave the resurrection message. John began with no messenger at all, but on Mary Magdalene's second visit she confronted two angels, although they were speechless. Finally she confronted Jesus himself, whom she mistook for the gardener. From Jesus she received the resurrection message.

Did the women see the risen Lord in the garden at dawn on the first day of the week? Mark and Luke said no. Matthew said yes. John said yes also, but he insisted that it was a little bit later. Where did the risen Christ appear to the disciples? Paul gave no hint of location in his list of appearances. Mark recorded no appearance stories,[2] but he hinted that there would be a meeting between the risen Lord and the disciples in Galilee. Matthew was quite specific, writing that the only time Jesus appeared to the disciples was in Galilee on a mountaintop, at which time he gave what we call the Divine Commission. Luke was equally specific but diametrically opposed to the Mark and Matthew tradition.

In Luke the risen Christ quite pointedly ordered the disciples to remain in Jerusalem until they were empowered by the Holy Spirit; that is, they were not to go to Galilee, as the angelic messenger in Mark had ordered and as Matthew had narrated. Luke then asserted that the only resurrection appearances that occurred took place in the Jerusalem area. For him the setting was in an upper room and in the village of Emmaus, some six miles away from Jerusalem. Luke implied that there was no Galilean appearance because for him appearances of the risen Lord ceased with the ascension that occurred just outside of Jerusalem. John said, in agreement with Luke, that the initial resurrection experiences took place in Jerusalem, but then, in disagreement with Luke, he went on to record a Galilean resurrection tradition in chapter 21.

There are many scholars who believe that the final chapter of John is not from the pen of the same man who wrote chapters 1 through 20, so the Galilean tradition in the Fourth Gospel does not rest on quite as firm a biblical base as it does in Mark and Matthew. However, it must be noted that John's Galilean tradition is not set on a mountaintop as it is in Matthew, but by a lake. It does seem strange that the experience of the risen Christ, which had to have been a moment of tremendous consciousness expanding and revelation, could not be located in one consistent place. Most of us remember where we were when a life-changing event occurred. The biblical narratives do not give evidence of a consistent tradition. When fundamentalists, in an attempt to smooth over these factual differences, argue that there were many resurrection appearances—some in Jerusalem and some in Galilee—their solution raises so many questions as to be inoperative. Did the disciples not talk to each other? Could the first experience of resurrection have been so insignificant that they did not remember whether it was in Galilee, as Mark implied and Matthew stated, or in Jerusalem, as Luke insisted and with which John concurred? The mystery deepens and the case for a literal understanding of Scripture totters perceptibly. But there are still more difficulties.

When did the risen Christ appear to the disciples? We are so accustomed to the reference to the third day in the recitation of the Creed that we think automatically that the Bible asserts that resurrection occurred on the first day of the week following the crucifixion on Friday. A careful reading of the biblical text, however, does not universally support the first day of the week as the moment when the risen Christ was seen. Careful reading also will raise questions about the length of time in which resurrection appearances were thought to occur.

The data are these. Paul asserted the first-day-of-the-week tradition for the first Easter appearance, but he stretched the time in which these manifestations of the living Christ occurred to include his own conversion moment. His "seeing" of the risen Lord differed in no way from the other appearance narratives, he asserted, save in that his was last (1 Cor. 15:8). That opens the time frame, as we have noted earlier, to a span of from one to six years after the events of the first holy week and Easter. Even if we take the earliest possible date of one year, it stretches considerably the common wisdom that surrounds the Easter tradition, and it calls into question anew the chronology of Luke that suggests that no more than fifty days marked the time of the resurrection appearance. It also means that either Paul or Luke is wrong. Paul regarded his conversion as a resurrection experience. Luke clearly did not, for he asserted that no resurrection experiences occurred after the ascension (Acts 1:3ff).

Mark, the earliest Gospel, recorded no appearance stories at all but hinted that such would occur at some unspecified later date, certainly not the first day of the week, for the disciples were told to return to Galilee to await the fulfillment of that angelic message. Matthew, though adding to Mark's story the appearance of the Easter Christ to the women at the tomb, suggested that the mountaintop experience, which was for Matthew Jesus' only appearance to the disciples, took place much later in Galilee. Luke made Jerusalem and the first day of the week the time and place of his narrative. He did, however, bring the disciple band into this experience only in the evening of that day after his narrative of Emmaus (Luke 24:29, 33, 36). John agreed with Luke but added his own unique twist. He made the first-day-of-the-week appearance at dawn in the garden to be a preascension appearance (John 20:17ff) to Mary Magdalene alone. The disciples were not granted the resurrection vision until the evening of that day (John 20:19). Recall that the Jews reckoned time from sundown to sundown, not from midnight to midnight. Therefore evening on the first day was the beginning of the second day for them. When the Christ did appear in John's narrative, he was the already ascended Lord who could breathe on them and present them in this way with the gift of the Holy Spirit. In the final chapter of John, the Galilean tradition was dated days or weeks later. The disciples had returned to their homes and had resumed their careers (John 21:3ff).

This last reference in the Fourth Gospel to the relationship of resurrection to ascension and Whitsunday or Pentecost raises still another level of conflict in the literal text. Who was the Christ that they saw? Was he resurrected but not yet ascended? That was Luke's answer and that was John's conclusion, but only in regard to Mary Magdalene in the garden. Was it the already ascended Lord or the not yet ascended Lord who appeared on the mountaintop in Matthew? Did he appear out of heaven or did he, like the disciples, trudge up the mountainside? Did Pentecost come after ascension, as Luke clearly stated (Acts 1, 2), or was Pentecost and even ascension part of the total Easter experience, as John implied? There is no agreement. Literally they are mutually exclusive and therefore mutually contradictory.

If textual inerrancy is to be maintained as a virtue in the study of Holy Scripture, we must face the fact that inerrancy cannot survive even an analysis of the moment of Easter, in which the Christian movement clearly had its origin. Those Easter Christians who come to church once a year do not have to face these issues. At such a service they will hear but one small section of one of the Gospels read. The contradictions exist only when all of the resurrection accounts are placed side by side. The Easter churchgoer can blissfully ignore the other biblical traditions of which he or she might be only vaguely aware.

As I stated in the discussion of the birth narratives, it is not within the scope of this book to analyze in detail the Easter narratives of the New Testament.[3] My purpose here is quite different. I seek once more to separate experience from narration. The narratives that seek to convey the experience cannot be literalized without drowning their very integrity in a sea of contradictions.

The experience of Jesus as risen Lord, the breaker of the barrier of death, the living, empowering presence in the life of the church underlies every verse of the Christian writings. There is no question about the reality of Easter as a source of power or the centrality of Easter in the life of the believer.

222

Obviously something happened after the death of Jesus that had startling and enormous power. Its power was sufficient to reconstitute a scattered and demoralized band of disciples. Its reality was profound enough to turn a denying Peter into a witnessing and martyred Peter, and to turn disciples who fled for their lives into heroes willing to die for their Lord. Easter was so intense that it created a new holy day, the first day of the week, and in turn a new liturgical act, the breaking of bread, turning both into a weekly celebration of the presence of the living Lord in their midst. Easter was of such power that Jewish disciples taught from the time of their cradle that God alone was holy, that God alone was to be venerated, prayed to, and worshiped now could no longer conceive of God apart from Jesus of Nazareth. They could also no longer look at Jesus of Nazareth without seeing God. Whatever Easter was literally for the disciples, it meant that Jesus had been taken into God and vindicated by God. It also meant that Jesus had transcended death and was therefore ever present to the disciples as the animating Spirit. That was what the word *Easter* came to stand for in this faith community.

The words that gave rational form to that experience came later. These words varied widely and interpreted this reality quite differently. To treat these words literally is to hurl the believer into an abyss of contradictions and irreconcilable assertions. To go beyond the literal words, indeed to use those words as the vehicle for entering the experience of the resurrection, is, however, the purpose for which we Christians today pore over our Scriptures with such intensity and such seriousness.

I can only hint at where that study is leading the church. It does appear, however, that resurrection, ascension, and Pentecost were originally three ways of describing the same reality. In time narratives formed around each aspect of this single experience. Over the years, in the retelling, these narratives wrenched this experience into three parts that lodged in the mind of the church and to this day are celebrated liturgically in the church year in this way.

An analysis of the earliest Easter traditions will reveal that originally passive verbs only were used to describe the Easter event. The Easter story was the narrative of a God who *raised* Jesus. The implication of that passive verb *raised* was that God raised him not back into life but into heaven. Resurrection-ascension was one act at God's initiative, and before the two aspects were split apart, the word *exaltation* covered both. When Paul was writing to the Philippians, he used a text that many scholars think was part of a very early Christian hymn. It is revealing in what it does not say.

> Have this mind among yourselves which is yours in Christ Jesus, who though he was in the form of God, did not count equality with God a thing to be grasped, but emptied himself, taking the form of a servant, being born in the likeness of men. And being found in human form he humbled himself and became obedient unto death, even death on a cross. *Therefore God has highly exalted him* [italics are mine] and bestowed on him the name which is above every name, that at the name of Jesus every knee should bow, in heaven and on earth and under the earth, and every tongue confess that Jesus Christ is Lord, to the glory of God the Father. (Phil. 2:5-11)

In this passage, which may well be the most ancient part of the New Testament, there is no mention of resurrection. The words move directly from death on the cross to exaltation into heaven. God raised Jesus from death to the heavenly realm, to the side of God, into the very being of God. In that place the eyes of faith perceived Jesus as victorious over death, and the believers knew themselves to be filled with the Christpower,[4] the Holy Spirit of God. This ancient hymn also included the original and, I believe, still the best creed that has ever come out of the Christian church—"Jesus is Lord."

When in the telling and retelling of the Easter story resurrection and ascension were split into two separate actions, the language evolved to accommodate the change. The passive "raised" was associated more and more with what came to be called the ascension. An active verb that implied that Jesus

224

himself did the rising came to be associated with the resurrection. Resurrection was resurrection back into life and was attributed to Jesus, and ascension was exaltation into heaven and remained the action of God.

When the experience of Easter was first put into words, it was simply a proclamation without narrative. Jesus lives! Death cannot contain him! Proclamations, however, never remain simply proclamations; they inevitably create a narrative to explain them. Jesus lives! became "we have seen the Lord" and gave rise in time to all of the appearance stories. "Death cannot contain him" was expanded first into such shouts as "O death, where is your sting?" "O grave, where is your victory?" (1 Cor. 15:55). Then later the concept was encapsulated into narratives about a tomb that was empty and a grave that had been escaped. The essence of the gospel is never found in the narrations, but all of the irreconcilable contradictions are. In the telling and retelling of the story, the facts were bent, twisted, and even changed.

The biblical literalist wants to claim inerrancy for what is in fact a narrative two steps removed from the reality it seeks to narrate. Behind the narrative is an unnarrated proclamation. Behind the proclamation is an intense life-giving experience. The task of Bible study is to lead believers into truth, a truth that is never captured in mere words but a truth that is real, a truth that when experienced erupts within us in expanding ways, calling us simultaneously deeper and deeper into life and, not coincidentally, deeper and deeper into God. Our Christ has come, said the Fourth Gospel, that we "may have life, and have it abundantly" (John 10:10).

Human life alone could not produce that which we have experienced in Jesus the Christ. He is of God, so the Christmas story points to truth, but the words used to describe or capture that truth are not themselves true in any literal sense. The power of Easter is, for me, both real and eternal, but the words used by human beings to narrate that truth can themselves only point to that truth. They can never capture it. To literalize the biblical narrative in all cases is to distort and ultimately to destroy its truth. In the specific instance of Christmas and Easter, this conclusion is easily documented. Perhaps if we could lead this generation beyond the words of these narratives into the truth to which these narratives point, we would not be so prone to change the Christ child into a Santa Claus, the manger into a Christmas tree, the heavenly host into Rudolf the red-nosed reindeer, the risen Christ into a prolific Easter bunny or a hatching Easter egg, and Pentecost into a birth-of-the-church celebration.

There is more to our story—ever so much more than is contained in these limiting narratives, but until we free the Scriptures from the killing straitjacket of literalism, fundamentalism, and inerrancy and free the church from every claim of infallibility, that wondrous life-giving "more" will never be known, engaged, or integrated into our lives in Christ. Christmas and Easter both cry out to be discovered anew. In a human life God has been met and known, even in a human life that was once a helpless infant. In a human life the limits of finitude have been broken, including the ultimate barrier of death. That is the story we have to tell. It is, I believe, a story that men and women are eager to hear. It is a pity that this truth cannot be heard until the Bible is freed from the hands of those who are in fact destroying Christianity with their literalistic claims even though in their naïveté they believe themselves to be serving the Bible faithfully.

14

Who Is Christ for Us?

Who is Christ for our day?

This question was first framed for me by Dietrich Bonhoeffer from his prison cell in Flossenburg, Germany, in 1945. This seminal Lutheran thinker had turned that cell into a worldwide pulpit as he awaited his execution at the hands of the Nazis. His question was not, Who is Christ? but rather, Who is Christ for us, for our day?[1] Bonhoeffer recognized, as so many religious people fail to do, that anything we say about Christ is subjective. We do not capture Christ. Our minds do not embrace Christ. Our words point to Christ. Our images interact with Christ. But our words and our images are products of our world, our cultural realities. They are not objective. They will not endure forever.

What is true of our words and images is also true of the words and images of every previous era, including the words and images of that century which experienced Christ in history. That century was not universal. The early Christians were not universal men and women. They thought in the frame of reference peculiar to the first century. Their minds were formed by the way first-century people comprehended reality. They were bound by the limits and subjectivity of their own language, their own history, and their own way of life. When they

227

came to put their experience of Christ into words, they had to use the only language available to them. The Christ experience was captured and distorted and frozen in the subjectivity of that era.

The Christian revelation was thus forever stamped with a first-century bias. It was a powerful and controlling bias, and it continues to be operative in our day in religious circles. One Episcopal seminary dean in a letter to me claimed for his rather strange and antiquated point of view the authority of such words as "biblical" and "apostolic."[2] The more he could bend his mind into a first-century form, the more authentically Christian he could consider himself to be. More important, the more he could banish from his religious world the sounds of modernity, which challenged so deeply his view of both God and reality, the happier he would be.

It was the first century that gave the verbal form to the Christian experience. Into the words of Mark, Matthew, Luke, and John the Christ event was placed. By these words the universality of that experience was instantly compromised. The words of the first century became the normative and defining words for Christianity itself. So powerful was the experience of Christ that to the words that told of the experience was attached the reality of the experience itself. The treasure of the experience was confused with the earthen vessel that articulated the experience. The essence of Christ was confused with the form in which that essence was communicated.

The experience of Christ was proclaimed by men and women who bore their witness and shared their faith. First there were leaders like Peter and Paul, who in the light of their meeting with Christ addressed the issues that concerned the first Christians in the form of letters to the churches. In this way the Epistles were born. Later the memory of Jesus, his sayings, his parables, and stories about him achieved the status of treasured, remembered, repeated words. Finally they were gathered by authors and editors and placed into written form. In this way the Gospel narratives entered history. In turn these books that slowly but surely obtained the status of Scripture began to define the only legitimate way to talk about the Christ event, and as such they helped to create the words and phrases of the Christian creeds.

Despite assumptions that were made and efforts that were exerted, these creeds did nonetheless change the biblical images dramatically. The question is never, Who is Christ? as if there were some pure objective human capacity to capture truth for all time. The question is, Who is Christ for us? How do we as subjects carried along in the stream of history, whether we are conscious of it or not, apprehend the reality of Jesus and appropriate that reality for our time?

The framers of the creeds, like us, were removed from the original Jewish context that marked most of the biblical narrative. They were answering the question, Who is Christ *for us?* in their own way as Hebrew roots faded and Greek philosophical thinking became dominant. They admitted, for example, a dualism that would never have been natural to the Hebrew mind with its understanding of creation. They dealt with words that the original Jewish Christians could not have fathomed. Far more than the church fathers recognized, they were moving the Christ experience far beyond its original vocabulary.

Contrary to the unhistorical view of creedal fundamentalists and biblical literalists, there never was a moment when the Christ experience was captured to be normative for all time. So many of our classical theological understandings are distinctly nonbiblical. But we have fused them so deeply into Christian tradition that we do not separate creedal concept from biblical content. Indeed, we tend to read the Bible through creedally formed Greek and Western eyes. Yet Mark would never have understood a word like *incarnation*. Paul quite obviously was not a trinitarian. Each generation spoke of the way they saw Christ in their day. Mark saw a cosmic struggle in the supernatural realm between demonic forces and the intervening God. Matthew saw a new and greater Moses fulfilling the expectations of the Hebrew Scriptures. Luke saw a new and greater Elijah reaching toward a universalism that would embrace gentiles as well as Jews. John saw Christ in terms of the preexistent deity who was Being itself, the great I Am. Each of these images participated in the truth of Christ. None of them bound Christ forever inside their images.

This process has continued for two thousand years. Each generation stands in the midst of its concepts and values and uses a vocabulary tainted by the tribal experience of those people who developed that particular language. The knowledge available to Christians in any age was and is nothing more or less than the common knowledge of that era.

Christ and the divine power that is met in that figure continues to erupt as the years flow by. Christ is indeed "the hero of a thousand faces."[3] He was the divine judge and the helpless infant. He was the life-denying monastic and the political revolutionary. He was the soft Jesus who sat on a hillside and invited the children to come to him and the liberationist and radical organizer who drove money changers from the temple. Christ has been and still is many things to many people. All of them are Christ and none of them is Christ. Freeze any image and idolatry is the sure result. Allow no concrete images to emerge and the Christ will disappear from our consciousness.

Who is Christ for our day? What images can we employ that will enable us to be the body of Christ with integrity while remaining women and men of relevance in our generation? A Christianity that is not changing is a Christianity that is dying. A Christianity that cannot restate in a radical and new way the essence of its truth is a Christianity destined to live only on our library shelves or in the museums of antiquity. Is there truth in Christ to which our words can point, into which our world can enter, and by which this generation can live? These are the issues and concerns to which we now turn.

Interpreting Christ According to Our Experience

The clue to this pursuit of the truth of Christ for us does not lie in words and images. They are always limited by the age

230

that produced them. We must journey beyond words and images into the experience that produced those words. In this endeavor it is helpful to employ an active imagination.

Let us assume for a moment that the Christ was not a first-century event but a twentieth- or even twenty-first-century event. To be more specific, let us assume that the Jesus in whom God was experienced as uniquely present was born in the last decade of the twentieth century. Since God is an ultimate truth and reality, my assumption is that the God experience in the first century would not be different from the God experience in the last decade of the twentieth century. But when the experience is put into words and concepts, an astonishing variation would appear. That variation would be so wide that many would argue that the experience could not have been even similar, much less identical.

To freeze the interpretation of the experience in the words of any era, including our own, would be to guarantee the eventual loss of the truth of the experience. One generation cannot finally get inside the words and the concepts of another time. It would be like the refreshing biblical story of the young lad David, who volunteered to fight the giant Goliath (I Sam. 17:31ff). The men of war of that era insisted that David be clothed in the familiar armor of soldiers, in the style of the previous generation. David, weighted down and immobile under the burden of that style of battle, declined to go forward until he could do it his way. So much of Christian theology today is not unlike the armor of the past that the elders wanted to place upon David as he journeyed to engage the realities of his world. This is not to denigrate that armor or that theology, for it may have served well in another era where it was appropriate to the circumstances that existed at that time. But that does not mean that it is appropriate to us or our time. We read it to understand how our ancestors in faith dealt with the issues of their day, how they interpreted truth in categories that were alive for them. We do not make their understanding of truth a straitjacket into which our minds must be placed.

231

I am not interested in preserving the doctrine of the incarnation. I am interested in understanding the truth to which the doctrine of the incarnation points. I am eager to enter the experience out of which the doctrine of the incarnation emerged so that my generation can, with different words and different images, begin to appropriate the truth that is present in this historic doctrinal affirmation.

Similarly, I am not interested in preserving the doctrine of the Trinity. I do not believe that the ultimate truth of God has been captured in the trinitarian formula. I am passionately interested in understanding why the doctrine of the Trinity was a life-and-death issue during the early centuries of Christian history. I am eager to embrace the experience out of which the doctrine of the Trinity was forged and the truth to which this doctrine points. There is, however, nothing sacred or eternal for me about the words previous generations chose to be the bearers of their truth.

Ecclesiastical claims to possess infallibility in any formulated version of Scripture and creed or in the articulations of any council, synod, or hierarchical figure are to me manifestations of idolatry. Such claims do not serve the truth. They serve only the power and control needs of the ecclesiastical institution. The church must embrace the subjective and relative character of everything it says and does. If the church provides security, it cannot provide truth. This is the choice that faces Christians today. I vote for insecurity and the pursuit of truth. The alternative, I believe, is security and the creation of a doomed idolatry.

The seminary in which I was trained had as its motto "Seek the truth—come whence it may, cost what it will."[4] For me those words are a call to walk into the truth of Christ. Alas, even that seminary seems today to be more interested in propaganda than in education, more concerned about orthodoxy than truth, more afraid of the future than welcoming of it, and more defensive for its version of Christianity than it is open to the leading of the Holy Spirit that the Bible suggests is the way into future truth. Like every institution, its primary concern is its own survival and viability. This is the inevitable result of institutional religion.

Yet having issued that criticism, let me also state that the institutionalization of our religious heritage made that heritage available to us today. We Christians would long ago have perished from the earth if there had been no Bible in which to ground our experience, no creeds through which to articulate our common heritage. My quarrel is not with Bible and creeds but with the freezing of these instruments in time or with the assumption that somehow the Bible or the creeds escaped the subjectivity of the era that created them. The Bible and the creeds are windows into truth. They are not themselves the truth. They are valued documents in the faith journey of the people of God. They set parameters and call us to take those parameters seriously. But neither Bible nor creeds are to be taken literally or treated as if somehow objective truth has been captured in human words. Until that barrier of understanding has been crossed, the Bible and the creeds of Christianity have no chance to be live options or respected sources of truth as the twenty-first century dawns.

My quarrel with fundamentalist and conservative Christians is not their right to believe as literally as they wish to believe. It is rather with their attempt to define Christianity so narrowly that only fundamentalists or conservatives can be included within the definition. It is their need to impose their truth on all Christians as the only truth that I resent. At this point biblical fundamentalism and the official position of the Roman Catholic church with its defined orthodoxy and papal claims to infallibility are remarkably similar, if not in form at least in intention. Both are, in my opinion, remarkably wrong and remarkably destructive to Christian truth and to a Christian future.

But who is Christ for us? How would we tell the Christ story if Jesus had been a reality of this contemporary period of human history? Surely it would not be in terms of the anthropomorphism of the first century. We do not envision God as a superhuman man who dwells beyond the sky. To talk of a

233

Father God who has a divine-human son by a virgin woman is a mythology that our generation would never have created and, obviously, could not use. To speak of a Father God so enraged by human evil that he requires propitiation for our sins that we cannot pay and thus demands the death of the divine-human son as a guilt offering is a ludicrous idea to our century. The sacrificial concept that focuses on the saving blood of Jesus that somehow washes me clean, so popular in evangelical and fundamentalist circles, is by and large repugnant to us today. This understanding of the divine-human relationship violates both our understanding of God and our knowledge of human life.

To see human life as fallen from a pristine and good creation necessitating a divine rescue by the God-man is not to understand the most elementary aspect of our evolutionary history. To view human life as depraved or as victimized by original sin is to literalize a premodern anthropology and a premodern psychology.

Yet historic Christianity has traditionally been understood in terms of these categories. Baptism to wash away the stain of Adam's sin in the newborn child is just one practice that emerges out of that understanding. To frighten parents into baptism by suggesting that their unbaptized infants might be damned to an eternity apart from God is insulting primarily to God. Who among us could worship such a deity? To traffic in guilt as the church has done, to take the beauty and life-giving quality of sexual love and distort it with layer after layer of sexual guilt is simply no longer defensible, if it ever was. Surely the experience of the Christ in this moment of history would not result in a use of these words and concepts to give rational form to the reality of that experience.

If we saw an epileptic person being healed, we would not assume that the demons had gone out of the victim. If we saw a herd of swine stampeding to their deaths in a lake, we would not interpret it as the result of demonic spirits having entered the herd. If we wanted to assert that human life could not have

234

produced the presence of God that is met in Jesus, we would not do so by telling a virgin birth story. We do not believe, as the first century seemed to believe, that the entire genetic makeup of the new life was carried in the spermatozoan of the male. A virgin birth story that deletes the male would not result for us in the divine-human life of Jesus.

If we wanted to assert that in Jesus all barriers, including the barrier of death, have been set aside, we would not do so by turning the parable of Lazarus and Dives, recorded only in Luke, into a historic account of the raising of Lazarus from the dead, as the Fourth Gospel seems to do. In Luke's parable the narrative concludes as Abraham denies the rich man's request that Lazarus return from the dead to warn his brothers. "If they do not hear Moses and the prophets," says Abraham, "neither will they be convinced if someone should rise from the dead" (Luke 16:20ff). That is exactly what happened, argued the Fourth Gospel. Lazarus was called back into life and still no one believed. Indeed, the raising of Lazarus resulted, according to this Gospel, in the crucifixion itself (John 11:1ff).

We could not retell the story of God providing manna in the wilderness by suggesting that the divine nature of Jesus allowed him to expand loaves and fish in a supernatural way, as the stories of Jesus feeding the multitude suggested. We could not talk of resurrection as if it were physical resuscitation, as some parts of the resurrection narratives suggest. We would not turn the proclamation "death cannot contain him" into empty-tomb stories of Easter, complete with angels, earthquakes, soldiers falling over like dead men, and temple veils that kept human beings separated from the holy of holies being ripped open. We would not transform the ecstatic Easter cry of "He is risen," "we have seen the Lord" into a series of ghostlike appearance stories that fight with each other as to whether or not this risen Christ is physical or spiritual.

Did this risen Lord ask for and eat food and invite the inspection of his wounds—suggesting a real physicality that can chew, swallow, digest, and feel? Or did he appear and disappear at will and enter rooms where the doors and windows were locked and barred—behavior that would suggest a nonphysical spirit.

We would never in our day of space travel and knowledge of the vastness of the universe try to assert that the God experienced in Jesus has been reunited with the God who was presumed to dwell just beyond the sky by telling the story of the cosmic ascension. We do not assume either the flatness of the earth or the centrality of this planet that the ascension story assumed. Our task is neither to dismiss these narratives as prescientific, and therefore to be without truth, nor to seek to wrap our twentieth-century brains around a first-century cosmology. Rather, we probe the story, go beneath the words, and seek to enter the experience that produced the words.

There is a consistency to the experience of God in every age. The inconsistency, indeed the fallacy, is in the words used to articulate the experience, for words are both limited and dated. Literalized words always distort experience, and if these words are frozen so firmly they cannot change with the times, then finally literal words will render inaccessible in another time the meaning they once conveyed.

We today do not think in natural / supernatural categories. God is not for us a human parent figure. We do not see human life as created good and then as fallen into sin. Human life is evolving, not always in a straight line, but evolving nonetheless into higher and higher levels of consciousness. We do not need the divine rescuer who battles the demonic forces of a fallen world in the name of the creator God. We are not likely to turn the Christ story into the mythological tale that begins with a virgin birth and ends in the cosmic victory over death. None of these elements of our faith story is wrong, but all of them are sorely limited by the worldview of the first century.

That worldview has passed away. It no longer lives. Unless the experience of our faith story can be separated from the words and concepts of a dead worldview, it will be a dead faith story. Those who literalize the ancient biblical text guarantee this fate to the very religious system they think they are fighting to save. When they try to impose their literalized version of the truth on the whole church, they violate the integrity of the gospel and the meaning of Scripture. They render the experience out of which our faith story rises to be nonsensical. They thus unwittingly become the enemies of Christ.

But if Christ is to be real for us, we must find words through which that reality can be articulated. This is not to suggest that our words will endure forever. Like the words of every age, our words will in time prove to be limited by our age, our ability to apprehend reality, and our time-oriented language. The German New Testament theologian Rudolf Bultmann, writing in the 1920s, was wrong, I believe, when he suggested the word *demythologize* as the tool for bringing Christian truth out of the past and into the present. Bultmann seemed to assume that the present is free of "mythology." This reflects, I believe, the arrogance of modernity. What we need to do is to demythologize in order that we might remythologize. We must seek the truth that lies beneath the mythology of the distant past so that we might experience that truth. But when we put that experience into words in our day, we will not escape the use of the subjective, inadequate words in our modern mythological understanding of reality, for we have no objective words. We will have succeeded only in remythologizing the truth of the Christ event. Our efforts will serve us but for a time. Our remythologizing process will capture truth no more eternally than did the creators of Scripture or the framers of creeds.

Yet we must do this or we stand to lose forever what we Christians believe to be an ultimate truth—namely, that somehow in and through the person of Jesus of Nazareth the reality of God has become an experience in human history that is universally available.

What We Can Claim about Jesus

The experience of Jesus was an experience of love. This love was a powerful life-affirming reality. It was love that broke every human barrier and that swept over every human prejudice. It was love that would not be confined by the Jewish limits in which it was born. It embraced the Syro-Phoenician woman and the Samaritan. It was love that put human life before religious rules (The Sabbath was made for man, not man for the Sabbath). It was love that transcended the religious definitions of what was thought to be clean and unclean. Not only gentiles but lepers, prostitutes, tax collectors, and thieves were transformed with the power of that love.

No barriers could be erected around that love of God that was seen in the life of Jesus. It was a terrifying, barrier-free love that rendered our religious security systems no longer operative. Such a love called for profound changes in the human psyche. Such love called for openness, for the death of prejudice, for the radical insecurity of a fully accessible humanity, for the end of any human isolation. Such love could not be tolerated; rather, it had to be eliminated. The cross was a necessity if human life was unwilling to be opened this widely, and human life was, in the first century, quite unwilling to be made so vulnerable.

Human life still is unwilling to be so vulnerable. Every assault on human or religious prejudice today elicits anew that incredible human anger of an insecure creature. We clutch our defining limitations to our breasts like sweet sicknesses from which we dare not be purged. For years we convinced ourselves of the subhuman status of black people, women, lefthanded people, homosexual people. We reacted to those persons with AIDS as our spiritual ancestors had reacted to the lepers. We built churches to house the righteous while relegating the sinners to the ranks of the rejected as our pharisaic forebears did so many years ago.

We cannot, however, escape the power of the fact that Jesus means love—divine, penetrating, opening, life-giving, ecstatic love. Such love is the very essence of what we mean by God. God is love. Jesus is love. God was in Christ. This was the experience that sought to find verbal forms in such creedal concepts as the Holy Trinity, the incarnation, the virgin birth. It is not the creedal words that are sacred but the reality of the experience that lies behind the words. That is where holiness is met. The God who is love cannot be approached in worship except through the experience of living out that unconditional quality of love. That is why the church must be broken open and freed of its noninclusive prejudices. That is why slavery, segregation, sexism, bigotry, and homophobia tear at the very soul of the church.

A church that calls itself the body of Christ cannot reject or oppress or define pejoratively one who is the recipient of the overwhelming love of God. To do so is to deny Christ. It is to play church. When that occurs, the marks of death are seen in that institution. Those marks are present when the refusal to upset the religious folk becomes a higher priority for the church than the search for truth or the demand for justice. Those marks are present when the church bends to accommodate the racists without hearing the cries of the rejected victims of racism. They are present when the church compromises its truth in order to accommodate those whose sexism refuses to allow women access to ecclesiastical positions of power without hearing the pain in the generations of women who have been defined as auxiliary to the church. The marks of death are present when the church rejects lesbian and gay persons because they do not fit the narrow homophobic definition of "normal" humanity and do not hear the pain of the oppressed and rejected homosexual community. These are the signs that death awaits the Christ experience.

When the love of God is contained inside human barriers, it dies. It ceases to be the demanding, searing, opening love of God. It has become instead the perfume of human respectability, sprinkled on the cesspools of human negativity. Perfume will never last into another generation. A contained, curtailed, domesticated, tamed love of God will never lead to the cross of Calvary. Jesus is the love of God that opens us and makes us vulnerable. The power of this Jesus can be met and known in every age. I have experienced this Christ when I've walked the edges of the ecclesiastical world and opened myself to the

239

victims of the rejection of those who claim to be the church of God. On those edges Jesus is still present. He is powerful, alive, loving, probing, embracing. There is an eternal reality about the love of God that is present in the historic crucified life of Jesus of Nazareth. Behind the words of Scripture that love is seen.

The experience of Jesus was also an experience of life, by which I mean whole life. Jesus was alive. Jesus was present with those whom he engaged. There was, in the words of Paul Tillich, an "eternal now"[5] about his life. People around him felt engaged by him. He was alive to the woman of the street who interrupted dinner in the house of Simon the Pharisee to wash Jesus' feet with her tears and to dry them with her hair (Luke 7:36ff). He was present to Zaccheaus, who, being short in stature, climbed the tree to get a better view, only to discover himself hosting Jesus at dinner (Luke 19:2ff). He was present to the Samaritan woman at the well, who tried to divert his energy into theological debate but who discovered that his life was undivertable (John 4:7ff). He was also present to the woman whose only desire was to touch the hem of his garment (Luke 8:43ff). He was present to the crowds who covered his path with palm branches (Mark 11:1ff), as well as to the soldiers who drove the nails of crucifixion (Luke 23:34). He was present to the penitent thief and to his grieving mother (John 19:26ff) even as his life force was being emptied. Jesus showed the meaning of life so deeply, so richly, and so completely that the very source of life seemed to be present in him.

Behind the words, the parables, the stories of Jesus in Scripture, there is a life that is appealing, transcendent, open, full, and free. It is the portrait of a life that is in touch with a reality so powerful that it has escaped all human limits. It is a picture of life so deeply loved that it has expanded to the point where it presses against every human limitation. It is this life, said the experience of the first Christians, that tested the human barrier of finitude and broke it open. Death could not and cannot contain the divine life-giving love. That was the reality behind the resurrection narratives. It does not reduce the resurrection to subjectivity, as the literalists claim; it rather invites us into the timeless Christ experience where resurrection is not so much an event of history as it is an experience of transcendence, ever available to those whose ability to live reflects the presence of the love that is God.

Jesus was alive, totally alive, and in that vibrant, vital life God was experienced. This God was perceived in Scripture and creed as a human form who lived just beyond the sky, who manipulated life by entering it and by withdrawing from it. That limited view has faded. This God is now perceived as the presence of life that animates the universe, that reaches self-consciousness in Homo sapiens, and that breaks open to the essence of transcendence in Jesus of Nazareth. In the fullness of this life we enter the same experience of God that marked the life of Jesus. We worship this God and acknowledge the saving power of this Jesus when we dare to live openly, fully, completely—affirming the life of God that is within us. The God whom Paul asserted was in Christ is also in those of us who acknowledge that presence with a commitment to live.

Finally, the experience of Jesus was an experience of *Being*. It was the Greek world that self-consciously used the philosophical concepts of ontology, or being, to talk about God. Yet its echoes are found, as we have noted, in the ancient Hebraic name for God, recorded in the book of Exodus. *YHWH* was a word that derived its meaning and its power from the verb "to be." God and being somehow were bound up together in every human language and in every religious system. When Paul Tillich used the phrase "the ground of all Being" as his favorite name for God, he was in fact reflecting the religious sensitivities of the ages.

If God is the *Ground of Being*, how does that which is relate to the ground of all? This is the ultimate religious question. How does one worship the God who is Being? What was the experience that led the people of the first century to see Jesus as a human and yet complete expression of the Being of God?

Once more we need to travel behind and beneath the words of both Scripture and creeds and to seek entry into the

241

experience that created the words contained in both. Words are always but a human vehicle through which ultimate meaning seeks to find expression. The words cannot be identified with the ultimate meaning. How did Jesus reflect this ground of being, which caused people to see in this life the very Being of God? The biblical record reveals a Jesus who had the courage to be himself. It is the portrait of one who did not need flattery. He could endure the ultimate abuse of having his life taken from him, but his "being" remained intact. His being did not seem to waver, regardless of the external circumstances. Somehow in a unique way Jesus was what God created him to be. In Jesus the full meaning of creation seemed to break forth. He both lived out the meaning of the Ground of Being in his own life and through his love gave to others the capacity to enter their own being at deeper and deeper levels. He still does this, for the Christpower we meet in Jesus is an eternal presence of the Holy God.

To be a Christian, said Dietrich Bonhoeffer in his letters from prison, is not to be religious—it is just "to be."[6] Religion is but one more mask that insecure people put on to cover their sense of personal inadequacy. The call of Christ is an eternal call to the affirmation of that which is. In the words of the popular commercial, it is a call to be all that one can be.

To have the courage to be oneself, to claim the ability to define oneself, to live one's life in freedom and with power is the essence of the human experience. "I came that they may have life, and have it abundantly," said the Christ of the Fourth Gospel (John 10:10). True Christianity ultimately issues in a deeper humanism. That is why any attitude that kills the being of another person is an affront to the meaning of Christ. To be a humanist is to affirm the sacredness of life. Jesus touched the depth of being, and the Christ experience is nothing less than our call to be who we are, inside the love of God. I worship this Jesus when I claim my own being and live it out courageously and in the process call others to have the courage to be themselves.

It is scary to be a follower of Jesus. It even elicits great anger from the religious establishment. It loosens the power of religious institutions to control behavior. It opens one to the immensity of human life, to new dimensions of consciousness and transcendence. To follow Jesus is to be called to walk into the very Being of God.

Who is Christ for us today? I cannot answer this question for everyone. No one can do that. I can only bear witness to what I believe the Christ event is. Jesus is the point in the human enterprise where, for me, the divine and the human flow together perfectly, revealing God as the Source of love, the Source of life, and the Ground of Being. Jesus is human being where the essence of the divine life breaks forth with a peculiar intensity. Jesus reveals God in loving totally, living fully, and being all that he can be. I worship the God I meet in Jesus by risking love, by daring to live, and by having the courage to be myself—my best, deepest, and holiest self. As I walk to the edges of life and bump into the meaning of transcendence, I find God over, under, around, and through all that I know and all that I am.

So the call of Christ to me is an eternal call to love, to live, and to be. It is an invitation to work for those things that create life and to oppose those people, those attitudes, and those systems that distort life. It is to become aware of the freeing, exhilarating, consciousness-raising experience of the Holy God. That God calls me into ever-new possibilities. I have never met God by retreating from life. I seem to meet God only when I enter deeply into life. That is the God that I confront when I look deeply at Jesus of Nazareth. When I enter this experience, I turn to the words of Scripture and to the phrases of the creeds and I no longer find the sterile choice between literalism and nothing. I find rather an expression in dated words and time-warped symbols of the same reality that I am in touch with today at the edges of my human limits and in the dawning moments of a transcendent awareness. Then suddenly the ancient biblical story becomes my story, and its ancient symbols interpret my life. I know then that I have touched divinity, a divinity that is the same yesterday, today, and forever. I breathe that divinity in and I worship its source and I commit myself anew to live "in Christ," as Paul would say, by living, loving, and being, as one who has been transformed by the infinite and eternal presence of God. Christianity becomes for me not an empty and outdated set of scriptural and creedal concepts but a new adventure in living as I walk side by side with the Christians of the ages who, with me, have journeyed into the meaning of God.

I will speak of Christ as I have experienced Christ, and thus I will add to the words of the ongoing story. My words will not last any more than I will last, but they will form a link or, even better perhaps, a chapter in an eternal narrative. Beneath my words is an eternal truth. I will express that truth for my time. Those who come after me will have to express that truth for their time. All of us will be glad that men and women in every age gave rational form to their experience with Christ so that we can be enriched and inspired by the witness of the ages that includes both Scripture and creeds. Enriched and inspired becomes our experience and our reality when the Scriptures are opened in this way. Bound and straitened by the words of yesterday becomes our terror when the Scriptures are literalized. The former gives life and keeps the tradition alive. The latter gives death and guarantees a religious idolatry that will finally be overthrown.

As the words of the Book of Joshua suggested long ago, there is set before us today life and death. In the name of the living Christ, I choose life.

Epilogue

This very brief journey through Holy Scripture has now come to an end. I hope I have punctured pomposity, exposed ignorance, opened windows to truth, and titillated the imagination of my readers. Above all else, it has been my purpose to call people into a love of Scripture for what it is—a chronicle written by our ancestors in faith as they walked through history in the presence of their God.

I believe that the key to understanding how the Bible is the Word of God is found not by studying the literal text but rather by entering the experience out of which the literal text came to be written. Those ancient words that have been employed to interpret the experience are themselves not holy. Indeed, they have frequently even blinded us from seeing and entering the experience they seek to describe because these words are always limited by their time, their culture, and their apprehension of reality.

I also write to challenge mainline church members to take the Bible seriously. I find the biblical ignorance that marks the lives of churchgoers to be beyond my capacity to exaggerate. In preaching today, the speaker cannot illustrate with a biblical example without telling the story in full detail because the knowledge of biblical content is no longer something that permeates the lives of even churchgoing individuals in any meaningful way.

I recall visiting a church in my diocese one Sunday and speaking to the assembled host of approximately 180 persons on the subject of the Ten Commandments. I began the sermon by asking, "How many of you think the Ten Commandments are important?" There was an almost universal response of raised hands. "Yes, sir," they were saying, "that is the basic standard of ethical behavior. We all think ethical behavior and the Ten Commandments are important!" Pleased with this enthusiastic endorsement of this time-honored code, I went on to say, "Well, if you agree that the Ten Commandments are important, then obviously you must know what the Ten Commandments say. Let's see if you can name them." There was an embarrassed squirming, and all 180 people together could not come up with the ten!

There is clearly a gulf between the values to which we give lip service and the values in which our lives are invested. The Bible for most of us is, I fear, in the same category as the Ten Commandments were to this congregation. We say it is an important book and worthy of respect. Yet our lives are not organized in such a way as to demonstrate that we really hold this sacred text in either honor or high esteem.

I am not impressed by what passes for adult education in most churches. Many a church adult Bible class is little more than the pooling of ignorance. Few clergy that I observe are willing to give the time necessary to become competent teachers of the Bible in their congregations. When they do, the biblical ignorance of the ages rises up to haunt them, for scholarship challenges the pious, simple faith of those who do not want to be bothered by disturbing truth. By not doing the hard task of teaching, the clergy have relegated our holy book to either oblivion or to the "Babylonian captivity of the fundamentalists." I use this expression aware that those who do not know anything about biblical history will also not understand it.

246

I love the Bible. When I was a parish priest, I used an adult Bible class to excite and empower my congregation and as the primary means of evangelization. I know it can be done. I have spent much of my life poring over the words of the Bible, understanding its background, studying the issues that gave rise to the writings of the particular books, and learning the nuances of the biblical drama that help me to differentiate, for example, between a passage in Chronicles and a passage in Kings, or to recognize a Gospel story as coming from John or Mark or Luke without being told its source. This love of the Bible was a gift to me from the fundamentalism of my Presbyterian mother. I honor fundamentalism's demand that the Bible be taken seriously.

I write with the passion of one who believes that the time is short. That is not to revert to an eschatological warning based upon yet another prediction of the end of the world. It is rather the recognition that we have no more than one generation left, in my opinion, before the dying embers of the values that were based on Bible reading and a biblical view of life will be cold. There is still time for those embers to be fanned into bright, contagious flames once more. If we do not succeed in this last opportunity, the ignorance of mainline Christians will increase and the absurdity of fundamentalist Christians will reach a new crescendo. The result will be a revulsion that will accelerate the total secularization of the life of this society, putting an end completely to the religious traditions of our past. That process will move us beyond the reach of a revival. One can revive that which is dormant. One cannot revive that which has ceased to be. That requires a new creation.

So I hold the Bible before my readers seeking boldly to free it from the clutches of a mindless literalism and, at the same time, presenting it as a dramatic and exciting document whose relevance for our day is both mighty and real. My witness is consistent. I have met the living God in my engagement with Scripture and I have heard the living Word of this God speaking to me through the words of Scripture. It is that God and that Word to which I want my life and this book to point.

247

When I seek to give content and form to that living Word, I find myself saying very traditional things. The Word of God in Scripture confronts me with the revelation that all human beings are created in God's image and reflect God's holiness. All human beings means all human beings . . . *all human beings.* Men and women, homosexual persons and heterosexual persons, all races, nationalities, and persons of any ethnic background, all communists and capitalists, rich and poor, old and young, religious and nonreligious, Christians, Moslems, Jews, Buddhists, and Hindus, atheists and agnostics—all persons reflect the holiness of God, for all are made in God's image. How can I enslave, segregate, denigrate, oppress, violate, or victimize one who bears the image of the Holy One? That is the Word of God I meet in the Bible. That is also what I mean when I say I believe in God the Father, almighty creator.

The Word of God in Scripture also confronts me with the fact that God loves all that God has made. God loves every person my prejudice would reject. There is nothing one can do or be that places that person outside the boundaries of God's love. God loves even those whose lives seem intent on killing the love of God when that love is incarnate in human history. If I continue to hate one whom God has loved, I place myself in the peculiar position of claiming for myself a moral righteousness that is beyond the righteousness I attribute to God. Since God, by definition, is still loving me even in that stance, I learn something of love's inescapability. That is the Word of God to me that I meet especially in the second covenent recorded in the Bible and that is what I mean when I say I believe in Jesus Christ, God's only Son, our Lord.

Finally, I confront the living Word of God in the realization that God calls all of God's creation into the fullness of life. Each of us is created, loved, and invited by the Source of life into the fullness of life, into a heightened consciousness, into having the courage to be ourselves—all of the selves that we are. The more significantly human we are, the more we reveal the meaning of divinity. So every force that dehumanizes, diminishes, or distorts life must be confronted by the Word of God in judgment so that the image of God may be freed and the love of God experienced. That is what it means to be the church and that is what I mean when I say I believe in the Holy Spirit, the Lord and giver of life.

Yes, for me the Bible is the means through which I hear, confront, and interact with the Word of God. No, the words of the Bible are not for me the words of God. That distinction is, for many, a narrow edge, but it is an edge that must be walked consciously and deliberately if the Word of God is to be heard in this generation.

That we might "read, mark, learn and inwardly digest" the words of the Scripture is the prayer of the church on what was once called Bible Sunday. It is the prayer of this bishop that this volume will assist that to occur.

2 9 9 23

Notes

Chapter 3. The Pre-Scientific Assumptions of the Bible

1. Jerry Falwell, *Finding Inner Peace and Strength*, 26.

Chapter 4. The Formation of the Sacred Story

1. Buckminster Fuller, *The Critical Path* (New York: St. Martin's, 1981), 3–24.
2. James Breasted, *The Dawn of Conscience* (New York: Scribners, 1933), 350–52.
3. Many of these questions are raised in Sigmund Freud's book *Moses and Monotheism*

Chapter 5. Prophets, Psalms, Proverbs, and Protest

1. Jerry Falwell, *Finding Inner Peace and Strength* 126, 127.
2. John S. Spong, *Born of a Woman* (HarperSanFrancisco, forthcoming). My primary teacher in regard to the birth narratives is Raymond E. Brown, whose book *The Birth of the Messiah* is available from Garden City, New York: Doubleday, 1977.
3. That impact will be spelled out in more detail in chapter 11.
4. Found in the Apocrypha.
5. This concept permeates the thought of Jung, but is given an autobiographical treatment in the chapter, "Confrontation with the Unconscious" in the book *Memories, Dreams and Reflections*.

Chapter 6. Forming the Second Covenant

1. This appears to occur as early as Paul (1 Cor. 16:2). It also finds reference in Acts 20:7 and Rev. 1:10. The first day of the week was called by early Christians "The Lord's Day." For a fuller exposition see my chapter "A New Holy Day" in the book *The Easter Moment*.
2. There are some New Testament scholars who doubt the Pauline authorship of Colossians, and they would suggest that Philippians is his final letter. I do not share that conclusion.
3. Edward Schillebeeckx, *Jesus* (New York: Crossroad Press, 1981), 410ff.

Chapter 7. The Man from Tarsus

1. Second Corinthians 6:14–7:1 might be a piece of the first epistle referred to in 1 Cor. 5:9. Second Corinthians 10–13 appears to be part of the third letter. This would, of course, make what we call 1 Corinthians the second letter, and the balance of 2 Corinthians would really be the fourth letter.
2. Arthur D. Nock, *St. Paul* (New York: Harper & Bros., 1937).
3. C. H. Dodd, *The Epistle of Paul to the Romans* (London: Hodder & Stoughton, 1949).
4. Arthur D. Nock, *St. Paul* (New York: Harper & Bros., 1937), 233.

Chapter 8. Christ, Resurrection, Grace: The Gospel of Paul

1. Robert Young, *Analytical Concordance to the Bible* (Grand Rapids, Michigan: Wm. B. Eerdmans, 1955).

Chapter 9. Mark: Beyond Mythology to Reality

1. Eusebius, *Church History* III, *The History of the Church* (Minneapolis: Augsburg-Fortress, 1975), 39:15.
2. D. E. Nineham, *Mark*, The Pelican series (Baltimore: Penguin, 1963).
3. Edward Schillebeeckx, *Jesus: An Experiment in Christology* (New York: Seabury Press, 1979), 33.

Chapter 10. Matthew: The Story of Jesus from a Hebrew Perspective

1. For a fuller discussion of this issue, see my book *Born of a Woman* (HarperSanFrancisco, forthcoming).
2. Various Christian bodies have divided them quite differently to achieve this round number. Some divided the first commandment about God into (1) You shall have no other Gods and (2) You shall make no graven images. They are identical in meaning. Others divided the last commandment into (1) You shall not covet your neighbor's house and (2) You shall not covet your neighbor's wife. They are obviously two aspects of the same injunction. The number ten, however, served the didactic purpose of teaching.
3. This is an informed guess. See chapter 13.

Chapter 11. Luke: The Story of Jesus from a Gentile Perspective

1. Many scholars believe that Isaiah 56–66 is the work of a third person and not, technically speaking, part of Second Isaiah. In Jesus' day or in Luke's day, however, no such distinction was made.

Chapter 12. The Fourth Gospel: In the Beginning—I Am

1. John S. Spong, *This Hebrew Lord*, rev. ed. (San Francisco: Harper & Row, 1987).
2. I am aware that many scholars do not regard John 21 as authentic. I do not believe, however, that this changes the argument substantially.
3. It is Raymond E. Brown more than any other New Testament scholar who opened these ideas to me for the first time. See his *Gospel According to John*, "Introduction," Anchor Bible series (New York: Doubleday, 1966).

Chapter 13. Christmas and Easter: Ultimate Truth and Literal Nonsense

1. Virginia Ramey Mollenkott, review of *Living in Sin? A Bishop Rethinks Human Sexuality*, by John S. Spong, *Letters of Ruth*, Summer 1989.
2. New Testament scholars are unanimously agreed that the original text of Mark ended with verse 8 of chapter 16. The material beyond verse 8 is a much later addition to Mark's Gospel.
3. See John S. Spong, *The Easter Moment* (San Francisco: Harper & Row, 1980 and 1986).
4. Christpower, written as one word, has become for me a way to describe the Christ life that is the gift of the Spirit, the mark of membership in the Christian community. The word was coined for me by Lucy Newton Boswell and it became the title of a book of theological poetry on which Lucy N. Boswell and I collaborated. It was published by Thomas Hale, Richmond, Virginia, in 1975.

Chapter 14. Who Is Christ for Us?

1. Dietrich Bonhoeffer, *Prisoner for God* (New York: Macmillan, 1959), 123.
2. The Very Reverend John Rogers, dean of Trinity School for Ministry, Ambridge, Pennsylvania.
3. From the book title by Joseph Campbell.
4. Virginia Theological Seminary, Alexandria, Virginia.
5. This is the title of one of Professor Tillich's important books.
6. Dietrich Bonhoeffer, *Prisoner for God* (New York: Macmillan, 1959), 123.

Bibliography

Albright, William F. *Some Canaanite-Phoenicial Sources of Hebrew Wisdom.* Pg 1–15. An essay, in a collection of essays called: *Wisdom in Israel and in the Ancient Near East.* Edited by M. Noth and D. Winton Thomas. Leiden: Brill, 1955.

Anderson, Bernhard W. *Understanding the Old Testament.* 4th ed. Englewood Cliffs, NJ: Prentice-Hall, 1986.

Barrett, Charles K. *Essays on John.* Philadelphia: Westminster Press, 1982.

Batchelor, Edward J., Jr. *Homosexuality and Ethics.* New York: Pilgrim Press, 1980.

Bonhoeffer, Dietrich. *Letters and Papers from Prison.* 2d English ed. London: SCM Press, 1956. Also published under the title *Prisoner for God* by Macmillan in New York, 1959.

Brown, Raymond. *The Birth of the Messiah.* Garden City, NY: Doubleday, 1977.

————. *The Gospel According to John.* Vols. 1 and 2. Garden City, NY: Doubleday, 1966–70.

Bultmann, Rudolf. *The Gospel of John: A Commentary.* Translated by G. R. Beasley. Oxford: B. Blackwell, 1971.

Caird, G. B. *St. Luke.* Pelican series. Baltimore: Penguin Books, 1963.

Campbell, Joseph. *The Hero with a Thousand Faces.* New York: Pantheon Books, 1949.

Campbell, Joseph, with Bill Moyers. *The Power of Myth.* New York: Doubleday, 1988.

Childs, Brevard. *The Book of Exodus: A Critical Theological Commentary.* Philadelphia: Westminster Press, 1974.

Conzelman, Hans. *The Theology of St. Luke.* London: Faber & Faber, 1960.

Coote, Robert B., and Mary P. Power. *Politics, and the Making of the Bible.* Philadelphia: Fortress Press, 1990.

Dodd, Charles H. *The Epistle of Paul to the Romans.* London: Hodder & Stoughton, 1949.

_____. *The Interpretation of the Fourth Gospel.* Cambridge: Univ. Press, 1968.

Easton, Burton S. *The Gospel According to St. Luke.* New York: Scribners, 1926.

Eissfeldt, Otto. *The Old Testament, An Introduction.* New York: Harper & Row, 1965.

Ellis, Earle E. *The Gospel of Luke.* New Century Bible. London: Thomas Nelson & Sons, 1966.

Erikson, Erik H. *Identity and the Life Cycle.* New York: International University Press, 1959.

Eusebius. *The History of the Church.* Minneapolis: Augsburg-Fortress, 1975.

Evans, Rod L., and Berent, Irwin M. *Fundamentalism: Hazards and Heartbreaks.* La Salle, IL: Open Court Press, 1988.

Falwell, Jerry. *Finding Inner Peace and Strength.* Garden City, NY: Doubleday, 1982.

Freud, Sigmund. *The Future of an Illusion.* Translated by James Strackey. New York: W. W. Norton, 1961, 1975.

_____. *Moses and Monotheism.* Translated by Katherine Jones. New York: Vantage Books, 1967.

_____. *Totem and Taboo.* New York: W. W. Norton, 1950.

Fuller, R. Buckminster. *Critical Path.* New York: St. Martin's Press, 1981.

Fuller, Reginald. *The Formation of the Resurrection Narratives.* New York: Macmillan, 1971.

Habel, Norman C. *The Book of Job.* London: SCM Press, 1985.

Haenchen, Ernst. *The Acts of the Apostles, A Commentary.* Philadelphia: Westminster Press, 1971.

Harnack, Adolph. *The Expansion of Christianity in the First Three Centuries.* Translated by James Moffett. Freeport, NY: Books for Libraries Press.

Hick, John. *God and the Universe of Faith.* London: Macmillan, 1973.

Hoskyns, Sir Edwin. *The Fourth Gospel.* London: Faber & Faber, 1947.

James, Fleming. *Personalities of the Old Testament.* New York: Charles Scribner's Sons, 1955.

Jung Carl G. *Memories, Dreams, Reflections.* New York: Vintage, 1965.

Küng, Hans. *On Being a Christian.* Garden City, NY: Doubleday, 1976.

MacGregor, G. H. C. *The Gospel of John.* New York: Doubleday, 1929.

Manson, William. *The Gospel of Luke.* London: Hodder & Stoughton, 1963.

Nineham, D. E. *Mark*. Pelican series. Baltimore: Penguin Books, 1963.

Nock, Arthur D. *St. Paul*. New York: Harper & Brothers, 1937.

Noth, Martin. *Exodus, A Commentary*. Philadelphia: Westminster Press, 1962.

Pagels, Elaine. *The Gnostic Gospels*. New York: Random House, 1979.

Pannenberg, Wolfhart. *Jesus, God and Man*. Philadelphia: Westminster Press, 1968.

Parrinder, Geoffrey. *Sex in the World's Religions*. New York: Oxford Univ. Press, 1980.

Perrin, Norman. *The Resurrection According to Matthew, Mark and Luke*. Philadelphia: Fortress Press, 1977.

Pope, Marvin H. *Job*. The Anchor Bible Commentary. New York: Doubleday, 1965.

Ramsey, A. Michael. *The Resurrection of Christ*. Philadelphia: Westminster Press, 1956.

Robinson, John A. T. *The Human Face of God*. Philadelphia: Westminster Press, 1973.

_____. *The Priority of John*. London: SCM Press, 1985.

Romer, John. *Testament—The Bible and History*. New York: Henry Holt, 1988.

Rowley, Harold H. *Job*. New Century Bible. London: Thomas Nelson & Sons, 1970.

Sagan, Carl. *Cosmos*. New York: Random House, 1980.

Sandmel, Samuel. *The Genius of Paul*. New York: Farrar, Straus & Cudahy, 1958.

Schillebeeckx, Edward. *Jesus: An Experiment in Christology*. New York: Seabury Press, 1979.

_____. *Christ: The Experience of Jesus as Lord*. New York: Seabury Press, 1980.

Smith, Norman H. *The Book of Job: Its Origin and Purpose*. Napeville, IL: Alec R. Allenson, 1968.

Spong, John S. *The Easter Moment*. Reprint. San Francisco: Harper & Row, 1987.

_____. *Into the Whirlwind: The Future of the Church*. San Francisco: Harper & Row, 1983.

_____. *Living in Sin? A Bishop Rethinks Human Sexuality*. San Francisco: Harper & Row, 1988.

_____. *This Hebrew Lord*. Reprint. San Francisco: Harper & Row, 1987.

Spong, John S., with Denise G. Haines. *Beyond Moralism: A Contemporary View of the Ten Commandments*. San Francisco: Harper & Row, 1986.

Tannehill, Robert C. *The Narrative Unity of Luke/Acts*. Philadelphia: Fortress Press, 1986.

Taylor, John V. *The Go-Between God*. Philadelphia: Fortress Press, 1973.

Taylor, Vincent. *The Gospel According to Mark*. London: Macmillan, 1953.

Temple, William. *Readings in St. John*. New York: Macmillan, 1945.

Tillich, Paul. *The Courage to Be*. New Haven: Yale Univ. Press, 1952.

————. *The Eternal Now*. New York: Charles Scribner's Sons, 1963.

————. *The New Being*. New York: Charles Scribner's Sons, 1935.

————. *The Shaking of the Foundations*. New York: Charles Scribner's Sons, 1948.

Toynbee, Arnold J. *Christianity Among the Religions of the World*. New York: Charles Scribner's Sons, 1957.

Tur-Sinai, N. H. *The Book of Job, A New Commentary*. Jerusalem: Kiryath Sepher, 1957.

Von Rad, Gerhard. *Genesis, A Commentary*. London: SCM Press, 1972.

————. *Old Testament Theology*. Vols. 1 and 2. New York: Harper & Row, 1962–65.

Warner, Marina. *Alone of All Her Sex*. New York: Alfred A. Knopf, 1976.

Wilberforce, William. *A Practical View of the Prevailing Religious System of Professed Christians in the Higher and Middle Classes Contrasted with Real Christianity*. American Tract Society, 1978.

Index

13, 14, 97; **14:34, 35,** 6, 101; **14:35,**
91, 101; **15,** 209; **15:8,** 220; **15:9,** 98;
15:17, 217; **15:50,** 218; **15:55,** 225
2 Corinthians: **3:6,** 184; **3:15,** 104;
5:14, 122; **6:8–10,** 109; **7:5,** 111;
10:10, 99; **11:6,** 99; **12:1–5,** 95;
12:7–9, 118
Cosmology, pre-scientific, 25–26,
29–31, 129–30, 132–33, 184, 210,
227–28, 233–34, 236
Covenant, 47, 49, 71, 77–90
Creationism, 9, 32
Cromwell, Oliver, 103

Daniel, 57, 61, 163; **7:14,** 163; **12:3,**
162
Darwin, Charles, 9
David, 40, 46, 59, 60, 62, 74, 127,
154, 156, 162, 173, 213, 231
Death, 15, 18, 28, 75, 121, 125, 133,
226, 235, 239, 244; of Christianity,
31–33; cosmic victory over, 236;
and divine love, 240; Jesus and,
164; and life, battle between, 144;
life after, 61; Paul on, 110, 113,
118, 122; sacrificial, 5
Democracy, 47
Deuteronomy, 43, 50–53; **4:12,** 51; **5,**
23; **6:16,** 161; **8:3,** 161; **10:12–13,**
20; **14:21,** 20
Dietary laws, 54, 92
Diocletian (emperor), 175
Dionysius, 193
Dispensation, 77
Divine election, theory of, 20
Divine inspiration, theory of, 78–79
Dodd, C. H., 97

Easter, 81–82, 136, 154, 163, 167–68,
180, 182, 186, 209, 216, 235; Mark
on, 141, 146; Palm Sunday
procession to, 87; story, true, 217–
26
Eden, Garden of, 32, 35
Einstein, Albert, 25
Elijah, 179–83, 198, 229
Elohist narration, 43, 46–50, 51, 53,
58

Ephesians, 89, 94, 95; **2:12–17,** 126;
2:21, 22, 127
Epilepsy, 119, 143, 234
Episcopal Church, 5, 11
Ethics, 16–17. *See also* Morality
Ethnic purity, 71–72
Eucharist, 148
Evangelism, 1, 3, 171; audiences
addressed by, 83–84; and birth
narratives, 213; and the Gospel of
Luke, 82, 172, 179; and Hell,
concept of, 155; and slavery, 102;
television, 4, 25–26
Eve, 32, 45, 64
Evil, 4, 34, 111, 234; and adultery,
17; God and, 68–69, 129, 132, 138,
140, 144, 155; and good, 132, 138;
Job and, 68; Paul and, 112, 113,
116, 117, 120, 123; problem of, 68;
and slavery, 102; and tribal
culture, 65
Evolution, 32, 34, 38–39
Excommunication, 9, 201
Exile, 48–54, 60–61, 148, 156; and
the Book of Daniel, 57; and the
chosen people, notion of, 70, 72;
and the covenant, unfaithfulness
to, 71; and the Psalms, 62
Exodus, 53, 241; **1:8,** 48; **2:11ff,** 16;
3:1ff, 46; **3:13ff,** 204; **9:27,** 17;
11:4–6, 17; **11:7,** 17; **12:35–36,** 17;
14:21ff, 157; **15,** 18; **16:4ff,** 54, 157;
19ff, 157; **20,** 23, 54; **20:4–6,** 65;
21:1ff, 156; **21:15, 17,** 18; **22:20,** 18;
24:8, 49; **24:9–11,** 49; **32,** 17; **34,**
23, 46; **34:29–35,** 160
Ezekiel, 2, 53, 65, 66–67, 164; **10,**
60; **18:2–4,** 2; **18:46,** 65; **37,** 60

Fall, the, 34–35
Falwell, Jerry, 2, 58
Farmer, James, 103
Feminism, 6, 75, 104
Ferraro, Geraldine, 101

Galatians, 80, 81, 89, 94, 95, 99–100;
1:9, 91; **1:12ff,** 98; **1:13ff,** 115; **1:14,**
98; **1:22,** 98; **2:9,** 100, 192; **2:20,**

260

122; **3:8**, 104; **3:17**, 104; **3:28**, 100, 145; **4:12, 19**, 118–19; **4:13**, 118; **4:15**, 118; **4:19**, 119; **5:12**, 91; **15–21**, 100
Galileo, 9, 26
Genesis, 25, 26–32, 46; **1:1–2:4**, 21; **2:4–25**, 44–45; **2:5ff**, 23; **2:7**, 45; **2:8**, 45; **2:18–23**, 45; **2:23**, 64; **2:46–4:26**, 44; **3**, 32; **3:8**, 45; **3:9**, 45; **3:21**, 45; **7:11**, 29; **7:19, 20**, 29; **9:20**, 44; **9:25–27**, 1; **12:3**, 45; **17:17**, 40; **19:8**, 7; **19:24–25**, 40; **19:26**, 40; **19:30–36**, 7, 44; **19:30–38**, 45; **20:1ff**, 45; **20:1–18**, 17; **22**, 40; **25:29–34**, 45; **27**, 47; **27:1ff**, 47; **28:10–17**, 47; **29:15ff**, 48; **29:17**, 48; **30:7**, 49; **30:9**, 51; **32:22–32**, 47; **35:16–20**, 156–57; **36:1**, 45; **37**, 16; **37:3**, 48; **37:20ff**, 48; **37:25**, 23; **37:28**, 23; **37:35**, 31; **38**, 17; **42**, 48; **46**, 156; **47**, 48
Geology, 32, 38–39, 54, 74
God, 11, 23–24, 39–40, 59, 108; anger of, 28; and the Canaanites, 42; covenant with, 47, 49, 71, 77–90; and cruelty, 2, 17–18, 21; as "deep within us," 33; divine will of, 138; and Easter, 223, 224–25; and evil, 68–69, 129, 132, 138, 140, 144, 155; false, 18; and Genesis, 5, 27, 28, 29, 31, 32; as the Ground of Being, 241–42, 243; and homosexuality, 7; "I Am" as the name of, 204–05; invitation to "come unto," 5; and Jesus, 5, 119, 121, 122–27, 132, 143, 151–52, 156, 159, 162, 163, 165, 170, 176, 183, 184, 204, 215–16, 231–34, 237. 238–44, 248; and Joseph, 214–15; "journey into," 170; judgment of, 58; and justice, 67; Kingdom of, 76, 84, 98, 116, 138, 142, 145, 157, 177; and love, 4, 72, 75–76, 109, 121, 125–26, 238–43, 248; as male, 28, 101; as a "man of war," 18; as omnipresent, 184; Paul and, 112, 121, 122; and plagues, 17; power of, 49, 67, 69, 70, 75, 109, 198;

and pre-scientific beliefs, 28–36, 211–12; as the "Prince of Peace," 18; and punishment, 28, 155; and segregation, 3; and sexism, 6; and slavery, 2, 18; in the Torah, 23; as a tribal deity, 41; true, 18–19; union with, 75; and universalism, 41, 45; wind (*ruach*) of, 60; and the world, 66. *See also* Word of God; Yahweh
Good Friday, 78, 154
Goodness, 33, 34; and evil, 132, 138; God and, 67, 68; and the Sabbath day command, 53
Grace, 106, 114, 117, 120–23, 126, 127
Graf-Welhansen school, four-document theory of, 43

Harnack, Adolph, 100
Hinduism, 165
History, 74, 75, 129, 228–29; Jewish, 42–55, 57; and the New Testament, 77–79, 80–88, 93; "objective," 37–38; oral, 85, 88–90, 95, 100; philosophy of, 51; and the study of John's Gospel, 190; and the words of Jesus, in the Bible, 78–79
Homosexuality, 1, 7–8, 20, 75, 104, 165, 238–39, 248; Paul and, 116–18, 119, 120, 125–26
Hosannah (we pray), 84, 180
Hosea, 50, 59, 161

Incarnation, 229, 232, 238
Individualism, 61, 65–66, 68–69
Industrial Revolution, 103
Isaac, 17, 42; in Elohist narratives, 47, 49; in Yahwist narratives, 44, 45
Isaiah, 50, 58, 213–14; **1–39**, 59; **2**, 178; **6:9–10**, 162; **7:11**, 31; **7:14**, 60, 214; **11:1**, 161, 164; **40–55**, 61; **42:1**, 157, 178; **42:1–4**, 162; **42:6**, 178; **52:10**, 178; **53:9**, 163, 196; **56:7**, 178; **58:6**, 178; **61:1**, 178
Israel, 2, 17, 18, 30, 39; history of,

261

42–55, 157; judgment of kings in, 59; messianic vocation of, 65; and Moses, 41, 42; national identity of, 157; political interests of, 42

James, 39, 90, 152, 160, 172, 180, 192, 218
Jeremiah, 50, 60, 161
Jerusalem, 40, 81, 89, 99; destruction of, by the Romans, 70, 95, 147, 199; in Deuteronomic narratives, 50, 51, 53; in Elohist narratives, 49, 50; Jesus in, 139, 147, 180, 182, 213, 220, 221; and missionaries, 125; in Priestly narratives, 52–54; reign of Solomon in, 43; and warring kings, 60; in Yahwist narratives, 43–46
Jesus, 11, 21–23, 35–36, 51, 69, 78, 83, 227–44; arrest of, 87; ascension of, 15, 30–31, 124, 180, 181, 182, 184, 221, 223, 224–25, 226–27; baptism of, 157, 178; birth of, 14, 57, 58, 60, 80, 81, 151, 161, 167, 176, 210–17; body of, 13, 127, 154, 165, 239; as the Bread of Life, 158; church of, birth of, 183; crucifixion of, 80, 82, 105, 109, 112, 123, 129, 142, 153, 163, 180, 182, 192, 216, 220, 240; death of, 15, 58, 70, 80, 122, 137, 180, 223, 224, 225; and demonic forces, 129; exaltation of, 123–27; experience of, as an experience of Being, 241; and the first dispensation, 77; God and, 5, 119, 121, 122–27, 132, 143, 151–52, 156, 159, 162, 163, 165, 170, 176, 183, 184, 204, 215–16, 231–34, 237, 238–44, 248; historical, 13, 15–16, 104, 130–31, 143, 186; and "I am" statements, 203–7, 230; identification of, with the Son of Man, 150–51, 152, 159, 197, 204; and the invitation to "come unto" God, 5; in Jerusalem, 138, 147, 180, 182, 213, 220, 221; and Judaism, 139, 147–48, 156–58, 159–66, 187–89, 190, 191, 199–207,

229; and love, 125–26, 238–44; and the male/female dyad, 100; as the Messiah, 201; ministry of, 80, 85, 137, 186; murderers of, 121; negative portraits of, 21; resurrection of, 15, 105–6, 107–27, 151, 153–54, 167, 180, 187, 206, 209, 215–16, 217–26, 235, 240; righteousness of, 122, 126, 160; seen in the context of universal human experience, 119; suffering of, 135–36; temptation of, 86; words of, interpretation of, 16
Jews, 18, 28, 95, 147–48, 172–77, 248; as the chosen people, 69–70; and circumcision, 53; of the Dispersion, 199, 200; history of, 43–55, 57; identity of, 92; separatism of, 92, 148; tradition of, and Jesus, 139, 147–49, 156–66, 187–89, 191, 199–207, 229. *See also* Antisemitism; Israel; Judaism
Job, 64–69, 74
John, 22, 25, 82, 89, 90, 100, 152, 160, 180, 185–207, 217, 219, 221, 228, 229–30; **1**, 186; **1:1ff**, 202; **1:6ff**, 188; **1:14**, 197; **1:17**, 196; **1:29**, 188; **1:47**, 201; **2:13ff**, 186; **2:13–17**, 85, 186; **3:3**, 187; **3:4**, 187; **3:16**, 185; **3:18–20**, 22; **3:31**, 197; **4**, 188; **4:7**, 240; **4:10**, 187; **4:11**, 187; **4:33**, 188; **5:10**, 22; **5:14**, 197; **5:46**, 196; **6:33, 34**, 188; **6:35**, 205; **6:38**, 197; **6:42**, 188; **6:52**, 188; **7:28, 37**, 197; **7:33ff**, 188; **7:34**, 198; **7:35**, 201; **7:37**, 205; **7:42ff**, 195; **8:6**, 79; **8:21**, 198; **8:22**, 188; **8:23**, 188; **8:32**, 205; **8:39–44**, 22; **8:44**, 22, 189; **8:50**, 197; **8:57**, 80, 205; **8:57–59**, 205; **9**, 201; **9:22, 34**, 201; **9:36**, 197; **10:7**, 205; **10:10**, 225, 242; **10:11**, 205; **10:19, 24, 31, 33**, 22; **10:30**, 186; **10:36**, 186; **11:1ff**, 235; **11:4**, 197; **11:25**, 206; **11:35**, 185; **11:43**, 187; **12:42, 43**, 201; **12:44**, 197; **13:1–9, 12–16**, 85; **13:2**, 87; **13:30**, 140; **13:33**, 197, 198; **14:1–2**, 185; **14:6**, 205; **14:22**, 87; **14:23**, 198;

263

264

Book of Proverbs, 66; Job and, 68; moral retribution, 66, 68; and slavery, 102. *See also* Ethics

Moses, 16, 17, 127, 156–58, 164, 177, 179, 198, 203–4, 229, 235; death of, 41; in Deuteronomic narratives, 50, 196; in Elohist narratives, 48, 49; historic, 41–42; Law of, 132; and the Midianites, 19, 23; Pharaoh-, infancy story, 214; in Priestly narratives, 54; and the Torah, 23, 78, 104; in Yahwist narratives, 44, 46

Moslems, 165, 190, 199, 248

Mythology, 237

Nazism, 227

Nehemiah, 3, 53, 57, 71

Nephesh (spirit), 29, 45

Nero (emperor), 135, 137, 148, 174–75, 176

New Covenant, 76, 157

New Testament, 21, 77–90, 144; ancient documents that underlie Matthew and Luke, 85–88; disagreement among the Gospels in, 84–85; Falwell on, 58; lack of kosher laws in, 77; Lord's Prayer in, 86; and Quelle, 85–88, 95; Second Isaiah in, echoes of, 178; time frame of, 80–83; words of Jesus in, historicity of, 78, 90. *See also* specific books

Newton, Isaac, 9

Nicodemus, 187, 206

Nineham, D. E., 141

Noah, 1, 29, 44, 54

Numbers, 53; 5–11ff, 18; 6:2, 6–8, 164; 16:30, 31; 21:9, 196; 25:1–6, 18; 30:1–5, 19; 30:8, 19; 31:1, 2, 19; 31:7, 19; 31:9, 19; 31:10, 19; 31:15, 19

O'Connor, Sandra D., 101

O'Hair, M. M., 10–11

Old Testament, 104; earliest continuous written material in, dating of, 40; and Elohist narratives, 47, 50; Falwell on, 58; and Priestly narratives, 54. *See also* specific books

Passover, 51, 85, 186, 187

Patriarchy, 39, 42, 73, 101, 158; and the all-male priesthood, 6; and creation stories, 29

Paul, 6, 8, 13, 14, 22, 78, 80–82, 89, 91–127, 148, 172, 173, 174, 176, 192, 199, 205, 216, 217–19, 221, 224, 228, 241, 244; and the body, 110–11, 112–13, 117–23, 126; on death, 110, 113, 118, 122; and evil, 112, 113, 116, 117, 120, 123; and homosexuality, 116–18, 119, 120, 125–26; and Judaism, 96–98, 113, 114–15, 117, 119–20; and knowledge of God, 112; and love, 116, 121–22; and marriage, 115, 116, 117; and sin, 109–10, 111, 113, 115, 121, 122; and slavery, 93, 100, 101–02, 127; and women, 100–101, 115, 127

Pentecost, day of, 180, 182, 184, 222, 226

Peter, 6, 81, 89–90, 135, 137, 141, 148, 152, 160, 162, 172, 174, 184, 192, 195, 223, 228

Pharaoh, 17, 48, 49, 156

Philemon, 89, 94, 100, 102

Philippians, 89, 94, 115; 2:5–11, 123, 224; 3:2, 91; 3:4–6, 97; 3:12, 119; 3:13, 14, 119

Prayer, 4, 5, 28, 109, 200

Priesthood: all-male, 5–6; and the covenant with God, 49; Jewish, 4, 43, 46, 49, 51–55, 70–71; and women, 101

Priestly narration, 43, 52–54

Prostitution, 3, 17, 63

Protestantism, 10, 35, 58, 165, 199

Protest literature, 55, 72–74

Proverbs, 4, 62, 63, 65, 66–69, 196, 197, 198; 1:20–21, 197; 8:17, 198; 8:22, 23, 197; 8:31, 197; 8:32, 33, 197; 9:10, 66; 11:30–31, 67; 13:24, 4

Psalms, 15, 23, 52–64, 154; 22, 15,

265

58, 163, 164, 195–96; **24:1**, 63; **33:8**, 63; **95:4, 5**, 63; **109:25**, 163; **137**, 52; **137:7–9**, 18

Quelle, 85–88, 95

Race, 72, 183, 248
Racism, 2–3, 102
Rationality, 108, 123, 160, 223
Relativity, theory of, 25
Robinson, Janet, 14
Romans, 14, 89, 94; **1:3, 4**, 81; **1:24–25**, 112; **4:25**, 122; **5:14, 18**, 104; **6:9**, 122, 218; **6:12**, 110, 122; **6:19**, 110, 122; **6:21**, 110; **7:13**, 110; **7:14, 15**, 109, 111; **7:15**, 112; **7:18**, 109, 111; **7:21–24**, 113; **7:23**, 111; **7:24**, 113; **7:25**, 111, 113; **8:10**, 122; **8:31–39**, 97, 122; **8:38–39**, 105; **9:15**, 104; **10:5**, 104; **10:19**, 104; **11:8, 22**, 91; **11:13, 14**, 91; **13:1–4**, 102–03
Runcie, Robert, 5
Ruth, 64, 69–74

Sagan, Carl, 31
1 Samuel, 49, 51, 231
2 Samuel, 51, 59
Schillebeeckx, Edward, 86, 143
Science, 25–36, 61, 93, 133; and Genesis, 25–31, 38–40; and history, 38–43
Second Isaiah, 60–61, 65, 177–78
Segregation, 1–3, 5, 239
Sexism, 6, 239. *See also* Patriarchy
Sexuality, 1–11, 15, 17, 75, 116, 234; Paul and, 110–11, 112, 113, 115–17
Sin, 3–4, 157, 234; David and, 59; and the Fall, 34–35; and patriarchy, 6; Paul and, 109–10, 111, 113, 115, 121, 122; and Satan, 2; and the soul, 2
Sirach, 196; **4:11**, 197; **6:18**, 197; **6:20–26**, 198; **6:27**, 198; **24:8**, 197; **24:9**, 197
Slavery, 1–2, 42, 44, 54, 157, 239, 248; abolition of, 75, 77, 103; affirmation of, Paul and, 93, 100,

101–02, 127; of the Jews, 42, 43, 44, 48, 54, 63, 70; and the Law of God, 18; and tribal culture, 17, 65–66
Socialism, 62
Solomon, 173, 196; in the Book of Kings, 63; death of, 46; and polygamy, 77; Wisdom of, 66
Song of Songs, 62, 63, 64, 66
Soul, 2, 29, 34, 45
South Africa, 102
Supreme Court, 2
Swaggert, Jimmy, 3, 4

Ten Commandments, 15, 17, 23, 158, 246; Elohist version of, 49; Priestly version of, 54; Yahwist version of, 46
Tertullian, 22
Thatcher, Margaret, 101
1 Thessalonians, 80, 94; **2:18**, 105; **4:5**, 113
2 Thessalonians, 80, 91; **3:10**, 91
Tillich, Paul, 240
1 Timothy, 89, 94
2 Timothy, 89, 94
Torah, 8, 17, 18, 23, 73, 117, 214; authorship of, 23, 40, 78, 104; as the binding force of Jewish identity, 92; and chauvinistic nationalism, 20; and dietary laws, 54; interpretations of, and Jesus, 140; and Matthew, 160–61; and Paul, 97–98; penalty for homosexuality in, 118; and womanhood, 19
Tutu, Desmond, 103

Universalism, 41, 115, 119, 229
Ussher, James, 38

Vietnam War, 103–04
Virginity, 16, 111, 213–14, 215, 234–35, 238

War, 20, 43, 103–04
Washington, George, 103, 215
Wilberforce, Samuel, 9

266

Wisdom, 197; **6:12**, 198; **6:16**, 197; **6:17, 18**, 198; **6:22**, 197; **7:24, 25,** 198; **7:25**, 197; **7:26**, 197; **9:10**, 197; **9:16–18**, 197

Women, 5, 93, 158, 238, 239, 248; definition of, 6, 7; original creation of, 45; Paul and, 100–101, 115, 127; and the Torah, 19; and tribal cultures, 17, 18, 19. *See also* Feminism

Word of God, 6, 62, 77, 132, 245–49; and ancient cultural traditions, 54; and antisemitism, 23; and divine inspiration, theory of, 78–79; Jesus as the embodiment of, 216–17; and literalism, 10, 14, 20, 23, 38, 74; and male-inspired law, 18; and Paul, 92, 101–6, 126; in protest literature, 74–76

Yahweh, 43–46, 51, 70, 71, 190, 195, 204, 241

Yahwist narration, 43–46, 47, 51–52, 53

Zechariah, 61, 161, 162, 164